JOURNEY OF THE SOUL

*A fresh look at
life, death, and
the rest—in peace*

D1254672

JLI

JEWISH LEARNING INSTITUTE

CHAIRMAN
Rabbi Moshe Kotlarsky

PRINCIPAL BENEFACTOR
Mr. George Rohr

EXECUTIVE DIRECTOR
Rabbi Efraim Mintz

AUTHOR
Rabbi Naftali Silberberg

CURRICULUM DEVELOPMENT TEAM
Rabbi Mordechai Dinerman
Rabbi Yakov Gershon
Mrs. Rochel Holzkenner
Rabbi Eli Raksin
Rabbi Yanky Raskin
Mrs. Chava Shapiro
Dr. Casey Skvorc, PhD
Rabbi Shmuel Super

COORDINATOR
Mrs. Rivki Mockin

ADMINISTRATORS
Mrs. Chana Dechter
Mrs. Naomi Heber

Printed in the United States of America
© Copyrighted and Published 2020
by **THE ROHR JEWISH LEARNING INSTITUTE**
822 Eastern Parkway, Brooklyn, NY 11213

Cover Art: *The Cemetery Gates*, Marc Chagall,
oil on canvas, 1917. (Private Location)

(888) YOUR-JLI/718-221-6900
WWW.MYJLI.COM

The Rohr Jewish Learning Institute
gratefully acknowledges the pioneering
and ongoing support of

George and Pamela Rohr

Since its inception, the Rohr JLI has been
a beneficiary of the vision, generosity, care,
and concern of the Rohr family.

In the merit of the tens of thousands of hours
of Torah study by JLI students worldwide,
may they be blessed with health, *Yiddishe
nachas* from all their loved ones, and
extraordinary success in all their endeavors.

ENDORSEMENTS

This course will be of interest to any human being, since we all think about dying, death, and the afterlife. The course presents both more abstract theoretical points of view and, also, practical strategies for thinking about, and preparing for, death. The Jewish tradition offers unique answers to the intellectual issues and also strategies for coming to terms with death. I highly recommend this course.

JOHN MARTIN FISCHER, PHD

Distinguished Professor of Philosophy, UC Riverside
University Professor in the University of California
Director, The Immortality Project (2012–15)
Author, *Death, Immortality, and Meaning in Life* and nine other titles.

Your course description of *Journey of the Soul* does look to be a fascinating integration of ancient views on death primarily from the Jewish tradition with modern psychological understandings of the role of death perspectives in managing our anxieties about mortality. Thank you for sharing, and I would certainly encourage people in the communities offering the course to challenge themselves to consider these existential questions covered in your course.

RICHARD G. TEDESCHI, PHD

Distinguished Chair, Boulder Crest Institute for Posttraumatic Growth, Bluemont, VA
Faculty, Posttraumatic Growth Research Group, University of North Carolina, Charlotte
Coauthor, *Posttraumatic Growth: Theory, Research, and Applications* and four other titles

Attachment and love are fundamental to human existence. Without them, we can neither survive nor thrive. Alas, it is these very same conditions and the very same persons who are so important to us—that leave us vulnerable to the pain and dislocation of loss and bereavement. The human encounter with loss and grief is universal, but the particular ways in which people mourn and make sense of their loss is highly variable. Culture, religion, community and family all have a role to play in shaping the encounter with death. *Journey of the Soul* is both a timely and timeless opportunity. It aims to bring philosophical and psychological approaches to the field of thanatology into dialogue with insights from the wisdom of the Jewish faith tradition. In so doing, it cannot help but deepen our appreciation of human connections and the way in which we find and make meaning in life.

SIMON SHIMSHON RUBIN, PHD

Professor of Clinical Psychology,
Director, International Center for the Study of Loss, Bereavement and Human Resilience,
University of Haifa, Israel
Author, *Working with the Bereaved: Multiple Lenses on Loss and Mourning*

The Rohr Jewish Learning Institute's adult education course, *Journey of the Soul,* addresses philosophical issues surrounding death including why we die, facing death, what happens after death, social justice and death, and fears of dying and death. As one who has taught courses in death and dying since 1970, I find this course to be intriguing, timely, and worth taking. In this time of COVID-19, economic crises, social isolation, dying alone, and having isolated services for the dead, it is vital to examine the issues of death. While offering a Jewish perspective, this course allows the student to examine his or her own thinking by learning from the thoughts of others. It includes conceptual developments in thanatology, including "continuing bonds," creating therapeutic environments, and positive communications, and offers models for mourning. This course offers a scientific, research-based understanding of death while incorporating Jewish and philosophical understandings. It offers the opportunity to examine one's own thinking and ability to cope with death. An excellent opportunity to learn!

GERRY R. COX, PHD

Center for Grief and Death Education
Professor Emeritus, University of Wisconsin-La Crosse
Author and Coauthor, *Making Sense of Death* and seven other titles

It is one of life's great ironies that mortality is one of the few things we share with every other person, and yet when we are dealing with it ourselves, it's the loneliest feeling in the world. This course helps detoxify death by placing it in a spiritual context.

Combining ancient wisdom with modern psychological concepts, it encourages a thoughtful exploration of what can be a very scary but important subject. After all, it is the specter of death that compels us to find a sense of meaning and purpose in our lives.

MINDY GREENSTEIN, PHD

Clinical Psychologist and Psycho-oncologist,
Author, *Lighter as We Go: Virtues, Character Strengths, and Aging*

The Rohr Jewish Learning Institute's newest course, *Journey of the Soul*, examines death—and Jewish life—with an uplifting blend of Torah-based scholarship and contemporary psychological perspectives. Inspirational and thought-provoking text materials provide insight into understanding life's purpose. Highly recommended, especially for members of the helping professions.

CASEY SKVORC, PHD, JD

Medical Psychologist
National Institutes of Health

In these challenging times, it is important to know how our faith, community and culture can provide us with solace, strength and meaning. *Journey of the Soul* promises a journey through both ancient philosophy and modern scientific thought addressing the greatest mystery we will all face.

KATHLEEN R. GILBERT, PHD, FT
Professor Emerita, Applied Health Science
Indiana University Bloomington, School of Public Health
Author, *Coping with Infant or Fetal Loss* and other titles

Awareness of death provides us with a valuable opportunity to identify and address our fears about our own death—which can help to demystify and lessen those fears—and to discuss our concerns with the people around us, who can make a difference to our experience of death. A course such as this has never been more important, at a time when we risk losing sight of the value of death as an opportunity to explore who we are and to connect on a profound level with those we love.

BIANCA NOGRADY
Author, *The End: The Human Experience of Death*

This course strikes me as a very fine juxtaposition of ancient theological wisdom with contemporary empirical science. My sense is that this would be an interesting and rewarding educational and personal experience.

SHELDON SOLOMON, PHD
Professor of Social Psychology, Skidmore College
Coauthor, *In the Wake of 9/11: The Psychology of Terror*
Coauthor, *The Worm at the Core: On the Role of Death in Life*

It seems clear to me that this will be a very valuable course that will help people come to grips with their mortality, a topic that is too often avoided. By addressing this critical aspect of being human head-on, people can lead more thoughtful, focused, and enriched lives, and this course looks to be an excellent path toward doing so.

JEFF GREENBERG, PHD
Professor of Psychology, University of Arizona
Coauthor, *In the Wake of 9/11: The Psychology of Terror*
Coauthor, *The Worm at the Core: On the Role of Death in Life*

FOREWORD

"THE HEART OF THE WISE IS IN A HOUSE OF MOURNING;
THE HEART OF THE FOOLS IS IN THE HOUSE OF MERRYMAKING."
—ECCLESIASTES 7:4

Judaism provides no shortage of festivals and occasions for rejoicing. It strongly encourages maintaining a joyful disposition at all times and rejects the toxicity of excessive sadness and morbidity. That said, it also offers intellectual curveballs such as the above quote from Judaism's wisest, King Solomon, which spreads a shroud as a cloud across our perspective of life. Is he urging us to keep our mortality in mind to the point of minimizing merriment?

The thought of death can either drag us down or uplift and motivate us—depending entirely on our perspective of mortality. It is undeniable that to one degree or another, we all contemplate death and it actively influences our choices. For that reason, it is critical to ensure that our perspective is accurate and that it will bring us benefit through productively guiding our decisions and emotional reactions.

To that end, the Rohr Jewish Learning Institute (JLI) is proud to release a groundbreaking six-week course that examines mortality from every angle of the spectacular prism of Jewish thought and tradition: *Journey of the Soul: A Fresh Look at Life, Death, and the Rest—in Peace.*

This course draws from the depths of the Torah's ageless wellsprings of wisdom, crafting a perspective so transformative that it can originate only with the traditions imparted by the Provider of life, Who also redeems souls from bodies at a life span's end. It also incorporates insight and tools provided by modern-day psychology that oftentimes facilitate an enhanced application of the teachings of the Torah and Jewish mysticism.

The Jewish approach to death heavily informs the many rituals and practical customs that surround the funeral and mourning processes. It sheds light on their deeper purpose of assisting a mourner in mourning properly and productively and then—having fully processed the loss—reemerging functionally into life.

Journey of the Soul is designed to calibrate and significantly enhance your approach to death and the afterlife. Perhaps most importantly, it promises to reinvent your approach to the time you have been allotted on this cozy planet and motivate you to spend it wisely and happily.

With this latest addition to JLI's expanding catalog of original courses, we are delighted to debut our newly redesigned and upgraded full-color textbook. In addition to its aesthetic advantage, it will make your study easier and more intuitive. We hope you will enjoy this upgrade, and we encourage you to provide feedback on the new design—or on anything JLI-related—at flagship@myjli.com.

CONFLICT OF INTEREST DISCLOSURE POLICY

The **"Conflict of Interest Disclosure Policy"** of Albert Einstein College of Medicine—Montefiore Medical Center requires that faculty participating in any CME activity disclose to the audience any relationship(s) with a pharmaceutical, product, or device company. Any presenter, whose disclosed relationships prove to create a conflict of interest with regard to their contribution to the activity, will not be permitted to present.

Albert Einstein College of Medicine—Montefiore Medical Center also requires that faculty participating in any CME activity disclose to the audience when discussing any unlabeled or investigational use of any commercial product or device not yet approved for use in the United States. Albert Einstein College of Medicine—Montefiore Medical Center, CCPD staff, has no conflicts of interest with commercial interests related directly or indirectly to this educational activity.

AMERICAN DISABILITY ACT STATEMENT

Albert Einstein College of Medicine and Montefiore Medical Center fully comply with the legal requirements of the Americans with Disabilities Act. If you require special assistance, please submit your request in writing thirty (30) days in advance of the activity, to continuingeducation@myjli.com.

DISCLOSURE OF COMMERCIAL SUPPORT AND THE UNLABELED USE OF A COMMERCIAL PRODUCT

These activities are receiving NO commercial support.

DISCLOSURE: No member of the planning committee and no member of the faculty for this event has a financial interest or other relationship with any commercial product.

The members of the Planning Committee are:

Edward I. Reichman, M.D.—*Reviewer*
Professor of Emergency Medicine and Epidemiology & Population Health, Albert Einstein College of Medicine
Disclosure: Dr. Reichman presents no relevant conflict of interest.

Simon A. Rego, Psy.D.—*Reviewer*
Associate Professor of Psychiatry and Behavioral Sciences
Chief of Psychology, Department of Psychiatry and Behavioral Sciences
Director of Psychology Training, Department of Psychiatry and Behavioral Sciences,
Albert Einstein College of Medicine
Disclosure: Dr. Rego presents no relevant conflict of interest.

Casey Skvorc, PhD, JD—*Course Editor*
The Rohr Jewish Learning Institute
Disclosure: Dr. Skvorc presents no relevant conflict of interest.

Mindy Wallach—*Course Administrator*
The Rohr Jewish Learning Institute
Disclosure: Mrs. Wallach presents no relevant conflict of interest.

NOTE: Each individual location/activity will receive the faculty presenter's COI disclosure

ACCREDITATION

Montefiore — Albert Einstein College of Medicine

This activity was developed through a collaboration of Albert Einstein College of Medicine—Montefiore Medical Center and The Rohr Jewish Learning Institute.

Journey of the Soul provides Jewish cultural and psychological perspectives on end-of-life, death anxiety and grief.

Learning Objectives:

1. To define and discuss perspectives and methods that can help patients near end-of-life overcome death anxiety and help their families build a foundation for a healthy bereavement

2. To identify Jewish spiritual beliefs related to death and end-of-life to improve cultural sensitivity in communication with Jewish patients and their families.

Specific learning objectives for medical and mental health professionals can be found at www.myjli.com/continuingeducation.

JOINTLY ACCREDITED PROVIDER™
INTERPROFESSIONAL CONTINUING EDUCATION

ACCREDITATION STATEMENT

In support of improving patient care, this activity has been planned and implemented by Albert Einstein College of Medicine—Montefiore Medical Center and the Rohr Jewish Learning Institute (JLI). Albert Einstein College of Medicine—Montefiore Medical Center is jointly accredited by the Accreditation Council for Continuing Medical Education (ACCME), the Accreditation Council for Pharmacy Education (ACPE), and the American Nurses Credentialing Center (ANCC), to provide continuing education for the healthcare team. Continuing Education Credits have been designated for the following professionals:

PSYCHOLOGISTS

Albert Einstein College of Medicine—Montefiore Medical Center is approved by the **American Psychological Association** to sponsor continuing education for psychologists. Albert Einstein College of Medicine—Montefiore Medical Center maintains responsibility for this program and its content.

C.E. Credit 1.5*

PHYSICIANS, NURSE PRACTITIONERS, AND P.A.S

Credits Designation: Albert Einstein College of Medicine - Montefiore Medical Center designates this live activity for a maximum of *1.5 AMA PRA Category I Credits*™. Physicians should claim only the credit commensurate with the extent of their participation in the activity.*

*Credits designation is for each activity/lesson in the series.

SOCIAL WORKERS, FAMILY THERAPISTS, PROFESSIONAL COUNSELORS

The Jewish Learning Institute is a **Minnesota Board of Social Work** approved Continuing Education Provider (Sponsor number CEP-1161).

At the time this publication goes to print, an application is pending with the **State of Ohio Counselor, Social Worker and Marriage and Family Therapist Board.**

Social Workers, Licensed Marriage and Family Therapists and Licensed Mental Health Counselors in most states can satisfy their continuing education requirements with the aforementioned accreditations and approvals. For more information on eligibility in your state email continuingeducation@myjli.com.

FOR MORE INFORMATION and to register for credit, please go to www.myjli.com/continuing education.
Advance registration is required to receive credits.

CITATION TYPES

SCRIPTURE

The icon for Scripture is based on the images of a scroll and a spiral. The scroll is a literal reference; the spiral symbolizes Scripture's role as the singular source from which all subsequent Torah knowledge emanates.

TALMUD AND MIDRASH

The Talmud and Midrash are fundamental links in the chain of the Torah's oral tradition.

SAGES

Many generations of Jewish sages devoted their lives to expounding on and elucidating the texts of Scripture and the Talmud. The quill symbolizes the product of their toil.

MYSTICS

The mystics explore the inner, esoteric aspect of the Torah. The icon for mystical texts is based on the "*sefirot tree*" commonly present in kabbalistic charts.

LAWS & CUSTOMS

Ultimately, the teachings emerging from Scripture, the Talmud, and the writings of the later sages find expression in Torah law—known as halachah, "the way"—and the customs adopted by the various Jewish communities through the generations.

PERSPECTIVES

Personal perspectives expressed in essays, diaries, and other works make up a significant part of the total Jewish experience.

STORIES

Sometimes, the best way to illustrate an idea is by painting a picture through a story or a parable. Indeed, stories and parables, with their emphasis on the telling and listening experience, occupy an important place in Jewish teaching.

NOTE: Throughout this book, "G-d" and "L-rd" are written with a hyphen instead of an "o" (both in our own translations and when quoting others). This is one way we accord reverence to the sacred divine name. This also reminds us that, even as we seek G-d, He transcends any human effort to describe His reality.

CONTENTS

Lesson

1

DEMYSTIFYING DEATH

PERSPECTIVE ON LIFE AND BEYOND

Why are humans so anxious about death and dying? For many, the abrupt finality of death makes life itself seem futile. By exploring how our life force—our immortal soul—never ends but merely shifts roles, we begin to view life and death as two harmonious steps on the same journey.

I. THANATOPHOBIA

Welcome to an exploration of, and journey into, the Jewish traditions and insights surrounding the topics of death and the afterlife.

Our planet is populated by plenty of peoples, with a plethora of perspectives. Some fear death. Some actively embrace it. And others try to ignore it altogether and focus on the here and now. What is the unique *Jewish* perspective?

Since we are seeking the Jewish perspective, we'll begin the Jewish way, and answer our inquiry by first offering a further question: Why bother? Granted, there is a universal fascination with death and all that is associated with it. But is the phenomenon of human expiration truly important enough to warrant indulging that fascination?

EXERCISE 1.1

What attracted you to this course? Which specific topic(s) are you most interested in clarifying?

1. _____

2. _____

3. _____

4. _____

5. _____

QUESTION

Not everyone reacts the same way to discussions of death and mortality. Which feelings does this topic evoke in you?

MERRIAM-WEBSTER
DICTIONARY

THANATOPHOBIA [than-ət-ə-'fō-bē-ə]

noun:
fear of death

TEXT 1

A UNIVERSAL FEIR

A UNIVERSAL FEAR

IRVIN D. YALOM, *STARING AT THE SUN: OVERCOMING THE TERROR OF DEATH* (S. FRANCISCO: JOSSEY-BASS, 2008), PP. 1–2

IRVIN D. YALOM, M.D.
1931–

Psychiatrist. Dr. Yalom is an emeritus professor of psychiatry at Stanford University, as well as an author of both fiction and nonfiction. He was a pioneer in the area of existential psychotherapy, which emphasizes that mental health problems are frequently caused by struggles with existence. He defined four "givens" of the human condition—death, meaning, isolation, and freedom—that have become the basis for the field.

Mortality has haunted us from the beginning of history. Four thousand years ago, the Babylonian hero Gilgamesh reflected on the death of his friend Enkidu with the words . . . : "Thou hast become dark and cannot hear me. When I die shall I not be like Enkidu? Sorrow enters my heart. I am afraid of death."

Gilgamesh speaks for all of us. As he feared death, so do we all—each and every man, woman, and child. For some of us the fear of death manifests only indirectly, either as generalized unrest or masqueraded as another psychological symptom; other individuals experience an explicit and conscious stream of anxiety about death; and for some of us the fear of death erupts into terror that negates all happiness and fulfillment.

Want to learn more about Terror Management Theory? "How We Cope with Death," by *Nathan A. Heflick, PhD*, is a good place to start: *myJLI.com/soul*

FIGURE 1.1

FEAR OF DEATH STATISTICS

SURVEY OF U.S. ADULTS,
STATISTA, RESEARCH
DEPARTMENT, PUBLISHED
SEPTEMBER 16, 2020

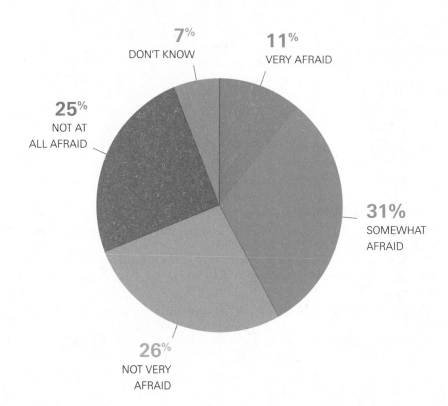

II. SOUL SURVIVOR

Is death the end of who we are?

The answer to this sobering question depends entirely on how
we identify ourselves.

So, the *first* question to ask ourselves is: Who are we?

TEXT 2

BODY GARB

RABBI CHAIM VITAL, *SHAAREI
KEDUSHAH* 1:1

**RABBI CHAIM VITAL
C. 1542–1620**

Lurianic kabbalist. Rabbi Vital
was born in Israel, lived in Safed
and Jerusalem, and later lived in
Damascus. He was authorized
by his teacher, Rabbi Yitschak
Luria, the Arizal, to record his
teachings. Acting on this mandate,
Vital began arranging his master's
teachings in written form, and
his many works constitute the
foundation of the Lurianic school
of Jewish mysticism. His most
famous work is *Ets Chaim*.

נוֹדַע אֶל בַּעֲלֵי מַדָּע, כִּי גוּף הָאָדָם אֵינֶנּוּ הָאָדָם עַצְמוֹ מִצַּד הַגּוּף . . . נִמְצָא
הָאָדָם הוּא הַפְּנִימִיּת, אֲבָל הַגּוּף הוּא עִנְיָן לְבוּשׁ אֶחָד תִּתְלַבֵּשׁ בּוֹ נֶפֶשׁ
הַשִּׂכְלִית אֲשֶׁר הִיא הָאָדָם עַצְמוֹ בְּעוֹדוֹ בָּעוֹלָם הַזֶּה.

The wise are aware that the human body
is not the human being. . . .
When we speak of the human being,
we are referring to the human's inner dimension.
The body is merely a garment
in which the soul is attired
during its sojourn in this world.

FIGURE 1.2

WHO AM I?

The real me is my soul, not my body.

QUESTION

Can you think of an analogy to depict the body-soul relationship?

TEXT 3A

HUMAN FORMATION

GENESIS 2:7

וַיִּיצֶר ה' אֱלֹקִים אֶת הָאָדָם עָפָר מִן הָאֲדָמָה וַיִּפַּח בְּאַפָּיו נִשְׁמַת חַיִּים. וַיְהִי הָאָדָם לְנֶפֶשׁ חַיָּה.

G-d formed the human of soil from the earth and breathed into his nostrils a *neshamah* (soul) of life. And the human being became a living being.

TEXT 3B

ANIMAL FORMATION

IBID 1:24

וַיֹּאמֶר אֱלֹקִים: "תּוֹצֵא הָאָרֶץ נֶפֶשׁ חַיָּה לְמִינָהּ בְּהֵמָה וָרֶמֶשׂ וְחַיְתוֹ אֶרֶץ לְמִינָהּ", וַיְהִי כֵן.

G-d said, "Let the earth bring forth living beings of differing species:

cattle, creeping things, and beasts of the earth according to their species." And it was so.

Can you identify the primary distinction between the creation of the human being and the creation of animal and other forms of life?

TEXT 3C

DEATH DEFYING

RABBI CHEZKIAH BEN MANO'ACH, *CHIZKUNI*, GENESIS 2:7

RABBI CHEZKIAH BEN MANO'ACH (CHIZKUNI) C. 1250–1310

French rabbi and exegete. His commentary on the Torah, *Chizkuni*, is based principally on the work of Rashi and, according to the author's testimony, also draws upon nearly 20 earlier sources that he collected during his travels. He focuses on elucidating the straightforward meaning of the text of the Torah.

וַיִּפַּח בְּאַפָּיו נִשְׁמַת חַיִּים: בִּנְפִיחָתוֹ שֶׁל הַקָּדוֹשׁ בָּרוּךְ הוּא שֶׁהִיא רוּחַ הַקוֹדֶשׁ, מַה שֶּׁלֹּא נָפַח בְּשׁוּם אַף בְּרִיָה... נְשָׁמָה שֶׁהִיא חַיָּה לְעוֹלָם וְאֵינָהּ מֵתָה בְּמוֹת הַגּוּף.

G-d did what He had not done
with any other creature:
He blew [into Adam] with His holy spirit
a *neshamah* that is immortal
and does not perish when the body does.

FIGURE 1.3

WHO AM I?

1. The real me is my soul, not my body.

2. The real me, the soul, is eternal. So I am eternal.

TEXT 4

SOUL RESISTANCE

MIDRASH, TANCHUMA, PEKUDEI 3

מִיַּד רוֹמֵז הַקָּדוֹשׁ בָּרוּךְ הוּא לַמַּלְאָךְ הַמְמֻנֶּה עַל הָרוּחוֹת
וְאוֹמֵר לוֹ, "הָבֵא לִי רוּחַ פְּלוֹנִי שֶׁהִיא בְּגַן עֵדֶן, שֶׁשְּׁמוֹ פְּלוֹנִי
וּתְאָרוֹ כָּךְ וְכָךְ". לְפִי שֶׁכָּל הָרוּחוֹת שֶׁעֲתִידִין לְהִבָּרְאוֹת כֻּלָּן הֵן
נִבְרָאוֹת מִיּוֹם שֶׁבָּרָא הָעוֹלָם עַד שֶׁיִּכְלֶה כָּל הָעוֹלָם . . .

מִיַּד הוֹלֵךְ הַמַּלְאָךְ וּמֵבִיא אֶת הָרוּחַ לִפְנֵי הַקָּדוֹשׁ בָּרוּךְ הוּא, וּכְשֶׁהִיא בָּאָה
מִיַּד כּוֹרַעַת וּמִשְׁתַּחֲוָה לִפְנֵי הַמֶּלֶךְ מַלְכֵי הַמְּלָכִים הַקָּדוֹשׁ בָּרוּךְ הוּא. אוֹתָהּ
שָׁעָה אוֹמֵר הַקָּדוֹשׁ בָּרוּךְ הוּא לָרוּחַ, "הִכָּנְסִי בְּטִיפָּה זוֹ שֶׁבְּיַד פְּלוֹנִי".

פָּתַח הָרוּחַ פִּיו וְאוֹמֵר לְפָנָיו, "רִבּוֹנוֹ שֶׁל עוֹלָם! דַּי לִי הָעוֹלָם
שֶׁהָיִיתִי דָר מִיּוֹם שֶׁבְּרָאתַנִי, לָמָה רְצוֹנְךָ לְהַכְנִיסֵנִי בְּטִיפָּה זוֹ
סְרוּחָה, שֶׁאֲנִי קְדוֹשָׁה וּטְהוֹרָה וַאֲנִי גְזוּרָה מִגִּזְרַת כְּבוֹדֶךָ?"

Forty days before the conception of a child, G‑d summons the angel in charge of souls and tells him, "Bring before Me a certain soul that is now in Paradise. Its name is such-and-such and its appearance is such-and-such." This is [possible] because all the souls that are born in this world were created on the day the world was created and exist until the end of time. . . .

TANCHUMA

A Midrashic work bearing the name of Rabbi Tanchuma, a 4th-century Talmudic sage quoted often in this work. "Midrash" is the designation of a particular genre of rabbinic literature usually forming a running commentary on specific books of the Bible. *Tanchuma* provides textual exegeses, expounds upon the biblical narrative, and develops and illustrates moral principles. *Tanchuma* is unique in that many of its sections commence with a halachic discussion, which subsequently leads into nonhalachic teachings.

The angel goes and brings the soul before G-d. The soul bows and prostrates itself before the supreme King of kings. G-d instructs the soul, "Please enter the seminal drop that is currently in the hands of [the angel in charge of pregnancy]."

The soul protests, "Master of the Universe! I am quite satisfied with the world I inhabited since the day You created me. I am holy and pure, hewn from Your Throne of Glory—why do You wish to cause me to enter this putrid drop?"

The Jewish view of the soul is not monolithic. In "The Anatomy of a Soul," *Rabbi Avrohom Bergstein* elaborates: *myJLI.com/soul*

▼ **SLEEPING CHILD**
Bernardo Strozzi (1581/2–1644), oil on canvas, first half 17th century. (Residenzgalerie Salzburg, Austria)

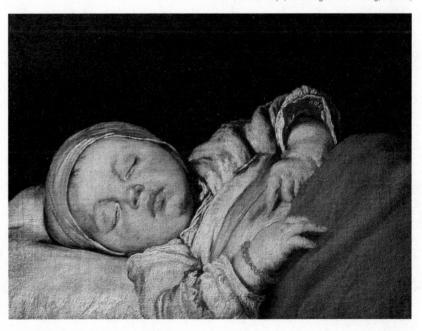

TEXT 5

PREPARING IN THE CORRIDOR

ETHICS OF THE FATHERS 4:16–17

ETHICS OF THE FATHERS (PIRKEI AVOT)

A 6-chapter work on Jewish ethics that is studied widely by Jewish communities, especially during the summer. The first 5 chapters are from the Mishnah, tractate Avot. Avot differs from the rest of the Mishnah in that it does not focus on legal subjects; it is a collection of the sages' wisdom on topics related to character development, ethics, healthy living, piety, and the study of Torah.

הָעוֹלָם הַזֶּה דּוֹמֶה לַפְּרוֹזְדּוֹר בִּפְנֵי הָעוֹלָם הַבָּא. הַתְקֵן עַצְמְךָ בַּפְּרוֹזְדּוֹר, כְּדֵי שֶׁתִּכָּנֵס לַטְרַקְלִין ...

וְיָפָה שָׁעָה אַחַת שֶׁל קוֹרַת רוּחַ בָּעוֹלָם הַבָּא, מִכָּל חַיֵּי הָעוֹלָם הַזֶּה.

This world is like a corridor
before the World to Come.
Prepare yourself in the corridor,
so that you may enter the palace. . . .

A single moment of bliss
in the World to Come
is greater than all of this world.

FIGURE 1.4

WHO AM I?

"What Is Life?" *Rabbi Manis Friedman's* penetrating explanation: *myJLI.com/soul*

1. The real me is my soul, not my body.

2. The real me, the soul, is eternal. So I am eternal.

3. The real eternal me is relatively unaffected by birth or death.

III. CULTURE OF LIFE

Does Judaism suggest a flippant or nonchalant approach to corporeal demise? After all, why should we be perturbed by the loss of the physical body if the soul—the real me—graduates to a far better and greater place?

No, Judaism certainly does *not* want us to consider the body and the material world insignificant nor to underrate the significance of entering or leaving this world.

However, in order to understand how the significance of corporeal life coexists with the priority of soul over body and the superiority of the afterlife, we will need to take our journey a little further. We need to understand why we come down here in the first place.

◄ **WOMAN AT A WINDOW**
Caspar David Friedrich, oil on canvas, Berlin, Germany, 1822. (Alte Nationalgalerie, Staatliche Museen zu Berlin)

TEXT 6

A TORAH TO LIVE BY

MAIMONIDES, *MISHNEH TORAH*,
LAWS OF THE FUNDAMENTALS
OF THE TORAH 5:1

**RABBI MOSHE BEN MAIMON
(MAIMONIDES, RAMBAM) 1135–1204**

Halachist, philosopher, author, and physician. Maimonides was born in Córdoba, Spain. After the conquest of Córdoba by the Almohads, he fled Spain and eventually settled in Cairo, Egypt. There, he became the leader of the Jewish community and served as court physician to the vizier of Egypt. He is most noted for authoring the *Mishneh Torah,* an encyclopedic arrangement of Jewish law; and for his philosophical work, *Guide for the Perplexed.* His rulings on Jewish law are integral to the formation of halachic consensus.

כְּשֶׁיַּעֲמֹוד גּוֹי וְיֶאֱנֹוס אֶת יִשְׂרָאֵל לַעֲבוֹר עַל אַחַת מִכָּל מִצְוֹת הָאֲמוּרוֹת בַּתּוֹרָה אוֹ יַהַרְגֶנּוּ, יַעֲבוֹר וְאַל יֵהָרֵג, שֶׁנֶּאֱמַר בְּמִצְוֹת (וַיִּקְרָא יח, ה), "אֲשֶׁר יַעֲשֶׂה אֹתָם הָאָדָם וָחַי בָּהֶם". "וָחַי" בָּהֶם, וְלֹא שֶׁיָּמוּת בָּהֶם.

If a non-Jew attempts to force a Jew to violate one of the Torah's commandments at the pain of death, the Jew should violate the commandment rather than be killed because the Torah states concerning the *mitzvot*: "A person shall do them and live by them" (LEVITICUS 18:5). One should *live by them* and not die because of them.

SABBATH ▶
Jankel Adler, mixed media: oil, sand on canvas, Dusseldorf, 1925. (Jewish Museum Berlin)

**TEXT 7
(CONCLUSION OF TEXT 4)**

G-D'S ENCOURAGING WORDS

MIDRASH, TANCHUMA, PEKUDEI 3

מִיָד אוֹמֵר הַקָדוֹשׁ בָּרוּךְ הוּא לַנְשָׁמָה, "עוֹלָם שֶׁאֲנִי מַכְנִיסְךָ בּוֹ יָפֶה יְהֵא לְךָ מִמַּה שֶׁהָיִיתָ דָר בּוֹ, וּבְשָׁעָה שֶׁיְצַרְתִּיךְ לֹא יְצַרְתִּיךְ אֶלָא לְטִיפָה זוֹ". מִיָד מַכְנִיסוֹ הַקָדוֹשׁ בָּרוּךְ הוּא לְשָׁם בַּעַל כָּרְחוֹ.

G-d hurries to reassure the [descending] soul: "The world to which I am bringing you will prove more beneficial than the one you presently inhabit. Indeed, I formed you exclusively for the purpose of [creating mortal life from] this [particular] drop [of seed]." With that, G-d forcibly installs the soul.

TEXT 8 (IMMEDIATELY PRECEDES TEXT 5)

GREATER THAN HEAVEN

ETHICS OF THE FATHERS 4:17

יָפָה שָׁעָה אַחַת בִּתְשׁוּבָה וּמַעֲשִׂים טוֹבִים בָּעוֹלָם הַזֶה, מִכָּל חַיֵי הָעוֹלָם הַבָּא.

A single moment of repentance and of good deeds in *this* world is greater than all of the World to Come.

QUESTION

How might we reconcile the value Judaism places on *bodily* life with its belief in the immortality of the *soul*?

TEXT 9

THE PRIMORDIAL CONDITION

TALMUD, SHABBAT 88A

BABYLONIAN TALMUD

A literary work of monumental proportions that draws upon the legal, spiritual, intellectual, ethical, and historical traditions of Judaism. The 37 tractates of the Babylonian Talmud contain the teachings of the Jewish sages from the period after the destruction of the 2nd Temple through the 5th century CE. It has served as the primary vehicle for the transmission of the Oral Law and the education of Jews over the centuries; it is the entry point for all subsequent legal, ethical, and theological Jewish scholarship.

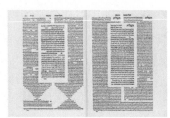

שֶׁהִתְנָה הַקָּדוֹשׁ בָּרוּךְ הוּא עִם מַעֲשֵׂה בְּרֵאשִׁית, וְאָמַר לָהֶם: "אִם יִשְׂרָאֵל מְקַבְּלִים הַתּוֹרָה, אַתֶּם מִתְקַיְּימִין; וְאִם לָאו, אֲנִי מַחֲזִיר אֶתְכֶם לְתוֹהוּ וָבוֹהוּ".

G-d created the universe on a condition:

"If the Jews accept the Torah,"

He told the universe,

"you will continue to exist.

If [they do] not,

I will return you to nothingness."

THE CREATION ▶
James Jacques Joseph Tissot, gouache on board, France; c. 1896–1902. (The Jewish Museum, New York)

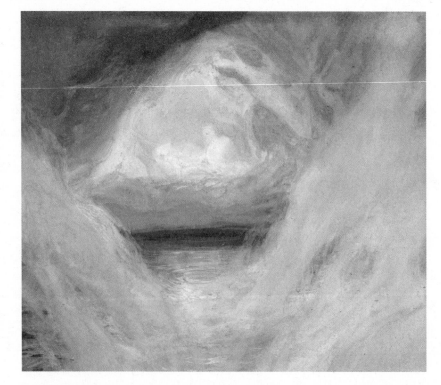

TEXT 10

A FORCED BEGINNING; A FORCED ENDING

ETHICS OF THE FATHERS 4:22

שֶׁעַל כָּרְחֲךָ אַתָּה נוֹצָר, וְעַל כָּרְחֲךָ אַתָּה נוֹלָד,
וְעַל כָּרְחֲךָ אַתָּה חַי, וְעַל כָּרְחֲךָ אַתָּה מֵת.

Against your will you are formed,
and against your will you are born.

Against your will you live,
and against your will you die.

FIGURE 1.5

SUMMARY

1. Death is not the end.

2. Nevertheless, we value life more than anything.

IV. THANATOPHOBIA RESOLUTION

We very much want to live, but at the same time, death fails to frighten us.

TEXT 11

A TERROR TACTIC THAT BACKFIRED

ADAPTED FROM RABBI YOSEF YITSCHAK SCHNEERSOHN, *SEFER HASICHOT* 5680, P. 4

RABBI YOSEF YITSCHAK SCHNEERSOHN (RAYATS, FRIERDIKER REBBE, PREVIOUS REBBE) 1880–1950

Chasidic rebbe, prolific writer, and Jewish activist. Rabbi Yosef Yitschak, the 6th leader of the Chabad movement, actively promoted Jewish religious practice in Soviet Russia and was arrested for these activities. After his release from prison and exile, he settled in Warsaw, Poland, from where he fled Nazi occupation and arrived in New York in 1940. Settling in Brooklyn, Rabbi Schneersohn worked to revitalize American Jewish life. His son-in-law, Rabbi Menachem Mendel Schneerson, succeeded him as the leader of the Chabad movement.

I arrived for interrogation at the offices of the Soviet GPU. However, in keeping with my principles, I was not very cooperative. One of the interrogators raised a revolver that sat on the desk before him. He looked me in the eye and mockingly said, "This small toy has incredible powers. It causes principles to melt away. It opens mouths. Under its spell, even mutes have become talkative."

I responded: "You are quite mistaken. That toy only has an effect on fainthearted nonbelievers, those with one world and multiple gods. We, on the other hand, have one G-d and two worlds. As such, I don't panic at the sight of your toy; it has no effect on me whatsoever."

TEXT 12

A REASON TO WEEP

TALMUD, KETUBOT 103B

כְּשֶׁחָלָה רַבִּי, נִכְנַס רַבִּי חִיָּיא אֶצְלוֹ וּמְצָאוֹ שֶׁהוּא בּוֹכֶה.
אָמַר לוֹ, "רַבִּי, מִפְּנֵי מָה אַתָּה בּוֹכֶה? וְהָתַנְיָא, 'מֵת מִתּוֹךְ
הַשְּׂחוֹק סִימָן יָפֶה לוֹ, מִתּוֹךְ הַבְּכִי סִימָן רַע לוֹ'" . . .
אָמַר לֵיה, "אֲנָא אַתּוֹרָה וּמִצְוֹת קָא בָּכִינָא".

When Rabbi [Judah the Prince] fell ill [and lay on his deathbed], Rabbi Chiya entered and found him weeping. "My Master!" exclaimed Rabbi Chiya, "Why do you weep? Was it not taught, 'If one dies smiling, it is a good sign for him; while weeping, it is a bad sign for him. . .'?"

Rabbi [Judah] replied, "I weep because of [my inability to study] the Torah and [observe] the commandments [after death]."

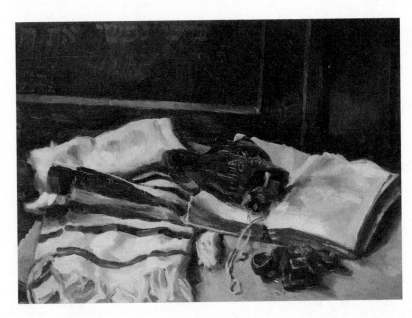

◄ "PRAISE THE L-RD, MY SOUL!" [PSALMS 104:1–2]
Ludwig Meidner, oil on board, Cologne, Germany, c. 1936–1937. (Jewish Museum der Stadt Frankfurt am Main)

V. LIFE BEYOND DEATH

In a way, our study of Judaism's approach to death holds greater significance for living life than for digesting demise. For a start, the ideas we presented impact and enhance life— because they reduce or even eliminate the fear of death. But there's a lot more to it than that. As we will demonstrate, these concepts are highly relevant to the choices that fill our daily existence.

TEXT 13

THE IMMORTALS

TALMUD, BERACHOT 18A

אֵלוּ צַדִּיקִים, שֶׁבְּמִיתָתָן נִקְרְאוּ חַיִּים.

After their demise, *tsadikim* [righteous people] are referred to as being alive.

THERE'S MORE...

For a related text, see Text 20 (in the Appendix section of this lesson), on p. 30.

QUESTION

What might be the Talmud's definition of "alive" in the above statement?

TEXT 14

SPIRITUAL LIFE

RABBI SHNE'UR ZALMAN
OF LIADI, *TANYA, IGERET
HAKODESH* 27

**RABBI SHNE'UR ZALMAN OF LIADI
(ALTER REBBE) 1745–1812**

Chasidic rebbe, halachic authority,
and founder of the Chabad
movement. The Alter Rebbe was
born in Liozna, Belarus, and was
among the principal students
of the Magid of Mezeritch. His
numerous works include the
Tanya, an early classic containing
the fundamentals of Chabad
Chasidism; and *Shulchan
Aruch HaRav*, an expanded and
reworked code of Jewish law.

שֶׁחַיֵּי הַצַּדִּיק אֵינָם חַיִּים בְּשָׂרִיִּים כִּי אִם חַיִּים
רוּחָנִיִּים, שֶׁהֵם אֱמוּנָה וְיִרְאָה וְאַהֲבָה.

כִּי בָּאֱמוּנָה כְּתִיב, "וְצַדִּיק בֶּאֱמוּנָתוֹ יִחְיֶה" (חֲבַקּוּק ב, ד);

וּבְיִרְאָה כְּתִיב, "וְיִרְאַת ה' לְחַיִּים" (מִשְׁלֵי יט, כג);

וּבְאַהֲבָה כְּתִיב, "רוֹדֵף צְדָקָה וָחֶסֶד יִמְצָא חַיִּים"
(מִשְׁלֵי כא, כא), וְחֶסֶד הוּא אַהֲבָה.

The life of the *tsadik* [righteous person] is not
corporeal but spiritual, consisting of faith,
reverence, and love [of G-d. This reality is
reflected in the following passages]:

Of faith it is stated (HABAKKUK 2:4):
"The *tsadik* lives by his faith."

Of reverence it is stated (PROVERBS 19:23):
"Reverence of G-d produces life."

Of love it is stated (IBID. 21:21): "He who
pursues charity and kindness will find
life"; and kindness is [rooted in] love.

How does death affect the way we
live? *Rabbi Manis Friedman* has a
2-minute explanation: *myJLI.com/soul*

TEXT 15

THE LIFE OF THE MATTER

RABBI SHALOM DOVBER
SCHNEERSOHN, *SEFER
HAMAAMARIM* 5670, P. 19

**RABBI SHALOM DOVBER SCHNEERSOHN
(RASHAB) 1860–1920**

Chasidic rebbe. Rabbi Shalom
Dovber became the 5th leader
of the Chabad movement
upon the passing of his father,
Rabbi Shmuel Schneersohn.
He established the Lubavitch
network of *yeshivot* called Tomchei
Temimim. He authored many
volumes of Chasidic discourses
and is renowned for his lucid
and thorough explanations
of kabbalistic concepts.

Can we transcend death? *Rabbi
Naftali Silberberg* explains how
we do so in "Attaining Immortality":
myJLI.com/soul

"רְאֵה נָתַתִּי לְפָנֶיךָ אֶת הַחַיִּים וְאֶת הַטּוֹב וְאֶת כו'" (דְּבָרִים ל, טו וְאֵילָךְ).

דְּפֵירוּשׁ "חַיִּים" וּ"מָוֶת" אֵין הַכַּוָּונָה בְּחַיִּים בָּעֵת שֶׁהַנִּבְרָא חַי, וּמָוֶת הוּא לְאַחַר פֵּירוּד הַחַיּוּת כו', דְּמִי זֶה פֶּתִי לֹא יִבְחַר בַּחַיִּים כו'?

רַק הַכַּוָּונָה שֶׁבְּכָל דָּבָר נִבְרָא, בָּעֵת שֶׁהוּא בְּחַיּוּתוֹ וְקִיּוּמוֹ, יֵשׁ בּוֹ חַיִּים וּמָוֶת. וְהוּא, שֶׁגַּשְׁמִיּוּת הַדָּבָר וְחוּמְרִיּוּתוֹ הוּא מָוֶת בְּעַצֶם, דְּהַיְינוּ שֶׁהוּא כָּלֶה וְנִפְסָד, וְכַאֲשֶׁר רוֹאֶה הָאָדָם הֶפְסֵד כָּל דָּבָר גַּשְׁמִי, וְכַאֲשֶׁר מַרְגִּישׁ גַּם בְּעַצְמוֹ כִּלְיוֹן הַכֹּחוֹת הַגּוּפָנִיִּים שֶׁלּוֹ שֶׁכָּלִים וְנִפְסָדִים מִזְּמַן לִזְמַן כו', וְהָרוּחָנִיּוּת וְהַכֹּחַ הָאֱלֹקִי הוּא הַחַיִּים שֶׁאֵין בָּזֶה כִּלָּיוֹן וְהֶפְסֵד חַס וְשָׁלוֹם, כִּי אִם הוּא בִּבְחִינַת קִיּוּם נִצְחִי כו'.

"Behold, I have set before you today life and goodness and [death and evil. . . . Choose life]!" (DEUTERONOMY 30:15, 19)

The term "life" in this verse does not refer to corporeal life, nor does "death" refer to the result of the soul's departure. For which simpleton needs to be instructed to choose to live?

Rather, each creation, while alive and fully existent, contains both life and death. The physicality of the object is intrinsically lifeless; it is in a constant state of decline and deterioration. We observe this decline in every physical object, as well as in ourselves—our physical capabilities and powers weaken with time.

By contrast, the spiritual and divine within each thing is alive, eternal, and not subject to destruction or deterioration, G-d forbid.

THERE'S MORE...

For a related text, see Text 21 (in the Appendix section of this lesson) on p. 31.

EXERCISE 1.2

1. Record one point from today's lesson that resonates with you most personally.

   _____

   _____

2. Identify an adjustment that you can introduce to your life for the sake of living in a manner that is more "alive" and consistent with your immortal soul.

   _____

   _____

◀ **STILL LIFE WITH A BOTTLE OF BENEDICTINE**
Mark Gertler, oil on canvas, 1908.
(Ben Uri Gallery, London)

KEY POINTS

1 The awareness of our mortality and the resulting natural fear of death influence many elements of our psyche, behavior, and life choices. Our perspective on death influences multiple areas of our lives.

2 The *neshamah* (human soul), the true essence of the human being, is eternal; it precedes the body and continues to exist after the body is gone. While still in Heaven, it does not desire to descend into a body, and when the time of death arrives, it resumes its native spiritual state.

3 The fact that the briefest spiritual experience of the next world is more *pleasurable* than all of this world does not diminish the reality that even a brief stay in this world is more *important* than all of the next. Therefore, Jewish law gives precedence to preserving life over nearly every mitzvah.

4 This perspective allows us to appreciate and value life—without fear of death.

5 While our corporeal needs and endeavors die with the body, our soul-focused aspirations and actions live on eternally. Thus, when we live and identify with eternal values, our current life continues even after the body's demise.

APPENDIX A

TEXT 16

BALANCED GRIEF

RABBI DAVID IBN ZIMRA,
METSUDAT DAVID, MITZVAH 70

**RABBI DAVID IBN ZIMRA
(RADVAZ) 1479–1573**

Noted halachist. Radvaz was born
in Spain and immigrated to Safed,
Israel, upon the expulsion of the
Jews from Spain in 1492. In 1513,
he moved to Egypt and served
as rabbi, judge, and head of the
yeshiva in Cairo. He also ran many
successful business ventures and
was independently wealthy. In
1553, he returned to Safed where he
would later be buried. He authored
what would later become a classic
commentary to Maimonides's
code of law, and wrote many
halachic responsa, of which more
than 10,000 are still extant.

וְטַעַם הַשְּׁרִיטָה עַל הַמֵּת לְפִי הַפְּשַׁט, כִּי הָעוֹשֶׂה מַעֲשֶׂה בָּזֶה
מוֹרֶה שֶׁאֵין לַמֵּת הַשְׁאָרַת הַנֶּפֶשׁ.
וְעוֹד, כִּי אֵין רָאוּי לְבַעַל הַשֵּׂכֶל וְהַתּוֹרָה
לְהִצְטַעֵר עַל מַעֲשֵׂה הָאֵ-ל וּמִשְׁפָּטָיו יוֹתֵר מִדַּאי.
וְכֵן אָמְרוּ רַזַ"ל, שֶׁאֵין לְהִתְאַבֵּל יוֹתֵר מִדַּאי,
וְזֶה דֶּרֶךְ הַגּוֹיִם שֶׁאֵינָם מַאֲמִינִים בְּהַשְׁאָרַת הַנֶּפֶשׁ.
וְרָאִיתִי הַיִּשְׁמְעֵאלִים מַרְחִיקִים דָּבָר זֶה הַרְבֵּה,
וַאֲפִילוּ הַקְּרִיעָה עַל הַמֵּת אוֹסְרִים.
וְהַמִּדָּה וְהַדֶּרֶךְ הַמְּמוּצָע לְעוֹלָם הוּא טוֹב כַּאֲשֶׁר כָּתַבְנוּ.
וּלְפִיכָךְ רָאוּי לְהִתְאַבֵּל אֲבֵילוּת מְמוּצָע.

The most basic understanding of the Torah's
prohibition against self-mutilation in response to a
loved one's passing is that such a reaction demonstrates
lack of belief in the soul's immortality. (Besides, it is
improper for an intelligent person who has studied
the Torah to be exceedingly pained over G-d's ways
and decisions.) Therefore, our sages cautioned against
excessive mourning, for such is the convention of
the nations who do not believe in the eternal nature
of the soul.

I have personally observed that the Ishmaelites
disproportionately oppose [displays of mourning],
to the extent of forbidding the rending of garments
[in grief].

TEXT 16 CONTINUED

The proper approach, however, is always the middle path: it is proper to mourn—but not excessively.

◀ **JEWS MOURNING IN A SYNAGOGUE**
Sir William Rothenstein, oil on canvas, 1906.
(Tate Galleries, U.K.)

APPENDIX B

One element of the fear of death that we have not explored in today's lesson is the fear of *premature* passing. Some are afraid of leaving this world too early, or fear that someone they care for deeply will die prematurely. This apprehension is addressed by the following texts:

TEXT 17A

AT THE RIGHT TIME

ECCLESIASTES 3:1–2

לַכֹּל זְמַן וְעֵת לְכָל חֵפֶץ תַּחַת הַשָּׁמָיִם.

עֵת לָלֶדֶת וְעֵת לָמוּת.

Everything has an appointed season,
and everything under the Heaven has a time.

[There is] a time to be born and a time to die.

TEXT 17B

PREORDAINED LIFESPANS

MIDRASH, *KOHELET RABAH* 3:4

KOHELET RABAH

A Midrashic text on the Book of Ecclesiastes. Midrash is the designation of a particular genre of rabbinic literature. The term "Midrash" is derived from the root *d-r-sh,* which means "to search," "to examine," and "to investigate." This particular Midrash provides textual exegeses and develops and illustrates moral principles. It was first published in Pesaro, Italy, in 1519, together with 4 other Midrashic works on the other 4 biblical *Megilot*.

"עֵת לָלֶדֶת", מֵעֵת לָלֶדֶת הִיא "עֵת לָמוּת". מִשָּׁעָה שֶׁאָדָם נוֹלָד הוּא נִגְזָר עָלָיו כַּמָּה שָׁנִים יִחְיֶה.

A time to be born and a time to die: From the time of birth, there already is a time to die, meaning that from the moment of birth, it is already determined how many years a person is destined to live.

JEWISH FAMILY ▶
Mark Gertler, oil on canvas, 1913.
(Tate Galleries, U.K.)

TEXT 18

SOLELY IN
G-D'S HANDS

RABBI BACHYA IBN PAKUDAH,
*DUTIES OF THE HEART, SHAAR
YICHUD HAMAASEH*, CH. 2

**RABBI BACHYA IBN PAKUDAH
11TH CENTURY**

Moral philosopher and author.
Ibn Pakudah lived in Muslim
Spain, but little else is known
about his life. *Chovot Halevavot*
(*Duties of the Heart*), his major
work, was intended to be a
guide for attaining spiritual
perfection. Originally written in
Judeo-Arabic and published in
1080, it was later translated into
Hebrew and published in 1161 by
Judah ibn Tibbon, a scion of the
famous family of translators. Ibn
Pakudah had a strong influence
on Jewish pietistic literature.

שֶׁיַּאֲמִין, כִּי הַתּוֹעֶלֶת וְהַנֶּזֶק אֵינָם בְּיָד (בַּעֲצַת) נִבְרָא
וְלֹא בִּיכָלְתּוֹ מִבִּלְתִּי רְשׁוּת הַבּוֹרֵא.

We believe that no created being has the ability
to benefit or harm us without the permission of
the Creator.

TEXT 19

"WHO SHALL LIVE AND WHO SHALL DIE"

UNETANEH TOKEF, HIGH HOLIDAY *MUSAF* LITURGY

בְּרֹאשׁ הַשָּׁנָה יִכָּתֵבוּן וּבְיוֹם צוֹם כִּפּוּר יֵחָתֵמוּן:

כַּמָה יַעַבְרוּן וְכַמָה יִבָּרֵאוּן,

מִי יִחְיֶה וּמִי יָמוּת,

מִי בְקִצּוֹ וּמִי לֹא בְקִצּוֹ,

מִי בַמַּיִם וּמִי בָאֵשׁ,

מִי בַחֶרֶב וּמִי בַחַיָּה,

מִי בָרָעָב וּמִי בַצָּמָא,

מִי בָרַעַשׁ וּמִי בַמַּגֵּפָה,

מִי בַחֲנִיקָה וּמִי בַסְּקִילָה.

מִי יָנוּחַ וּמִי יָנוּעַ, מִי יִשָּׁקֵט וּמִי יִטָּרֵף, מִי יִשָּׁלֵו וּמִי יִתְיַסָּר, מִי יֵעָנִי וּמִי יֵעָשֵׁר, מִי יִשָּׁפֵל וּמִי יָרוּם.

On Rosh Hashanah, it is inscribed [in Heaven], and on the fast of Yom Kippur, it is sealed:

How many shall depart and how many shall be born,

Who shall live and who shall die,

Who shall leave at his allotted time and who shall depart prematurely;

Who [shall perish] by water and who by fire,

Who by sword and who by wild beast,

Who by hunger and who by thirst,

Who by earthquake and who by disease,

Who by strangulation and who by lapidation.

Who shall be at rest and who shall wander;

Who shall be tranquil and who shall be harassed;

Who shall enjoy well-being and who shall suffer tribulation;

Who shall be poor and who shall be rich;

Who shall be humbled and who shall be exalted.

▼ **THE DAY OF ATONEMENT**
Jacob Kramer, pencil, brush, and ink on paper, U.K., 1919. (Ben Uri Gallery, London)

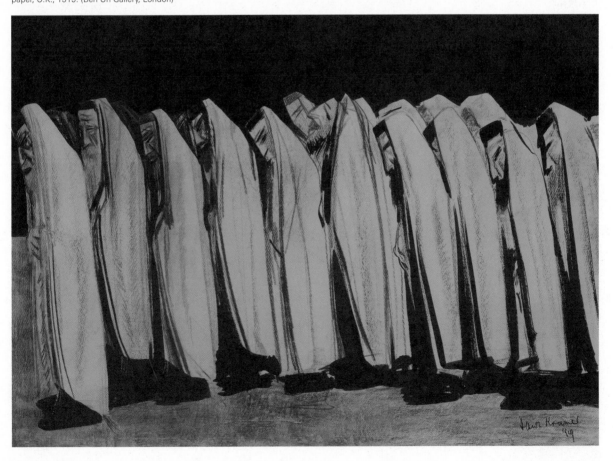

APPENDIX C

TEXT 20

WHEN TIME RUNS OUT

MIDRASH HAGADOL,
GENESIS 47:29

MIDRASH HAGADOL

A Midrashic work on the 5 books of the Pentateuch. Midrash is the designation of a particular genre of rabbinic literature usually forming a running commentary on specific books of the Bible. *Midrash Hagadol* quotes widely from Talmud and other earlier Midrashic works, serving as a valuable resource to reconstruct lost sections of Midrash. A traveler, Yaakov Sapir, first discovered the anonymous Midrash in Yemen in the middle of the 19th century. Some ascribe it to Rabbi Avraham, son of Maimonides.

"וַיִּקְרְבוּ יְמֵי יִשְׂרָאֵל" (בְּרֵאשִׁית מז, כט). רַבִּי שִׁמְעוֹן בֶּן לָקִישׁ אוֹמֵר: יְמוֹתֵיהֶן שֶׁל צַדִּיקִים מֵתִין וְהֵן אֵינָן מֵתִין. מַאי טַעֲמָא? "וַיִּקְרַב יִשְׂרָאֵל לָמוּת" אֵין כְּתִיב, אֶלָּא "וַיִּקְרְבוּ יְמֵי יִשְׂרָאֵל לָמוּת". וְכֵן בְּדָוִד: "וַיִּקְרְבוּ יְמֵי דָוִד לָמוּת" (מְלָכִים א, ב, א). וְכֵן בְּמֹשֶׁה: "הֵן קָרְבוּ יָמֶיךָ לָמוּת" (דְּבָרִים לא, יד).

"The days of Israel neared death" (GENESIS 47:29). Said Rabbi Shimon ben Lakish: The *days* of the righteous die, but they themselves do not die. This is indicated by this verse, which does not say that "Israel neared death," but that Israel's *days* neared death. A similar statement is made regarding David, "The days of David neared death" (I KINGS 2:1), and also regarding Moses, "[G-d told Moses,] 'Behold, your days are nearing death'" (DEUTERONOMY 31:14).

APPENDIX D

TEXT 21

HEAVEN ON EARTH

THE REBBE, RABBI MENACHEM
MENDEL SCHNEERSON, *TORAT
MENACHEM* 5715:1 (13), PP. 67–68

**RABBI MENACHEM MENDEL SCHNEERSON
1902–1994**

The towering Jewish leader of
the 20th century, known as "the
Lubavitcher Rebbe," or simply as
"the Rebbe." Born in southern
Ukraine, the Rebbe escaped
Nazi-occupied Europe, arriving in
the U.S. in June 1941. The Rebbe
inspired and guided the revival
of traditional Judaism after the
European devastation, impacting
virtually every Jewish community
the world over. The Rebbe often
emphasized that the performance
of just one additional good deed
could usher in the era of Mashiach.
The Rebbe's scholarly talks and
writings have been printed in
more than 200 volumes.

כְּתִיב (בְּרֵאשִׁית לג, יז), "וּלְמִקְנֵהוּ עָשָׂה סֻכֹּת". "מִקְנֵהוּ" - הֵם דְּבָרִים
הַנִּקְנִים ("אַיינגֶעקוֹיפְטעֶ זַאכְן"), דְּהַיְינוּ, כָּל הַדְּבָרִים הַגַּשְׁמִיִּים שֶׁהַנְּשָׁמָה
מִצַּד עַצְמָהּ אֵין לָהּ שׁוּם שַׁיָּיכוּת אֲלֵיהֶם, אֶלָּא שֶׁ"נִקְנוּ" וְנִיתוֹסְפוּ אֵצֶל הַנְּשָׁמָה
("אַ צוּגעֶקוּמעֶנעֶ זַאךְ") עַל יְדֵי יְרִידָתָהּ בְּגוּף. וְעַל זֶה נֶאֱמַר "וּלְמִקְנֵהוּ עָשָׂה
סֻכֹּת" - שֶׁכָּל הָעִנְיָנִים הַגַּשְׁמִיִּים צְרִיכִים לִהְיוֹת בְּאוֹפֶן דְּ"סֻכֹּת", בְּדֶרֶךְ
עֲרָאִי בִּלְבַד, וּכְמַאֲמַר רַז"ל "הָעוֹלָם הַזֶּה דּוֹמֶה לַפְּרוֹזְדוֹר בִּפְנֵי הָעוֹלָם הַבָּא,
הַתְקֵן עַצְמְךָ בַּפְּרוֹזְדוֹר כְּדֵי שֶׁתִּכָּנֵס לַטְּרַקְלִין", דְּהַיְינוּ שֶׁכָּל עוֹלָם הַזֶּה אֵינוֹ
אֶלָּא כִּ"פְּרוֹזְדוֹר".

וּמַה שֶּׁכָּתוּב "כְּדֵי שֶׁתִּכָּנֵס לַטְּרַקְלִין" - אֵין הַכַּוָּונָה לְאַחֲרֵי מֵאָה וְעֶשְׂרִים שָׁנָה
דַּוְוקָא, אֶלָּא עַל דֶּרֶךְ מַאֲמַר רַז"ל "עוֹלָמְךָ תִּרְאֶה בְּחַיֶּיךָ", דְּהַיְינוּ שֶׁכַּאֲשֶׁר הָאָדָם
נִמְצָא כָּאן לְמַטָּה צְרִיכִים הַדְּבָרִים הַגַּשְׁמִיִּים לִהְיוֹת אֶצְלוֹ בְּאוֹפֶן שֶׁל "אַרְעַי".

"Jacob constructed temporary huts for his cattle"
(GENESIS 33:17). The Hebrew term for cattle,
miknehu, also translates as "acquisitions" and refers
to all material things to which the soul has no innate
connection but are considered "acquired" as a result of
the soul entering a corporeal body. The verse teaches
us that we must make "temporary huts" for all these
acquisitions—we must treat all material matters as
fleeting. This is in accordance with the teaching of our
sages, "This world is like a corridor before the World
to Come. Prepare yourself in the corridor, so that you
may enter the palace."

TEXT 21 CONTINUED

It should be noted, however, that the phrase "so that you may enter the palace" does not necessarily refer to "after 120 years." Rather, as our sages tell us, it is possible for one to experience the hereafter while still alive. This is accomplished by considering all physical matters as "temporary" [and not of primary importance] even while living a mortal life.

◀ UNTITLED [CAPTIVE/FIGURE OF THIS WORLD—NEXT WORLD]
Paul Klee, oil and colored paste on primed burlap on burlap, Basel, Switzerland, c. 1940. (Fondation Beyeler, Basel)

ADDITIONAL READINGS

ESSENCE AND EXPRESSION

BY RABBI YANKI TAUBER

RABBI YANKI TAUBER
1965–

Chasidic scholar and author. A native of Brooklyn, N.Y., Rabbi Tauber is an internationally renowned author who specializes in adapting the teachings of the Lubavitcher Rebbe. He is a member of the JLI curriculum development team and has written numerous articles and books, including *Once Upon a Chassid* and *Beyond the Letter of the Law.*

Rabbi Yaakov would say: This world is compared to an antechamber before the world to come. Prepare yourself in the antechamber, so that you may enter the banquet hall.

He would also say: A single moment of repentance and good deeds in this world is greater than all of the world to come. And a single moment of bliss in the world to come is greater than all of this world.

—*Ethics of the Fathers, 4:16–17*

The Talmud relates that Rabbi Yaakov once witnessed the tragic death of a young man who, at that very moment, was engaged in fulfilling the very two *mitzvot* for which the Torah promises "long life."

"Honor your father and your mother," reads the fifth of Ten Commandments, "that your days be lengthened, and that good befall you."[1] The other *mitzvah* for which the Torah specifically promises reward is *shiluach hakan* ("dispatching the nest"): "If you happen upon a bird's nest . . . and the mother bird is sitting upon the young or upon the eggs, do not take the mother bird along with the young. Send away the mother bird, and you may then take the young for yourself, that good may befall you and that your days be lengthened."[2]

And yet, here was a man who was fulfilling both these commandments simultaneously. At his father's request, he had climbed a ladder to chase away a mother bird from her nest and collect the chicks. But no sooner had he done so that he slipped from the ladder and fell to his death.

"Where are this person's 'long days'?" asked Rabbi Yaakov. "Where is the 'good' he was promised? But, when the Torah says 'that your days be lengthened,' it is referring to a world that is wholly long; when the Torah says 'that good befall you,' it is referring to a world that is wholly good."[3]

"Rabbi Yaakov," concludes the Talmud, "is of the opinion that there is no reward for *mitzvot* in this world"—a view expressed in the *Ethics* by Rabbi Tarfon ("Know, that the reward of the righteous is in the World to Come"[4]) and reiterated by Maimonides in his codification of Torah law, the *Mishneh Torah.*[5]

Another talmudic sage, Rabbi Joshua ben Levi, quotes the verse "You shall keep the *mitzvah,* the decrees, and the laws, which I command you today to do them"[6]— "today to do them," Rabbi Joshua reads in the verse's meaning, "and not to do them tomorrow; today to do them, and tomorrow to receive their reward."[7]

In other words, the "present world" and "the world to come"

represent two entirely different modes of existence, which, for some reason, must each be confined to a world all its own. Our present existence is the environment for the deed and achievement, but lacks the possibility to enjoy the fruits of our labor. On the other hand, the "world to come" is a world of ultimate reward, bliss, and perfection, but one that precludes any further achievement on the part of man. The Talmud goes so far as to quote the verse, "There will come years of which you will say: I have no desire in them,"[8] and declare: "This refers to the days of the Messianic Era, in which there is neither merit nor obligation."[9]

Why this dichotomy? On the most basic level, this is a function of G-d's granting freedom of choice to man, without which our deeds would be devoid of moral significance. A world in which the benefits of obeying the Almighty's commandments are self-evident would obviously lack the challenge and the sacrifice which makes their observance worthy of reward. So in this world G-d created an environment in which neither He nor the divine nature of His commandments are openly manifest. A world in which surface appearances shroud and distort the divine truth—a world in which people engaged in life-lengthening *mitzvot* fall off ladders—challenging us to choose between good and evil, between faithfulness to our mission in life and its corruption. Only such a world can serve as the arena for meaningful accomplishment.

The Physics of Will

However, our material world's concealment of the divine truth is much more than an orchestrated moral challenge. On a deeper level, this concealment is significant to the nature of the *mitzvot* themselves.

The *mitzvot* are primarily physical deeds performed with physical objects: animal hides are fashioned into *tefillin* and wrapped around one's head and arm; flour and water become the instrument of a *mitzvah* in the form of the *matzah* eaten on Passover; a ram's horn is sounded on Rosh Hashanah; a citron and palm frond are taken on Sukkot. For the physical world is ultimately the most appropriate environment for the function of the *mitzvah* to be realized.

"*Mitzvot* relate to the very essence of G-d"[10] is a mainstay of chassidic teaching. But the very notion of something relating to another thing's essence is a philosophical oxymoron. The "essence" of something is the thing itself, as opposed to the manner in which it affects and is perceived by that which is outside of it. Hence the axiom: "The essence of a thing does not express itself or extend itself"[11] In other words, if you see it, it is not the thing itself that you see, only the manner in which it reflects light and imprints an image on your retina; if you understand it, then it is not the thing itself that you comprehend, only a concept that your mind has pieced together by studying its effect on other things, and so on.

Nevertheless, G-d desired to project His essence into the created reality. This is the function of the *mitzvot*: through observing His commandments and fulfilling His will, we "bring" the very essence of G-d into our lives. And this is why He chose the physical object as the medium of the *mitzvah's* implementation. Spiritual entities (e.g., ideas, feelings, etc.) intrinsically point to a source, a cause, a greater reality which they express and serve. Unlike the physical, whose deeper significance is buried deep beneath the surface of its corporeality, the spiritual readily serves as the expression of a higher truth. The spiritual is thus the natural medium for the various *expressions* of the divine reality that G-d chose to convey to us.

But when it comes to the projection of G-d's *essence,* the very "virtues" of the spiritual disqualify it: its capacity to convey, to reveal, to manifest, runs contrary to the introvertive nature of "essence." Here, the physical object, the most non-transcendental element of G-d's creation, is the most ideal vehicle for G-d's essence—capturing *mitzvot.*

A physical object merely *is:* "I am," it proclaims, "and my being is wholly defined by its own existence." As such, the physical object constitutes the greatest concealment of the divine truth.[12] Precisely for this reason, it is G-d's medium of choice for man's implementation of His will.

In other words, the object of the *mitzvah* is not a "manifestation" of the Divine. Were it to reflect Him in any way, were it to reveal anything of the "nature" of His reality, it would, by definition, fail to capture

His essence. But capture His essence it does, simply because He willed it to. G-d, of course, could have willed anything (including a manifest expression of His reality) to convey His essence, but He chose a medium that is most appropriate according to logical laws he established in creating our reality—a reality in which "essence" and "expression" are antithetical to each other. He therefore chose the material world, with its virtual blackout on any revealed expression of G-dliness, to serve as the "tool" with which we perform the *mitzvot* and thereby relate to His essence.

Better for Whom

"The reward of a *mitzvah* is a *mitzvah*,"[13] say our sages. For all pleasures and satisfactions (indeed, the very concepts of pleasure and satisfaction) were created by G-d. So what greater delight can there be than to experience the divine essence, the source of all pleasure? Were it possible for a human being to perceive what transpires each time he fulfills G-d's will in his daily life, he would experience the very essence of bliss.

But the very nature of what is accomplished by the performance of a *mitzvah* precludes the possibility of such "reward": as explained above, the concealment of the divine reality which categorizes our material-bound existence is what makes it the appropriate medium for the drawing down of G-d's essence. Reward can only come in a future world, a world that reveals rather than obscures its Creator. And yet, the world to come, precisely because of its manifest G-dliness, can serve only as the environment for the reward of the *mitzvah* but not for its implementation.

Thus, Rabbi Yaakov states in our *mishnah*: "A single moment of repentance and good deeds in this world is greater than all of the world to come. And a single moment of bliss in the world to come is greater than all of the present world."

Regarding the Almighty's purpose in creation—the drawing down of His essence into the physical creation[14]—a single positive act on the part of man is more meaningful than all the bliss experienced in the world to come. Yet the performer of the *mitzvah* remains in the dark. Although he may be aware of the value of what he is doing, he is unable to perceive it and experience it. On the experiential level, a single moment of bliss in the world to come is greater than all the joys of our present world.

The Banquet Hall

In light of this, one may ask: why bother with the reward at all? If G-d's purpose in creation is realized in our present-day lives, of what significance is our personal satisfaction?

One possible answer is that the need for a world to come is a function of G-d's commitment to justice and fairness. In the words of our sages, "G-d does not deprive any creature of its due."[15] If a man is instrumental in satisfying G-d's desire in creation, he deserves the satisfaction of enjoying the fruits of his labor.[16]

But this certainly does not describe the ultimate significance of the world to come. Rabbi Yaakov prefaces his above-quoted saying by comparing our world to an antechamber leading to the banquet hall, which is the world to come. Clearly, then, the World to Come is not a footnote to our world, but its purpose and goal, a theme that is reiterated by many sayings by our sages.

How, then, do we reconcile this with the concept that "the essence of a thing does not express itself or extend itself"? And that it is, therefore, our present world, *because* of its spiritual darkness and inexpressiveness that facilitates the drawing down of G-d's essence and thereby realizes His purpose in creation?

Truly Him and Truly Here

In applying terms such as "essence" and "expression" to the Almighty, we must bear in mind that it is He who created logic and its laws. Obviously, He is not governed or limited by any rational "axioms."

Nevertheless, He wishes to relate to our world as it is. So He chooses to make His relationship with us consistent with the basic "truths" that define our reality.

Indeed, since the purpose of creation is that the divine essence be drawn down into the physical reality, the objective is to do so on its (the physical reality's) terms, not by overriding them. So if the logical laws that govern our reality dictate that "expression" is incompatible with "essence," our bringing G-dliness into the world is to be achieved "blindly," without any perceptible manifestations of the divine essence.

On the other hand, however, if G-d's essence is truly to enter our reality, He must enter it as He is, without hindrance or inhibition. If *His* reality tolerates no limits or definitions, "revelation" must be no less conducive to His essence than "concealment."

In other words, for Him to be here implies two (seemingly contradictory) truths: if He is to be truly *here,* then His presence must be consistent with our reality; yet if it is truly *He* who is here, He must be here on His terms.

This is why the created existence has two distinct components: the present world and the world to come—the process and its culmination. The process of drawing down the divine essence into the created reality is carried out under an obscuring veil of corporeality, in keeping with the created rule that "the essence of a thing does not express itself or extend itself." At the same time, the product and end result of this process is a world in which G-d is uninhibitedly present, in which also the *expressions* of His reality fully convey the quintessence of His being.[17]

Beyond the Letter of the Law (Brooklyn, N.Y.: Vaad Hanochos Hatmimim, 1995), pp. 201–209.

Reprinted with permission of the publisher

Endnotes

1 Deuteronomy 5:16.

2 Deuteronomy 22:6–7.

3 Talmud, Kiddushin 39b.

4 *Ethics of the Fathers*, 2:16.

5 Mishneh Torah, Laws of Repentance 9:1.

6 Deuteronomy 7:11.

7 Talmud, *Eruvin* 22a.

8 Ecclesiastes 12:1.

9 Talmud, *Shabbat* 151b.

10 *Torat Shalom* pg. 190, see also *Tanya*, part IV, section 20.

11 *Guide for the Perplexed*, quoted in *Ki Shemesh U'magen* 5692.

12 Ultimately, however, this "I am, period" quality of the physical reflects on the wholly self-contained quintessence of its Creator. So while the most immediate function of the physical is to obscure the divine truth, a deeper contemplation of its qualities will yield insight into the very beingness of G-d, something that no spiritual expression of Him can convey. (It is told that following the Rosh Hashanah prayers one year, Rabbi Schneur Zalman of Liadi asked his son, Rabbi DovBer: "What did you think of during your prayers?" Rabbi DovBer replied that he had contemplated the meaning of the passage, "and every stature shall bow before You"—how the most lofty supernal worlds and spiritual creations negate themselves before the infinite majesty of G-d. "And you, father," Rabbi DovBer then asked, "with what thought did you pray?" Replied Rabbi Schneur Zalman: "I contemplated the table at which I stood.")

13 *Ethics of the Fathers* 4:2.

14 See *Wood Submerged in Stone*, pgs. 92–94; *Debating Truths*, pgs. 275–284.

15 *Midrash Mechilta*, Exodus 20:30.

16 See *The Resurrection of the Dead* on pg. 212.

17 Based on an address by the Rebbe, Tammuz 12, 5719 (July 18, 1959).

ETHICS FROM SINAI

BY RABBI IRVING M. BUNIM

RABBI IRVING M. BUNIM

1901–1980

Scholar and philanthropist. Rabbi Bunim was a prominent lay leader in the American Orthodox Jewish community. In the 1930s, he worked to establish the Young Israel movement, and over his lifetime, he was a major figure in many Jewish educational institutions.

He used to say: Better, finer is one hour [spent] in repentance and good deeds in this world than all of life in the world-to-come; and better, finer is one hour of spiritual pleasure in the world-to-come than all of life in this world.

R. Jacob goes on with his contemplation of the known world here on earth and the spiritual world-to-come, to consider how they compare and how they interrelate. This *mishnah* is thus a direct continuation of the previous one.

If this world is merely a foyer or waiting-room, a place to prepare and make ready, and the Hereafter is the great banquet hall, we might well assume that life on earth is of far lesser importance, not to be regarded or valued too highly. If R. Jacob has created any such impression through his first teaching, he corrects it now. True enough, for sheer spiritual bliss and thorough-going reward, the world-to-come is incomparably superior. But this world of ours has one overriding importance of its own: Only here is man able to will and act, to achieve, to repent and change for the better; in short, to develop and grow in spiritual maturity. "Whatever your hand finds to do by your strength," says Solomon the wise, "do it; for there is no work or thought, knowledge or wisdom in the nether-world, to which you are going."[1]

It is told that in his last moments, as he knew death to be approaching shortly, the Gaon of Vilna began to weep. His disciples, gathered by his bedside, could not understand. "O Master," they asked, "you have spent a lifetime preparing for the Hereafter. Now that you are about to enter it, why do you weep?" In reply he pointed to the *tzitzith*, the fringes at the four corners of a special white garment *(arba canfoth)* that he constantly wore. "This garment," he said, "I bought for such a little bit of money. Yet by wearing it each day, I was able to fulfill such precious *mitzvoth*. In the world-to-come, even so simple a deed will not be possible. I weep, for I will be deprived of any further chance for *mitzvoth*."

The Hereafter provides indescribable bliss, but it is a passive realm. There is no further chance for initiative, for conscious arousal to strive and achieve. The Midrash tells that ultimately, when the wicked stand in judgment before the Holy, Blessed One, they will plead, "Permit us, and we will repent." And the Holy One will reply, "You utter fools, the world in which you lived is like a Friday, and this realm is like a Sabbath. If a man does not prepare [food] on Friday, what will he eat on the Sabbath? Shall he then make his preparations on the Sabbath and thus desecrate it? Only one who has made his preparations beforehand can now eat. And do you not know that the world in which you lived is like the shore, while this realm is like the sea? If a man does not prepare for his meals while on shore, what will he eat at sea? Do you not know that this realm is like a wilderness, while the world from which you came is like a settlement? If a man does not prepare [food to take along] from the settlement, what will he eat in the wilderness? Again, the world in which you lived is like a sunny season, while this realm is like the rainy season. If a man does not plow in the sunny months, what will he eat when the rains descend?"[2]

The world-to-come is the realm of incomparable bliss, but this world of ours is the domain of incomparable achievement. Whatever ethereal joy the Hereafter may bring a person, there is one deep satisfaction it cannot give: the satisfaction of overcoming difficulties and making solid achievements. To see oneself grow spiritually, in faith, in religious observance, in Torah study, in deeds of kindness—this brings its own basic joy and contentment. In the Hereafter we can be wafted along on a cloud; in this world we can ourselves scale heights, knowing that our attainments will bring lasting compensation in the after-life.

On one point our Sages are firm and clear: that "there is no reward for a *mitzvah* in this world."[3] Scripture states, "Then you shall keep the commandment and the statutes and the ordinances which I command you this day to do them."[4] And the Talmud tersely comments, "*This day* [you are] *to do them,* but not this day [are you] to receive reward";[5] "you are to do them this day, but receive their reward tomorrow."[6] Again and again is this theme expressed: "The entire recompense of the righteous is held in readiness for them for the world-to-come.[7] The Holy, Blessed One has postponed the reward that the performers of *mitzvoth* receive, so that they should fulfill them in faith and trust."[8] In *Pirke Avoth* itself we learned, "Know that the reward of the righteous is granted them in the world-to-come."[9]

Yet this is in startling contradiction to the countless passages in our Written Torah that distinctly promise a reward of material goods and material well-being for observing the *mitzvoth.* In the *Sh'ma* that the devout Jew recites morning and evening, we read, "If you will carefully heed My commandments which I command

you this day, to love the Lord your G-d and to serve Him with all your heart and all your soul, then will I give the rain for your land in its [proper] season, the autumn rains and the spring rains, that you may gather in your grain, your wine and your oil. And I will make grass grow in your fields for your cattle, and you shall eat and be satisfied."[10] Interpret as we will, neither Heaven nor the Hereafter is mentioned directly here. In its literal meaning, the verse promises the Almighty's recompense in man's everyday life on earth.

First we might note the point that the *Rambam* makes. He concludes that where Scripture promises material rewards, it predicts them not as full and true compensation, but merely as means toward further goals and ends. If the Torah and its precepts are faithfully observed, there will be the kind of material rewards that will promote Torah living further. The rewards will tend to create economic, political, and social conditions in which it will be easier, more convenient to do *mitzvoth* and flourish in religious growth. The *intrinsic,* essential reward for *mitzvoth,* however, remains spiritual bliss in the world-to-come.[11] As the Talmud states specifically about certain *mitzvoth,* "a man enjoys the 'fruits' in this world [in modern terminology, we might say the dividends] while the principle remains for him [to enjoy] in the Hereafter."[12]

Why does the "principle," the core of true reward, remain for the world-to-come? Why is there "no reward for a *mitzvah* in this world"? As we have mentioned elsewhere, there is not enough true pleasure or treasure in this whole wide world for the reward that a *mitzvah* deserves. It is as though a person earns a check, a bank draft for his Divine merit, but there is no bank here on earth with funds enough to honor it. The reward for *mitzvoth* is so great and sublime that it can be given only in the "currency" or "wealth" of the world-to-come.

What is it like, then—we may ask in curiosity—to receive such recompense in the Hereafter? Try as we will, we cannot imagine or comprehend this kind of experience. Just as earthly goods cannot provide this blissful reward, human words and thoughts cannot describe it. When we sleep and perhaps dream, we are totally unaware of the passage of time; when we are awake and conscious, it is impossible for us to *break out* of the dimensions of time and space and become unaware of them. Then how can we perceive anything clear about eternity, a realm in which the laws of time and space do not exist? The *Rambam* gives analogies: A person blind [from birth] can have no concept whatever of color; the deaf can have not the slightest understanding of sound; live fish can never experience fire for they exist in water. Even so can we, living our normal lives here on earth, know nothing of the sublime joy of the Hereafter through the cognition of direct experience.[13] The best we can do is to use simile and metaphor, describing the joys of the Hereafter as "pleasure" or "bliss," concepts that are familiar within our range of experience, although such terms are certainly inaccurate and misleading. Perhaps for this reason our *mishnah* uses the term *korath ruah* to denote the happiness in eternity, rather than the more usual *oneg*: The word *korath* seems to be associated with the root *kar,* "cold"; thus it would suggest a cooling or soothing calmness of spirit, in direct contrast to the excitation of the senses associated with intense pleasure here on earth.

In a similar vein, *Mahzor Vitry* explains: Anger and grief (or deep mourning) are passions designated as "heat"; hence pleasure, satisfaction of spirit is called *korath,* "cooling"; the mind is soothed and calmed by great happiness and joy.

A Talmudic passage comes to mind: "There was a habitual saying always on the lips of Rav: Unlike this world is the world-to-come. In the world-to-come there is neither eating nor drinking, neither conjugal intercourse nor business activity, nor envy, hatred, or heated rivalry. Rather do the righteous sit crowned in glory, enjoying the lustre of the *sh'chinah,* the Divine Presence."[14] Without the needs and appetites that the earthbound human being shares with the animal; without the drive to compete, excel, outdo others; without the destructive emotions of envy and hate— the Hereafter indeed offers a glimpse of unparalleled, unimaginable serenity and soothing tranquility, a vista of a new dimension of bliss.

Better, finer is one hour of repentance and good deeds . . .

Once more we can note that the language of our Sages is not random or haphazard. R. Jacob specifies one hour, one brief span of time: for our tradition teaches that some may achieve immortality, a share of life in the Hereafter, in one hour, while others may have to toil a lifetime.[15] One heroic deed for G-d or man, one impassioned response to a crisis, one act of sincerity and sacrifice that brings blessed consequences, may effect a revolution within; to transform a person's entire character and faith. For ever after his vision may be lifted from this world, from hopes and ambitions centered on material gains, to value morality and spiritual growth. When he wins the key to immortal life, that can well be a man's finest hour.

But let us bear in mind that the reverse is also true. Our Rabbinic tradition records that it was R. Judah haNasi who stated that some may win life in the Hereafter in a brief hour, while others toil for years. And he wept as he said this. In one source we read that he added, "some can toil all their living days and lose their entire reward in one brief hour."[16] This indeed is cause for weeping. How tragic for a person to lose so swiftly, through one heinous act, what he may have toiled a lifetime to achieve.

A further nuance lies in these words of R. Jacob: "Better is one hour of repentance and good deeds *miccol* (than all) life in the world-to-come." The prefix *mi* also has the sense of "deriving from, stemming from."[17] Hence R. Jacob's teaching could connote that an hour of turning to religion and good deeds in this world is superior, when it derives from a realization, an awareness of the reality of life in the Hereafter. The way a man chooses to spend a free hour should reflect an entire way of thought about the value and purpose of his being in the world. It will be truly a fine hour if he makes it a stepping-stone on a clear-cut path through life, determined by an awareness of the Hereafter.

The Midrash gives an apt parable: An old man sat at a fork in the road, where two pathways spread out before him. One began smooth and fine, but eventually became a mass of thorns, cedars, and reeds.

The other was at first nothing but reeds, cedars, and thorns, but eventually it became a smooth path. And so he would warn the passers-by how each pathway ultimately was. Now surely (the Midrash concludes) the passers-by should be grateful to him, that he warned them for their own good, so that they could avoid exhausting [waste of time and energy]. So should mankind be grateful to Solomon, for he sits at the gateways of wisdom and warns . . . "I have seen everything that is done under the sun, and behold, all is vanity and a striving after wind"[18]—everything except repentance and good deeds.[19]

At every free hour that we can spend in leisure, two roads open before us: one, the way of earthly pleasure, immediate gratification, certainly seems smooth and easy; the other is the path of virtue, to serve Heaven and benefit people, and it may seem beset by difficulties like twisted brambles and thorns; to travel such a road may mean much discomfort and sacrifice. But the wise Solomon sums up the value of earthly goals and gains, like the mathematician who writes a long equation on the blackboard, full of complex terms, and then writes at the end: equals zero. Hence R. Jacob advises: It is fine to devote a free hour to religious return and good deeds, knowing that this thorny way leads to the most blessed path of all.

At any rate, here we have evidence, if evidence is needed, that our Sages did not blindly follow popular concepts or ways of thinking. Through the ages the hedonist approach has never lacked a large enthusiastic following. In the words of Scripture, their cry is, "Let us eat and drink, for tomorrow we die."[20] The quatrains of Omar Khayyam echo and re-echo the yearning for the pleasures of wine and love as long as life allows. And in our own day a popular song dinned into our ears the wise counsel: "Enjoy yourself; it's later than you think." Life on this earth, says the hedonist, should be devoted to pleasure (even if it kills you).

As for religious worship and good deeds, the popular idea would be that this is a matter for angels, winged creatures who fly about heaven. If someone wants to explain that he is not really a good person, he says, "I'm no angel." If someone is being coaxed to do something good or kind, he may be urged, "Be an angel." At best, religious devotion and selfless compassionate kindness are expected of someone who lives an "other-worldly" life as a mystic or saint, without mingling in the ordinary activities of ordinary people, feet on the ground.

R. Jacob teaches the very opposite: The place for pleasure is in the Hereafter. Enjoyments on this earth do not begin to compare to the bliss of eternity. And the place for religiosity and deeds of kindness is here on earth. In the Hereafter no one can take the initiative to do *mitzvoth*. You can only obey and reflect the Divine will. The finest way to spend an hour on this earth is to "be an angel," and fulfill His commandments. The best way to spend an hour in the world-to-come is to enjoy yourself, although there it is never later than you think.

Ethics from Sinai (New York: Feldheim Publishers, 1966), pp. 151–156.

Reprinted with permission of the publisher

Endnotes

[1] Ecclesiastes 9:10.
[2] Midrash Mishle, vi; Rabbah, Eccl. i 15; Yalkut Shim'oni II, Mishle § 938.
[3] T.B. Kiddushin 39b, Hullin 142a.
[4] Deuteronomy 7: II.
[5] T.B. Abodah Zarah 3a.
[6] T.B. Erubin 22a.
[7] Midrash Rabbah ii 3.
[8] T.J . Pe'ah i 1.
[9] Avoth ii 21.
[10] Deuteronomy 11: 13–15.
[11] Rambam, *Commentary to the Mishnah*, Sanhedrin x, introduction.
[12] T.B. Shabbath 127a.
[13] Rambam, *Commentary to the Mishnah*, Sanhedrin x, introduction.
[14] T.B. Berakoth 17a.
[15] T.B. Abodah Zarah 10b, 17a, 18a.
[16] Midrash Eleh Ezc'rah, on R. Hanina b. T'radyon (Beth haMidrash II p. 68).
[17] R. Abraham Azulai similarly interprets the prefix here as "because of": An hour of repentance, etc. is fine *because of* all the life in the Hereafter that it will earn.
[18] Ecclesiastes 1: 14.
[19] Midrash Rabbah to *ibid*.
[20] Isaiah 22:13.

Lesson

2

TAKING LEAVE
OUR EVOLVING RELATIONSHIP WITH THE DEPARTED

Is death painful for souls? Is my presence felt when I visit a grave? Judaism's pre-burial and burial rituals accompany the soul's gradual transition from a limiting physical life to a completely spiritual one. We discuss those rituals and how, once freed, the soul's connection to the living continues in new and powerful ways.

▲ TWO HEART
Edvard Munch, colored woodcut, Berlin, 1899. (Tel Aviv Museum)

I. UNTETHERED

This chapter will explore what happens during the interval between the moment a person passes away and interment. While exploring the topic of interment, we will also examine the subject of grave visitation.

A soul's departure from its body signals the onset of a new phase in its journey. It is no longer attached and tethered to the foreign world of materiality; the soul is now free to soar in its native habitat—the spiritual, heavenly realms.

What significance does Judaism give to that fateful moment of transition?

Two letters that were penned by two Chasidic masters—along with an exploration of two of the soul's five components—will allow us to discover the ramifications that the moment of passing carries for the soul itself, as well as for those it leaves behind.

FIGURE 2.1

SOUL COMPONENTS

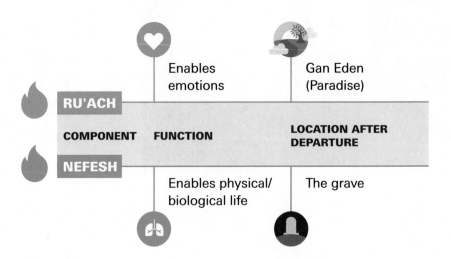

COMPONENT	FUNCTION	LOCATION AFTER DEPARTURE
RU'ACH	Enables emotions	Gan Eden (Paradise)
NEFESH	Enables physical/biological life	The grave

TEXT 1A

ESSENTIAL CONNECTION

RABBI SHNE'UR ZALMAN OF LIADI, *TANYA, IGERET HAKODESH*, CHAPTER 27

RABBI SHNE'UR ZALMAN OF LIADI (ALTER REBBE) 1745–1812

Chasidic rebbe, halachic authority, and founder of the Chabad movement. The Alter Rebbe was born in Liozna, Belarus, and was among the principal students of the Magid of Mezeritch. His numerous works include the *Tanya*, an early classic containing the fundamentals of Chabad Chasidism; and *Shulchan Aruch HaRav*, an expanded and reworked code of Jewish law.

Rabbi Yitzchak Schochet, in "Soul Connection," expounds upon the deceased's continuing relationship with his or her loved ones: *myJLI.com/soul*

כְּנוֹדָע שֶׁחַיֵּי הַצַּדִּיק אֵינָם חַיִּים בְּשָׂרִים כִּי אִם חַיִּים רוּחָנִיִּים, שֶׁהֵם אֱמוּנָה וְיִרְאָה וְאַהֲבָה...

וְהִנֵּה, בִּהְיוֹת הַצַּדִּיק חַי עַל פְּנֵי הָאֲדָמָה, הָיוּ שְׁלֹשָׁה מִדּוֹת אֵלּוּ בְּתוֹךְ כְּלִי וּלְבוּשׁ שֶׁלָּהֶם, בִּבְחִינַת מָקוֹם גַּשְׁמִי, שֶׁהִיא בְּחִינַת נֶפֶשׁ הַקְּשׁוּרָה בְּגוּפוֹ.

וְכָל תַּלְמִידָיו אֵינָם מְקַבְּלִים רַק הֶאָרַת מִדּוֹת אֵלּוּ וְזִיוָן הַמֵּאִיר חוּץ לִכְלִי זֶה עַל יְדֵי דִּבּוּרָיו וּמַחְשְׁבוֹתָיו הַקְּדוֹשִׁים. וְלָכֵן אָמְרוּ רַזַ"ל, שֶׁאֵין אָדָם עוֹמֵד עַל דַּעַת רַבּוֹ, וְכוּ'.

אֲבָל לְאַחַר פְּטִירָתוֹ, לְפִי שֶׁמִּתְפָּרְדִים בְּחִינַת הַנֶּפֶשׁ שֶׁנִּשְׁאֲרָה בַּקֶּבֶר מִבְּחִינַת הָרוּחַ שֶׁבְּגַן עֵדֶן שֶׁהֵן שָׁלֹשׁ מִדּוֹת הַלָּלוּ, לְפִיכָךְ יָכוֹל כָּל הַקָּרוֹב אֵלָיו לְקַבֵּל חֵלֶק מִבְּחִינַת רוּחוֹ שֶׁבְּגַן עֵדֶן, הוֹאִיל וְאֵינָהּ בְּתוֹךְ כְּלִי וְלֹא בִּבְחִינַת מָקוֹם גַּשְׁמִי...

הִלְכָּךְ, נָקֵל מְאֹד לְתַלְמִידָיו לְקַבֵּל חֶלְקָם מִבְּחִינַת רוּחַ רַבָּם הָעַצְמִיִּית, שֶׁהֵם אֱמוּנָתוֹ וְיִרְאָתוֹ וְאַהֲבָתוֹ אֲשֶׁר עָבַד בָּהֶם אֶת ה', וְלֹא זִיוָם בִּלְבַד הַמֵּאִיר חוּץ לַכְּלִי... כָּל אֶחָד כְּפִי בְּחִינַת הִתְקַשְּׁרוּתוֹ וְקִרְבָתוֹ אֵלָיו בְּחַיָּיו וּבְמוֹתוֹ בְּאַהֲבָה רַבָּה, כִּי הַמְשָׁכַת כָּל רוּחָנִיּוּת אֵינָהּ אֶלָּא עַל יְדֵי אַהֲבָה רַבָּה.

As is known, the life of the *tsadik* [righteous person] is not physical but spiritual; it consists of faith, reverence, and love [for G-d]. . . .

During the *tsadik's* lifetime on earth, these three attributes [that belong to the soul dimension of *ru'ach*] are constrained within their container and garb, namely, the *nefesh* that is bound to the corporeal body. This imposes the restraints of physical space upon these attributes.

As a result, all the *tsadik's* disciples receive but a glow of these *ru'ach* attributes, a mere ray that is emitted beyond the container by means of the

TEXT 1A CONTINUED

tsadik's holy words and thoughts. [The inability to receive directly from *ru'ach* is a revelatory handicap] and therefore, our sages stated that it takes forty years for students to fully plumb the depths of their master's teachings (TALMUD, AVODAH ZARAH 5B).

By contrast, after the *tsadik's* passing, the *nefesh* separates from the *ru'ach and* remains in the grave, while the *ru'ach* and its three attributes rise to Gan Eden. Consequently, whoever is close to the *tsadik* can receive directly from his *ru'ach* in Gan Eden because the *ru'ach* is no longer restrained in a container or confined to a physical space. . . .

There is now a straightforward path for the *tsadik's* disciples to connect with the *essence* of their master's *ru'ach*—the faith, awe, and love with which the *tsadik* served G-d—and not merely these attributes' outer glow that escaped beyond their container. . . . The disciples connect and receive commensurate to the degree of their loving connection and closeness to the *tsadik* during his lifetime and after his death. For the transmission of all things spiritual is always by means of great love.

What is the Jewish view on near-death experiences? In "Near-Death Experience," *Rabbi DovBer Pinson* offers some insights: *myJLI.com/soul*

TEXT 1B

A SPIRIT UNSHACKLED

THE REBBE, RABBI MENACHEM MENDEL SCHNEERSON, LETTER, 5 TAMUZ 5743 (1983)

RABBI MENACHEM MENDEL SCHNEERSON 1902–1994

The towering Jewish leader of the 20th century, known as "the Lubavitcher Rebbe," or simply as "the Rebbe." Born in southern Ukraine, the Rebbe escaped Nazi-occupied Europe, arriving in the U.S. in June 1941. The Rebbe inspired and guided the revival of traditional Judaism after the European devastation, impacting virtually every Jewish community the world over. The Rebbe often emphasized that the performance of just one additional good deed could usher in the era of Mashiach. The Rebbe's scholarly talks and writings have been printed in more than 200 volumes.

. . . It is also a matter of common sense that whatever the direct cause of the separation of the soul from the body (whether a fatal accident or a fatal illness, etc.), it could affect only any of the vital organs of the *physical* body, but could in no way affect the spiritual soul.

A further point, which is also understandable, is that during the soul's lifetime on earth in partnership with the body, the soul is necessarily "handicapped"—in certain respects—by the requirements of the body (such as eating and drinking, etc.). Even a *Tzaddik* whose entire life is consecrated to *HaShem* [G-d] cannot escape the restraints of life in a material and physical environment. Consequently, when the time comes for the soul to return "home," it is essentially a *release* for it as it makes its ascent to a higher world, no longer restrained by a physical body and physical environment. Henceforth the soul is free to enjoy the spiritual bliss of being near to *HaShem* in the fullest measure.

II. IN TRANSIT

No one would argue that the moment of a soul's departure is not a difficult experience for the relatives. Death is always difficult, and sometimes utterly crushing, for the deceased's loved ones.

But how does the *deceased* experience it? Is it difficult for a freshly departed soul as well?

As we will see, corporeal demise is indeed hard on the soul, despite the benefits and freedoms the soul gains by its departure (as explained previously).

In fact, the degree of distress that a soul experiences upon its return to the realm of the spirit directly mirrors the scale of suffering that its loved ones left to mourn its passing experience here on this world.

TEXT 2

A DIFFICULT FAREWELL

ZOHAR 3:88A

ZOHAR

The seminal work of kabbalah, Jewish mysticism. The *Zohar* is a mystical commentary on the Torah, written in Aramaic and Hebrew. According to the Arizal, the *Zohar* contains the teachings of Rabbi Shimon bar Yocha'i, who lived in the Land of Israel during the 2nd century. The *Zohar* has become one of the indispensable texts of traditional Judaism, alongside and nearly equal in stature to the Mishnah and Talmud.

וְלֵית לָהּ לְנַפְשָׁא קַשְׁיוּ בְּכֹלָּא כִּפְרִישׁוּ דִּילָהּ מִן גּוּפָא.

Nothing is as hard for the soul as its separation from the body.

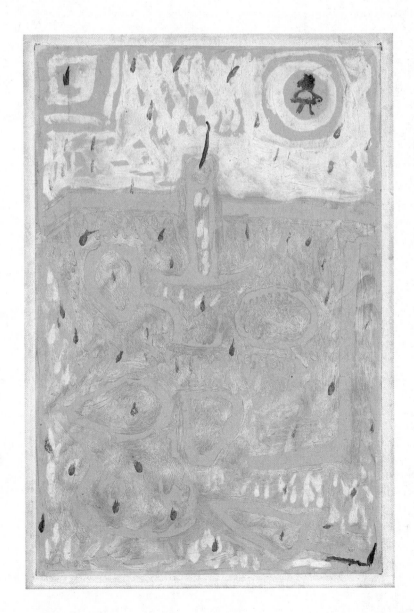

CANDLESTICK ▶
Paul Klee, oil on paper, 1937–1938.
(Ohara Museum of Art; Kurashiki, Japan)

FIGURE 2.2

PAINFUL SEPARATION

Three of the reasons why a soul experiences difficulty in parting from its body:

1. All transitions—even necessary and positive ones—are hard.

2. The soul can perform *mitzvot* only in this world. It mourns the loss of this opportunity.

3. The soul and body bond over time and develop an attachment. Breaking an attachment is traumatic.

TEXT 3

FIRST
THREE DAYS

JERUSALEM TALMUD,
MO'ED KATAN 3:5

JERUSALEM TALMUD

A commentary to the Mishnah,
compiled during the 4th and 5th
centuries. The Jerusalem Talmud
predates its Babylonian counterpart
by 100 years and is written in both
Hebrew and Aramaic. While the
Babylonian Talmud is the most
authoritative source for Jewish law,
the Jerusalem Talmud remains an
invaluable source for the spiritual,
intellectual, ethical, historical,
and legal traditions of Judaism.

כָּל תְּלָתָא יוֹמִין נַפְשָׁא טַיְיסָא עַל גּוּפָא,
סְבִידָה דְּהִיא חָזְרָה לְגַבֵּיה.
כֵּיוָן דְּהִיא חַמְיָא דְּאִישְׁתְּנֵי זִיוֵיהוֹן דְּאַפּוֹי,
הִיא שַׁבְקָא לֵיה וְאַזְלָה לָה.

For three days, the soul hovers above the body,
thinking that it can return to it.
[After three days,] when it sees that the body's
face has changed, it leaves the body and departs.

RIKUD HA'OR (THE DANCE OF LIGHT) ▶
Baruch Nachshon, acrylic on canvas,
Chevron, 2015. (nachshonart.com)

TEXT 4A

FIRST SEVEN DAYS

ZOHAR 1:218B–219A

כָּל ז' יוֹמִין, נִשְׁמָתָא אָזְלָא מִבֵּיתֵיהּ לְקִבְרֵיהּ וּמִקִבְרֵיהּ לְבֵיתֵיהּ וְאִתְאַבָּלַת עֲלוֹי דְּגוּפָא . . . בָּתַר ז' יוֹמִין גּוּפָא הֲוֵי כְּמָה דַהֲוָה, וְנִשְׁמָתֵיהּ עָאלַת לְדוּכְתָּא.

For seven days, the soul goes from the house where it lived to the grave, and from the grave back to the house, and it mourns its body. . . . After seven days, the body is subjected to its fate, and the soul ascends to its place.

TEXT 4B

FIRST THIRTY DAYS

ZOHAR 2:199B

כָּל אִינּוּן תְּלָתִין יוֹמִין,
אִתְדָנוּ נַפְשָׁא וְגוּפָא כְּחַדָא,
וּבְגִינֵי כָּךְ, אִשְׁתְּכַח נִשְׁמָתָא לְתַתָּא בְּאַרְעָא . . .
לְבָתַר, נִשְׁמָתָא סַלְקָא וְגוּפָא אִתְבְּלֵי בְּאַרְעָא.

For thirty days,
the soul and the body are judged as one,
and thus the soul is located down here, on earth. . . .
After that, the soul ascends while the body
erodes in the earth.

TEXT 4C

FIRST TWELVE MONTHS

TALMUD, SHABBAT 152B–153A

BABYLONIAN TALMUD

A literary work of monumental proportions that draws upon the legal, spiritual, intellectual, ethical, and historical traditions of Judaism. The 37 tractates of the Babylonian Talmud contain the teachings of the Jewish sages from the period after the destruction of the 2nd Temple through the 5th century CE. It has served as the primary vehicle for the transmission of the Oral Law and the education of Jews over the centuries; it is the entry point for all subsequent legal, ethical, and theological Jewish scholarship.

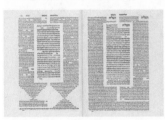

כָּל שְׁנֵים עָשָׂר חֹדֶשׁ גּוּפוֹ קַיָּם,
וְנִשְׁמָתוֹ עוֹלָה וְיוֹרֶדֶת.
לְאַחַר שְׁנֵים עָשָׂר חֹדֶשׁ הַגּוּף בָּטֵל,
וְנִשְׁמָתוֹ עוֹלָה, וְשׁוּב אֵינָה יוֹרֶדֶת.

For twelve months, the body still exists,
and the soul ascends and descends;
after twelve months, the body becomes null,
and the soul rises and no longer returns.

ALONE ▶
Jozef Israëls, oil on canvas, c. 1880–1881.
(The Mesdag Collection, The Hague)

TEXT 5

PHASED MOURNING

MAIMONIDES, *MISHNEH TORAH*,
LAWS OF MOURNING 13:11

**RABBI MOSHE BEN MAIMON
(MAIMONIDES, RAMBAM) 1135–1204**

Halachist, philosopher, author, and physician. Maimonides was born in Córdoba, Spain. After the conquest of Córdoba by the Almohads, he fled Spain and eventually settled in Cairo, Egypt. There, he became the leader of the Jewish community and served as court physician to the vizier of Egypt. He is most noted for authoring the *Mishneh Torah,* an encyclopedic arrangement of Jewish law; and for his philosophical work, *Guide for the Perplexed*. His rulings on Jewish law are integral to the formation of halachic consensus.

שְׁלֹשָׁה לִבְכִי,
שִׁבְעָה לְהֶסְפֵּד,
שְׁלֹשִׁים יוֹם לְתִסְפֹּרֶת
וְלִשְׁאָר הַחֲמִשָּׁה דְבָרִים.

Mourners observe three days of weeping;
seven days of eulogies;
and for thirty days, restrictions on haircuts
[and wearing freshly ironed clothing,
marrying, joining a celebration of friends,
and traveling on business].

A SON OF THE ANCIENT RACE ▶
Jozef Israëls, oil on canvas, Netherlands,
c. 1889. (The Jewish Museum, New York)

TEXT 6

EXTENDED MOURNING

RABBI YOSEF CARO, SHULCHAN
ARUCH, *YOREH DE'AH* 385:2

**RABBI YOSEF CARO
(MARAN, *BEIT YOSEF*) 1488–1575**

Halachic authority and author.
Rabbi Caro was born in Spain
but was forced to flee during the
Expulsion in 1492 and eventually
settled in Safed, Israel. He authored
many works, including the *Beit
Yosef, Kesef Mishneh*, and a
mystical work, *Magid Meisharim*.
Rabbi Caro's magnum opus, the
Shulchan Aruch (Code of Jewish
Law), has been universally accepted
as the basis for modern Jewish law.

הַמּוֹצֵא אֶת חֲבֵירוֹ אָבֵל בְּתוֹךְ ל' יוֹם, מְדַבֵּר עִמּוֹ תַּנְחוּמִין וְאֵינוֹ שׁוֹאֵל בִּשְׁלוֹמוֹ.
לְאַחַר ל' יוֹם, שׁוֹאֵל בִּשְׁלוֹמוֹ וְאֵינוֹ מְדַבֵּר עִמּוֹ תַּנְחוּמִים כְּדַרְכּוֹ, אֶלָּא מִן הַצַּד,
שֶׁאֵינוֹ מַזְכִּיר לוֹ שֵׁם הַמֵּת, אֶלָּא אוֹמֵר לוֹ: "תִּתְנַחֵם"...

וְעַל אָבִיו וְעַל אִמּוֹ מְדַבֵּר עִמּוֹ תַּנְחוּמִין כָּל י"ב חֹדֶשׁ; לְאַחַר י"ב חֹדֶשׁ מְדַבֵּר
עִמּוֹ מִן הַצַּד.

If you encounter an acquaintance within thirty days
of that person having lost a next of kin, offer words
of consolation and avoid the customary pleasantries.
If thirty days have elapsed since the relative's passing,
greet your acquaintance in the usual manner and offer
indirect words of consolation: avoid mentioning the
deceased by name, and extend a generic consolation,
such as, "May you be comforted."

If your acquaintance is mourning the loss of a parent,
you should offer direct messages of comfort for the
first twelve months, and only after that scale it back to
indirect consolation.

A "Letter of Condolence" penned
by *the Rebbe: myJLI.com/soul*

TEXT 7

MOURNING WITH THE UNMOURNED

TALMUD, SHABBAT 152A–B

מֵת שֶׁאֵין לוֹ מְנַחֲמִין, הוֹלְכִין עֲשָׂרָה בְּנֵי אָדָם וְיוֹשְׁבִין בִּמְקוֹמוֹ.

הַהוּא דְּשָׁכִיב בִּשְׁבָבוּתֵיה דְּרַב יְהוּדָה, לֹא הָיוּ לוֹ מְנַחֲמִין. כָּל יוֹמָא, הֲוָה דָּבַר רַב יְהוּדָה בֵּי עֲשָׂרָה וְיָתְבֵי בְּדוּכְתֵּיה. לְאַחַר שִׁבְעָה יָמִים אִיתְחֲזֵי לֵיה בְּחֶילְמֵיה דְּרַב יְהוּדָה וְאָמַר לֵיה, "תָּנוּחַ דַּעְתָּךְ שֶׁהֵנַחְתָּ אֶת דַּעְתִּי".

If a person dies and leaves no [next of kin] to be comforted, ten people should go and sit in the deceased's home.

A man died in Rabbi Yehudah's neighborhood. As there were no [mourners] to be comforted, Rabbi Yehudah assembled ten people every day, and they sat in the deceased's home. After seven days, the dead man appeared to Rabbi Yehudah in a dream and said, "May your mind be at rest, for you have set my mind at rest."

◀ **AT THE SICKBED**
Artur Markowicz, pastel on cardboard, Kraków, c. 1934.

III. HANDLING THE BODY

Until now, we have discussed the importance and centrality of our immortal souls. But where do our mortal bodies fit into the picture?

Is a lifeless body worthless? Once the soul's earthly "container" has been emptied of the soul's potent divine force, does its significance expire?

TEXT 8A

A STUNNING COMPARISON

TALMUD, MO'ED KATAN 25A

הָעוֹמֵד עַל הַמֵּת בִּשְׁעַת יְצִיאַת נִשָׁמָה חַיָּיב לִקְרוֹעַ,
הָא לְמָה זֶה דּוֹמֶה? לְסֵפֶר תּוֹרָה שֶׁנִּשְׂרָף.

One who is present at the time of a person's passing is required to tear their clothing.* This is because [a person's passing] is likened to the burning of a Torah scroll.

---

* Due to pragmatic reasons, this halachah is not practiced nowadays.

TEXT 8B

THE HUMAN TORAH

RABBI YOMTOV BEN AVRAHAM ASEVILLI, *CHIDUSHEI HARITVA*, AD LOC.

RABBI YOMTOV ASEVILLI (RITVA) C. 1250–1330

Spanish rabbi and Talmudist. Ritva was born in Seville. He is mostly known for his Talmudic commentary, which is extremely clear and, to this day, remains most frequently quoted and used.

וְהָרַמְבַּ"ן זַ"ל פִּירֵשׁ, שֶׁהַנֶּפֶשׁ בַּגוּף כְּאַזְכָּרוֹת בִּגְוִילִין.

Nachmanides points to the sacred names of G-d that are inked onto a Torah scroll's parchment as an analogy for the sacred soul that is installed within the corporeal body.

THE SCRIBE ▶
Alphonse Lévy, drypoint etching and mezzotint on paper, 1884. (Ben Uri Gallery, London)

TEXT 9

INDEPENDENTLY HOLY

RABBI YECHIEL MICHEL
TUCAZINSKY, *GESHER
HACHAYIM* 5:1

**RABBI YECHIEL MICHEL TUCAZINSKY
1874–1955**

Halachist. Rabbi Tucazinsky
was born in Lithuania. In 1882,
his family settled in Israel. He
studied in the Ets Chaim Yeshiva,
where he eventually became the
dean. He published many books
and articles on halachic issues,
including *Hayomom Bikadur
Haarets*, an effort to locate the
halachic dateline. His most famous
work is *Gesher Hachayim*, a classic
treatise on the laws of burial and
mourning that examines life as a
bridge between past and future.

כָּל מִתְעַסֵּק בְּמֵת צָרִיךְ לָדַעַת
שֶׁיֵּשׁ לוֹ עֵסֶק עִם דָּבָר קָדוֹשׁ:
גּוּפוֹ שֶׁל אָדָם הוּא לֹא רַק נַרְתֵּיק
שֶׁל קְדוּשָׁה שֶׁשִּׁמֵּשׁ לַנְשָׁמָה הָעִילָאִית,
אֶלָּא שֶׁהוּא עַצְמוֹ נִתְקַדֵּשׁ
גַּם בִּקְדוּשָׁה עַצְמִית, בְּדוֹמֶה לְסֵפֶר תּוֹרָה.

All who tend to a corpse must be aware
that they are handling a holy entity.
The human body is more than simply a sheath
to a sacred entity, a tool that serves a supernal soul.
Rather, it has itself become sanctified
with an independent holiness, similar to a Torah scroll.

TEXT 10

SOLEMN HONOR GUARD

RABBI YECHIEL MICHEL
TUCAZINSKY, IBID., 5:4

הַמֵּת צָרִיךְ שְׁמִירָה - אֲפִילוּ בַּיּוֹם, אַף בְּמָקוֹם שֶׁאֵין כָּל חֲשָׁשׁ לְהֶפְסֵד גּוּפוֹ.
וְהַשּׁוֹמְרוֹ עוֹשֶׂה מִצְוָה וּפָטוּר הַשּׁוֹמֵר מִשְּׁאָר מִצְוֹת . . . וּמִטַּעַם עוֹסֵק בְּמִצְוָה
פָּטוּר מִן הַמִּצְוָה. וּפְטָרוּהוּ גַם מִקְּרִיאַת שְׁמַע וּתְפִלָּה . . .

שְׁמִירַת הַמֵּת הִיא . . . מִשּׁוּם כְּבוֹדוֹ. שֶׁאִם יַנִּיחוּהוּ לְבַדּוֹ הֲרֵי זֶה כְּאִילוּ עֲזָבוּהוּ
כִּכְלִי אֵין חֵפֶץ עוֹד בּוֹ.

We are required to maintain constant watch over a
corpse, even during the daytime, and even if there
is no cause to suspect that something can happen
to the body. Those who maintain watch are actively
performing a mitzvah, to the extent that they are
meanwhile absolved from [many] other *mitzvot*, such
as reading the Shema and reciting the prayers [at the
appropriate times].

We maintain a watch over the dead . . . out of respect.
For if we were to leave the body alone, it would appear
as if we have abandoned it like a utensil that we no
longer require.

What is the Jewish way to treat
a body, and why? *Dr. Lisa Aiken*
briefly explains, in "Respecting
the Body": *myJLI.com/soul*

FIGURE 2.3

PRE-BURIAL RITES AND RULES

 The body is handled with extreme respect and dignity.

 The deceased is covered at all times.

 The body is gently cleansed and dressed in shrouds.

 The body is never placed face down.

 Lighthearted conversation is avoided in the presence of the deceased.

 A guard remains in proximity at all times, out of respect for the deceased.

"Praying with Gittel Rivka" is a heartwarming, firsthand account of a *taharah* (ritual preparation of a body for burial) by *Miriam Karp*: *myJLI.com/soul*

TEXT 11

THE SUM OF ITS PARTS

RABBI MOSHE SOFER,
RESPONSA CHATAM SOFER,
YOREH DE'AH 353

**RABBI MOSHE SOFER
(*CHATAM SOFER*) 1762–1839**

A leading rabbinical authority of the 19th century. Born in Frankfurt am Main, *Chatam Sofer* ultimately accepted the rabbinate of Pressburg (now Bratislava), Slovakia. Serving as rabbi and head of the yeshiva that he established, Rabbi Sofer maintained a strong traditionalist perspective, opposing deviation from Jewish tradition. *Chatam Sofer* is the title of his collection of halachic responsa and his commentary to the Talmud.

אֵין חִילוּק בֵּין סֵפֶר תּוֹרָה שָׁלֵם לְאוֹת אַחַת מִמֶּנּוּ,
וְהוּא הַדִּין נַמֵּי עֶצֶם מֵעַצְמוֹת הַקְּדוֹשִׁים
שֶׁנִּבְרְאוּ בְּצֶלֶם אֱלֹקִים, אָסוּר לִנְהוֹג בָּהֶם מִנְהַג בִּזָּיוֹן.

There is no differentiation [in reverential treatment] between a complete Torah scroll and a single letter [that has become detached] from a Torah scroll. Similarly, it is forbidden to handle with disrespect even a single bone [that has become detached] from a sacred body that was created in G-d's image.

PRAYING WITH TORAH ▶
Alex Levin, oil on canvas, Israel.

IV. BURIAL

When G-d recalls a soul to its celestial source in the heavens, it is our sacred duty to speedily return the body—intact—to the soil, which is the source from which G-d originally fashioned the human body.

From the dawn of our nation's history, and throughout its dissimilar stages over the course of four millennia, providing a Jewish body with a traditional Jewish burial, known as *kever Yisrael*, has remained a consistent feature and a highest priority. Stories both sad and inspiring woven throughout the annals of our history attest to the reality that Jews have consistently suffered supreme sacrifices to ensure a Jewish burial.

TEXT 12

SWIFT BURIAL

DEUTERONOMY 21:23

כִּי קָבוֹר תִּקְבְּרֶנּוּ בַּיּוֹם הַהוּא.

You shall surely bury him on the same day [as his death].

TEXT 13

EACH TO THEIR NATIVE HOME

ECCLESIASTES 12:5–7

כִּי הֹלֵךְ הָאָדָם אֶל בֵּית עוֹלָמוֹ, וְסָבְבוּ בַשּׁוּק הַסֹּפְדִים . . .

וְיָשֹׁב הֶעָפָר עַל הָאָרֶץ כְּשֶׁהָיָה, וְהָרוּחַ תָּשׁוּב אֶל הָאֱלֹקִים אֲשֶׁר נְתָנָהּ.

People proceed to their eternal abodes
and the mourners go about the streets. . . .

The dust returns to the earth, as it was,
while the spirit returns to G-d, Who bestowed it.

▼ **THE JEWISH CEMETERY**
Jacob Isaaksz van Ruisdael, oil
on canvas, 1654–1655, Haarlem,
Netherlands. (Detroit Institute of Arts)

TEXT 14

RETURNING THE DEPOSIT

RABBI CHAIM VITAL, *ETS HADAAT TOV* 358 (JERUSALEM, 2008)

RABBI CHAIM VITAL
C. 1542–1620

Lurianic kabbalist. Rabbi Vital was born in Israel, lived in Safed and Jerusalem, and later lived in Damascus. He was authorized by his teacher, Rabbi Yitschak Luria, the Arizal, to record his teachings. Acting on this mandate, Vital began arranging his master's teachings in written form, and his many works constitute the foundation of the Lurianic school of Jewish mysticism. His most famous work is *Ets Chaim*.

"כִּי עָפָר אַתָּה וְאֶל עָפָר תָּשׁוּב" (בְּרֵאשִׁית ג, יט).

כִּי גוּף הָאָדָם מִן הֶעָפָר הָיָה, וְדֶרֶךְ פִּקָּדוֹן הוּפְקַד בְּיַד הָאָדָם.

וּכְשֶׁמֵּת צָרִיךְ לְהַחֲזִיר הַפִּקָּדוֹן אֶל הֶעָפָר אֲשֶׁר מִמֶּנּוּ לוּקַח וְלִקְוֹבְרוֹ.

"For you are dust, and you will return to dust" (GENESIS 3:19). The body comes from the earth, and it is entrusted as a deposit to the individual's care. Upon death, the deposit must be returned to the earth from where it came, and buried there.

TEXT 15A

FINAL WISHES

TALMUD, TAANIT 21A

מִצְוָה לְקַיֵּם דִּבְרֵי הַמֵּת.

It is a mitzvah to implement the expressed [final] wishes of the deceased.

TEXT 15B

WHEN TO DISREGARD

MAIMONIDES, *MISHNEH TORAH*, LAWS OF MOURNING 12:1

אֲבָל אִם צִוָּה שֶׁלֹּא יִקָּבֵר אֵין שׁוֹמְעִין לוֹ, שֶׁהַקְּבוּרָה מִצְוָה, שֶׁנֶּאֱמַר, "כִּי קָבוֹר תִּקְבְּרֶנּוּ".

If a person requested not to be buried, we disregard the request. This is because burial is a mitzvah, as it is stated (DEUTERONOMY 21:23), "You shall surely bury him."

Do we always need to honor the deathbed wishes of the deceased? In "Honoring their Last Wish," *Rabbi Avrohom Bergstein* provides the halachic approach: *myJLI.com/soul*

V. GRAVE VISITATION

Interment does not spell the end of our connection to the soul of the deceased. In fact, it even fails to disconnect us from our loved one's *physical* remains. Therefore, visiting the graves of loved ones and righteous individuals has been a permanent, hallowed feature of Jewish tradition.

Our mystical traditions reveal that a gravesite is a communication port that allows us to commune with the souls above.

▼ OLD JEWISH CEMETERY
Natan Spigel (1886–1942), watercolor and pencil on paper, (Ben Uri Gallery, London)

TEXT 16

EVOKING THE SOUL'S EMPATHY

ZOHAR 2:141B

נֶפֶשׁ דָּא אִשְׁתְּכָּחַת גּוֹ קִבְרָא . . .
לְאִשְׁתַּכְּחָא גּוֹ חַיָּיא וּלְמִנְדַּע בְּצַעֲרָא דִּלְהוֹן,
וּבְשַׁעֲתָּא דִּי אִצְטְרִיכוּ, בָּעָאת רַחֲמֵי עֲלַיְיהוּ . . .

וְכַד אִצְטְרִיךְ לִבְנֵי עָלְמָא, כַּד אִינּוּן בְּצַעֲרָא וְאָזְלֵי לְבֵי קִבְרֵי,
הַאי נֶפֶשׁ אִתְּעָרַת וְאִיהִי אָזְלָא וּמְשַׁטְטָא וְאִתְּעָרַת לְרוּחַ . . .
וּכְדֵין קוּדְשָׁא בְּרִיךְ הוּא חָיִיס עַל עָלְמָא.

The *nefesh* remains present in the grave. . . .
Due to the fact that it remains among the living, it is
acquainted with their pain.
At their time of need, it pleads [with G-d] for mercy on
their behalf. . . .

When the inhabitants of the world are in need, when
they are in sorrow and visit the cemetery, the *nefesh* is
aroused [to their plight]. It ascends and awakens the
ru'ach [which, in turn, entreats G-d for mercy]. . . .
Consequently, the Holy One, blessed be He, has mercy
on the world.

Why do some place pebbles on
tombstones? In "The Right Place for
a Stone," *Rabbi Avrohom Bergstein*
sheds light: *myJLI.com/soul*

TEXT 17

VISITORS WELCOME

RABBI YEHUDAH BEN SHMUEL OF REGENSBURG, *SEFER CHASIDIM,* SECTIONS 709–710

RABBI YEHUDAH BEN SHMUEL OF REGENSBURG (RABBI YEHUDAH HACHASID) 1140–1217

Mystic and ethicist. Born in Speyer, Germany, he was a rabbi, mystic, and one of the initiators of *Chasidei Ashkenaz,* a Jewish German moralist movement that stressed piety and asceticism. Rabbi Yehudah settled in Regensburg in 1195. He is best known for his work *Sefer Chasidim,* on the ethics of day-to-day concerns.

קָהָל אֶחָד רָצוּ לָלֶכֶת לְמָקוֹם אֶחָד. בָּא מֵת לְאֶחָד בַּחֲלוֹם, וְאָמַר, "אַל תַּעַזְבוּ אוֹתָנוּ, כִּי יֵשׁ לָנוּ הֲנָאָה כְּשֶׁתֵּלְכוּ לְבֵית הַקְּבָרוֹת"…

בַּרְזִילַי הַגִּלְעָדִי אָמַר (שְׁמוּאֵל ב, יט, לח) "אָמוּת בְּעִירִי". כִּי הֲנָאָה יֵשׁ לַמֵּתִים שֶׁאוֹהֲבִים הוֹלְכִים עַל קִבְרֵיהֶם וּמְבַקְשִׁים לְנִשְׁמָתָן טוֹבָה, מְטִיבִים לָהֶם בְּאוֹתוֹ עִנְיָן. וְגַם כְּשֶׁמְּבַקְשִׁים עֲלֵיהֶם, הֵם מִתְפַּלְלִים עַל הַחַיִּים.

There was once a community that wished to relocate. One of the deceased [buried in the vicinity] appeared in a dream to a member of the community and pleaded, "Please do not abandon us, for we appreciate your visits to our cemetery." . . .

Barzilai the Giladite declared, "I would like to die in my own city" (II SAMUEL 19:38). He wished for this because the deceased appreciate when their loved ones visit their graves and request goodness for their souls; this improves their condition in Heaven. And when we pray on behalf of the deceased, they pray for us in turn.

VI. CONCLUSION

If there is one piece of writing that encapsulates the overarching theme that emerges from the above study—with a blend of insight, sensitivity, and practical direction—it is a 1958 letter sent by the Lubavitcher Rebbe to a grieving woman.

TEXT 18

A SCIENTIFIC ARGUMENT

THE REBBE, RABBI MENACHEM MENDEL SCHNEERSON, *CORRESPONDENCE*, 29 SIVAN, 5718 [JUNE 17, 1958]

Blessing and Greeting:

I received your undated letters, in which you write about your emotional upsets in connection with the passing of your mother, and the questions which are troubling you in this connection, involving also questions in regard to the passing of your father, peace unto them. . . .

Another fundamental point to remember, which has a direct bearing on your letter, is that all believers in G-d believe also in the survival of the soul. Actually, this principle has even been discovered in this physical world, where science now holds, as an absolute truth, that nothing in the physical world can be absolutely destroyed. How much more so in the spiritual world, especially in the case of the soul, which in no way can be affected by the death and disintegration of the physical body. It would be silly and illogical to assume that, because a certain organ of the body ceases to function, affecting other physical organs of the body, the spiritual soul would also be affected thereby. The truth is that when the physical body ceases to function, the soul continues its existence, not only as before, but even on a higher level, inasmuch as it is no longer handicapped by the restraints of the physical frame.

Thirdly, the attachment of children to their parents, and the general attachment between close relatives during life on this earth, is surely not a physical attachment by the respective physical bodies of the relatives. Essentially, the attachment is a spiritual one, due to the spiritual affinity between those concerned, and the qualities of the soul, including such spiritual things as character, kindness, goodness, etc., all of which are attributes of the soul, and not of the body. Therefore, also, every action on the part of a person in relation to a beloved person, and the desire to benefit that person, is not directed towards pleasing his physical body, his bones and tissue, for it is the spiritual pleasure that one is concerned with.

In view of the above, it is clear that even after the physical body has disintegrated and disappeared from view, it is still possible to bring joy and benefit to the soul, which, as noted above, not only survives, but does so on a higher level, and all the things which had previously brought joy and pleasure to one's parents, will continue to do so even after they are physically no longer here.

EXERCISE 2.1

1. Record the insight from this lesson that resonated with you most.

    _____

    _____

2. Is there a deceased person with whom you wish to strengthen your bond of love? What step can you take to do so?

    _____

    _____

KEY POINTS

1 *Nefesh* and *ru'ach* are two of the soul's components. After death, the *nefesh* remains with the body, while the *ru'ach* disengages and ascends to Gan Eden (Paradise).

2 Once the *ru'ach* is no longer limited to material existence, it is more accessible to all who wish to connect to it. Thus, when a person dies, our ability to spiritually connect with him or her is stronger and deeper than before.

3 Though the *nefesh* remains in the grave, it retains a connection with the higher levels of the soul. The gravesite is thus a portal where we can communicate with departed souls and ask them to intercede before G-d on our behalf.

4 Over the course of a lifetime, the soul and body integrate and bond; their separation at death is therefore painful for the soul.

5 The soul departs the body in stages. These stages correspond to the prescribed periods of mourning. When we mourn, we are mourning not only for the deceased but also *with* the deceased.

6 Dignity and sensitivity are the underlying principles that guide the care of a corpse and its preparation for burial. This is because even after death, the body retains its special status of having been the container for the soul.

7 Burial is of highest priority in Jewish tradition and culture. When G-d takes a person's soul, we are tasked to return the body to the place from which G-d fashioned it.

8 Burial affirms two fundamental Jewish beliefs: (a) our bodies aren't ours—they belong to G-d; (b) there will be a Resurrection of the Dead in the messianic era.

APPENDIX

TEXT 19

PROHIBITION AGAINST TATTOOS

LEVITICUS 19:28

וּכְתֹבֶת קַעֲקַע
לֹא תִתְּנוּ בָּכֶם.

Do not inflict a tattoo
on your bodies.

ADDITIONAL READINGS

END-OF-LIFE:

MANAGING
MENTAL AND
EMOTIONAL NEEDS

Complete end-of-life care also includes helping the dying person manage mental and emotional distress. Someone who is alert near the end of life might understandably feel depressed or anxious. It is important to treat emotional pain and suffering. Encouraging conversations about feelings might help. You might want to contact a counselor, possibly one familiar with end-of-life issues. If the depression or anxiety is severe, medicine may help.

A dying person may also have some specific fears and concerns. He or she may fear the unknown or worry about those left behind. Some people are afraid of being alone at the very end. This feeling can be made worse by the understandable reactions of family, friends, and even the medical team. For example, when family and friends do not know how to help or what to say, sometimes they stop visiting. Or, someone who is already beginning to grieve may withdraw.

Doctors may feel helpless because they can't cure their patient. Some seem to avoid a dying patient. This can add to a dying person's sense of isolation. If this is happening, discuss your concerns with the family, friends, or the doctor.

The simple act of physical contact—holding hands, a touch, or a gentle massage—can make a person feel connected to those he or she loves. It can be very soothing.

Warm your hands by rubbing them together or running them under warm water.

Try to set a comforting mood. Remember that listening and being present can make a difference. For example, Gordon loved a party, so it was natural for him to want to be around family and friends when he was dying. Ellen always liked spending quiet moments with one or two people at a time, so she was most comfortable with just a few visitors.

Some experts suggest that when death is very near, music at a low volume and soft lighting are soothing. In fact, near the end of life, music therapy might improve mood, help with relaxation, and lessen pain. Listening to music might also evoke memories those present can share. For some people, keeping distracting noises like televisions and radios to a minimum is important.

Often, just being present with a dying person is enough. It may not be necessary to fill the time with talking or activity. Your quiet presence can be a simple and profound gift for a dying family member or friend.

Spiritual Needs at the End of Life
People nearing the end of life may have spiritual needs as important as their physical concerns. Spiritual needs include finding meaning in one's life and ending disagreements with others, if possible. The dying

person might find peace by resolving unsettled issues with friends or family. Visits from a social worker or a counselor may also help.

Many people find solace in their faith. Others may struggle with their faith or spiritual beliefs. Praying, talking with someone from one's religious community (such as a minister, priest, rabbi, or imam), reading religious texts, or listening to religious music may bring comfort.

Family and friends can talk to the dying person about the importance of their relationship. For example, adult children can share how their father has influenced the course of their lives. Grandchildren can let their grandfather know how much he has meant to them. Friends can relate how they value years of support and companionship. Family and friends who can't be present could send a recording of what they would like to say or a letter to be read out loud.

Sharing memories of good times is another way some people find peace near death. This can be comforting for everyone. Some doctors think it is possible that even if a patient is unconscious, he or she might still be able to hear. It is probably never too late to say how you feel or to talk about fond memories.

Excerpted from https://www.nia.nih.gov/health/providing-comfort-end-life#emotional

SHE IS PURE

BY MIRIAM KARP

MIRIAM KARP

Writer and artist. Karp is an award-winning writer, artist, teacher, and lecturer. Her paintings explore intimate moments in Jewish life. She authored a personal memoir, *Painting Zaidy's Dream: A Memoir of a Searching Soul*, in which she shares her journey toward becoming Torah observant.

The years went on, the kids started to grow up. We gave away our last few disposable diapers, at long last. What a different phase, in so many ways. Little kids, little problems; big kids, big problems, the saying goes. It's true that as the children grew into more complex beings, their issues couldn't be solved with a lollypop and a kiss. I did miss the dizzy, delicious baby-on-the-hip days, much as it was a blur and hard to even believe that it had all transpired. But we savored and enjoyed the richness of our emerging people.

Finally, all the kids were in school—all day. I had time to branch out in new directions. A good friend regularly performed the *mitzvah* of *tahara*/purification, preparing a Jewish body for burial. I'd wanted to try this important task, but kept putting it off for . . . later. This wasn't one of the mitzvos that all observant people did such as keeping kosher, Shabbos, eating matzah on Passover, and so on. It was extra, voluntary— a *mitzvah* usually handled by more mature women, because of their freer schedules, and probably also because of their said maturity. As I rounded the corner on fifty, mortality wasn't a far off abstract notion that had little to do with me. My mom was struggling with dementia and decline. I had lost some close friends. So when Tamar asked if I might be willing to try this practice out, I gulped and hesitantly said yes. "Good," she said briskly. "Malka told me you were thinking about it. The first time you mostly just watch, and the women will help guide you. How 'bout tomorrow morning? We need a fourth. Na'ama will pick you up at 9:00. Okay?"

"Sure," I answered, sounding more confident than I was. Early the next morning, Na'ama honked right on time. She took side-roads for our half-hour trip, avoiding rush hour traffic. We pulled into the funeral home parking lot, going around to the back. Na'ama punched the code to the rear door, and we entered the quiet building. Several empty caskets were in the hallway. I followed the women into a utilitarian room, with a cupboard, sinks, and a concrete floor. We washed our hands, put on plastic aprons and latex gloves. They examined the name of the deceased, left on a piece of paper on the counter. I recognized it—I had visited her several times during her month of decline and knew her somewhat. Would it be easier or harder to do this on someone I had known?

There was no time to think. Ruth opened the heavy door of the walk-in refrigerated room that adjoined our work room. We entered. Two *meisim*/newly deceased lay in that chilly room, covered with sheets. I recognized Rachel's bulky shape.

Suddenly, everyone else faded into the background. I was only aware of her and me.

I took a deep breath and followed the three women. They wheeled Rachel into the preparation room. I followed, a bit nervously.

I had been touched and intrigued when I first heard about this ritual, back in the early days of Chassidic immersion. Soon enough, Yankel and I were busily pouring all our energies into building a Jewish homestead. I was focused on pregnancies and nursing—busy with the kids and their constant needs. I was nurturing life, not yet physically or emotionally ready to deal with its end.

But now, I felt more or less ready, and somewhat obligated to try. Obligated because purifying the deceased was a sacred ritual, performed with care by Jews all over the world. Some unknown *tahara* team had done it for my grandparents and in-laws, *alehem hashalom*. In our small community, we all shared the joys and responsibilities of Torah life, and every set of willing hands counted.

Alehem hashalom, may they rest in peace. According to Jewish law and tradition, the living helped the soul get ready to rest in peace, by preparing its earthly home—the body—with well-defined rituals of cleansing and dressing in simple shrouds.

These rituals were done with the utmost dignity, privacy, and respect. Rather than making an attractive façade for the funeral, they focused on purity and simplicity, each step suffused with deep Kabbalistic meaning.

I knew all this. In my head. But I still wasn't sure, could I really do it?

To be honest, I wasn't here just for altruistic reasons, beautiful and compelling as they were. Helping the dead was called *Chesed Shel Emes*—true kindness: you gave with no possibility of being paid back. I had my own reasons, beyond noble acts and shouldering my share of community responsibility; I wanted to expand my spiritual horizons.

Maybe I'd hone in on the real essence, become a truer wife and mother, waste less energy on trivialities; swallow and internalize a greater appreciation for the gift of life. Less kvetching even. Perhaps this encounter with mortality would make me a more sensitive artist and writer. I was now a reputedly respectable figure, a rabbi's wife and Jewish educator busily mining the treasures of Jewish mysticism and living. Every now and then, I still longed for those *wow man* really intense experiences, like *far out—awesome—extreme;* albeit in a Jewish way. Surely helping a soul and its body in this transition would meet the bill. The burial committee was traditionally called the *Chevra Kadisha*—the holy society. With a name like that, I reckoned, they must be privy to some deep, mysterious truths.

The *tahara* turned out to be like most of Jewish life, where searching for rarified or transcendent "Spirituality" wasn't exactly it—was kind of off the mark.

Was it profound, quiet, hushed; *Spiritual*? Yes—and no.

The *tahara* was surprisingly prosaic. Earthy. Even ordinary. Na'ama, the group leader, a brisk and efficient woman, helped dispel my initial discomfort by referring to Rachel as "her." "Move her over here," she instructed. "Hold up her head."

There was nothing macabre about the scene, though my subconscious offered up images from different horror movies, accompanied by a Gothic organ's pitched tone. It wasn't a staged "religious service," with the choir marching quietly in perfect formation. We were about to help a real woman, a she, a person. We had a job to do.

Watching my experienced partners' faces, for a cue in this new universe, I felt both humbled and relieved: humbled by their ability to just step up, assess the situation, and figure out the best way to proceed, with earnest and every day kind of caring. Relieved to see them show signs of compassion, even distress, at some of the bodily signs of the suffering Rachel must have endured these last few months. It was hard for them too. But they each took a breath and continued.

The first glance at her was hard. The first touch was hard.

The other women started washing Rachel with washcloths, keeping as much of her face and body covered as possible at any one moment, respecting her privacy, even now. Initially I stood back, watching with hands folded. I knew it would be best to jump right in, so as they turned Rachel to wash her back, I reached out tentatively and held her hand to keep it from flopping over.

The words dead weight and rigor mortis echoed through my mind. Rachel's hand was cold, heavy, and stiff. I imagined holding a living hand that had the pulse of life flowing through it. This was different.

I helped more and more, as we proceeded, following my friends' spoken and intuited guidance. As we gently washed her body, a body that had lived and loved and borne children, it seemed almost like bathing an infant, with its total dependence, as we hovered protectively around.

Trying to talk only as necessary, we gave each other instructions in subdued, focused voices. The quiet was punctuated by coughs, sighs, the sound of water filling the buckets, the snap of latex gloves.

We took off whatever bandages we could, along with other substances that would block the purifying water, so it could cover her as completely as possible. Removing her frosted pink nail polish was like stripping away her earthly life. I imagined a kind nurse or grandchild sitting patiently with Rachel and applying this reassuring slick coat of certainty and vanity on her worn, fading hand.

That was all behind her now.

In a non-broken sequence, Na'ama, Ruth, and Malka poured cascading buckets of water from the *mikveh*/ritual bath from her head to toe. "*Tahara hee*—she is pure," they intoned. Over and over in almost a chant—rhythmically, asserting, defining. The sound of the water splashing against the metal table accenting the words.

Pausing at several points, Na'ama murmured several prayers and parts of Psalms, the familiar sounds of the ancient Hebrew washing over Rachel and clothing her in a cocoon of comfort. We listened, understanding the intent, even if we couldn't translate each word. Our wishes for this woman cushioned and cloaked her as well.

Then, we gently patted her dry. Ruth brushed her hair. I watched the wet grey-white hair spring into soft, fine curls. This tender act was touching, like giving a small child that final mother's touch. Working together, we dressed Rachel in *tachrichim,* simple white linen garments: tunic, pants, gown, bonnet—each put on and tied in a special way.

We gently lowered her into the unadorned wooden casket. Fulfilling the Biblical declaration, "from the dust you came, to the dust you shall return," holes were drilled in the bottom of the casket, allowing the body contact with the dust of the earth.

Na'ama placed a shard of pottery on each of Rachel's eyes and on her mouth, symbolizing human frailty. Golden sand from the land of Israel was lightly sprinkled over her. We covered Rachel's face with a piece of the linen, and asked her to forgive us for any rough or disrespectful handling. We wished her a speedy journey to *Olam HaBah*—the world to come.

Lifting the heavy casket cover and positioning it onto its fastening pegs felt like an act of finality. Ruth opened the door to the refrigerated room. The whoosh and blast of cold air was startling, breaking the meditative mood. We wheeled Rachel inside, where she would wait for the next step of her voyage.

Stepping out of that quiet, windowless room into daylight, time, and schedules, we collected our purses and cell phones, and stepped back into our day; a sunny summer one.

The casual chatter on the drive home seemed strange after such intensity. But I soon relaxed, realizing the conversation offered a soothing transition. What we had shared did not really need to be put into words. Easing back to daily reality, I drew a blank when Malka asked me, "So, how was it for you?" I had to stop and think. How was what? Oh yeah. I just did a *tahara.* "It was okay," I said with a quiet smile, downplaying my inner relief that I'd made it through, which melded together with my sense of accomplishment.

I felt buoyed throughout the day. Catching up on the phone with Devora Leah, now a new mother, I told her, "I did my first *tahara.*"

She gasped. "Really?"

But, it wasn't a gasp type thing, not of horror, and not of an *Oh wow* mystical high. It was an ordinary, extraordinary thing to do. Rachel's image flittered though my mind once or twice. Not morbid. Just an image of a friend I was glad to have helped.

Early Thursday, I awoke and remembered her. I said *Modeh Ani,* expressing thanks for the new day. No rote recital this time; I really felt it.

Rachel was in her place in G-d's universe—stripped down to her essence, purified of her worldly concerns. And I was thankful to be in mine: unfinished business, chaos, imperfection, and all.

WHY DOES JEWISH LAW FORBID CREMATION?

BY RABBI NAFTALI SILBERBERG

NAFTALI SILBERBERG

Noted author and lecturer. Rabbi Naftali Silberberg is the codirector of curriculum for the Rohr Jewish Learning Institute and coeditor in chief of its Flagship division.

Question:

I'm in the process of making arrangements for my final resting place. In my family, some of my relatives have opted for a traditional Jewish burial, while others have chosen the route of cremation. While researching my options, I've discovered that Judaism is vehemently opposed to cremation. Can you please explain to me the origins and reasons for this stance?

Answer:

Before I respond to your question regarding the background of the Jewish prohibition against cremation, allow me to make some prefatory remarks:

In order to help clarify some of the issues, I am choosing to explain the topic "as is," i.e., as they appear in the "Big Books." Commenting on

the particulars of one's experience may need additional questions clarified and is often best done in person with a rabbi more familiar with the particular person or family.

Thus, if anything that I will write will come across as insensitive, I beg your forgiveness in advance. That is clearly not my intention.

The laws I will attempt to present here are a distillation of rabbinic writings over the years. In terms of some of the deeper reflection on the human body and its role that I hope to provide—that is distilled from deep Chabad discourses, though I can hardly assert that my distillation of this lofty concept is categorically correct.

Jewish law ("Halachah") is unequivocal that the dead must be buried in the earth.[1]

As a deterrent measure,[2] cremated remains are not interred in a Jewish cemetery.[3] Furthermore, we are told that many of the traditional laws of mourning are not observed after the passing of an individual whose body was cremated.[4] *Kaddish*, however, is recited for such individuals, and it is certainly appropriate to give charity and do *mitzvot* in memory of their souls.[5]

Responsibility for the deceased's proper burial lies with the next of kin.[6] While ordinarily Jewish law requires the deceased's children to go to great lengths to respect the departed's wishes,[7] if someone requests to be cremated or buried in a manner which is not in accordance with Jewish tradition, we nevertheless provide him/her with a Jewish burial.[8] It is believed that since the soul has now arrived to the World of Truth, it surely sees the value of a proper Jewish burial, and thus administering a traditional Jewish burial is actually granting what the person truly wishes at the moment. Furthermore, if anyone, all the more so your father and mother, asks you to damage or hurt their body, you are not allowed to do so. For our bodies do not belong to us, they belong to G-d.

[It is important to note that according to Jewish law, a person is only held accountable for his/her actions when they are done willingly, and with full cognizance of their implications.[9] Therefore, all the above does not apply to an individual who was cremated against his will. After the Holocaust, many conscientious Jews gathered ashes from the extermination camp crematoria and respectfully buried them in Jewish cemeteries. Recently, too, I heard of an instance where a hospital mistakenly cremated a Jewish body. With rabbinic sanction the ashes were put into a coffin and given a proper Jewish burial.

Furthermore, an individual who was raised in a non-religious atmosphere and was never accorded a proper Jewish education cannot be held responsible for his or her lack of observance.[10] This general rule applies to individuals who opt to be cremated because their education and upbringing did not equip them with the knowledge necessary to make an informed choice in this area. This assumption impacts some of the legal results presented above.]

The Biblical Commandment

Man's soul comes from Above, "He breathed into his nostrils the soul of life,"[11] and when its earthly mission has been accomplished it rises back to G-d, returning to its source.

The body, on the other hand, was taken from the ground—"the L-rd G-d formed man of dust from the ground"[12]—and must therefore return to the earth. This is expressed in the words that G-d tells Adam, the first man,[13] "For dust you are, and to dust you will return."

This concept is reiterated in Deuteronomy,[14] where we are commanded to bury the dead: "You shall bury him on that day." The Jerusalem Talmud[15] explains that this requires us to bury the body in its entirety, not after it has been diminished through cremation or in any other manner: "You must bury him in entirety, not partially. From this verse we extrapolate that the command was not fulfilled if the person was partially buried."

Cremating a body destroys most of the body, making burial of the flesh impossible, and thus violates the biblical command.

Our Responsibilities Vis-à-Vis the Human Body

In Jewish law, the human body belongs to its Creator. It is merely on loan to the person, who is the guardian of the body, but he or she has no right to deface it in any way.[16] The body must be "returned" in its entirety, just as it was given.[17]

Additionally, Man was created in "G-d's image and likeness."[18] Any violation of the human body is considered, therefore, to be a violation of G-d Himself.[19]

This general principle and law governs many of our laws, like those prohibiting self-mutilation[20] or tattoos,[21] and requiring us to do our utmost to keep ourselves from danger by maintaining proper hygiene and the like.[22] This principle applies after death, too; any mutilation of the dead is prohibited.[23]

This is also one of the reasons why Jewish law does not permit autopsies[24] other than in the most extenuating of circumstances.[25]

Utmost respect for the sanctity of the human body is also the overriding concern which pervades the process of preparing the deceased for burial. The funeral is scheduled for the earliest possible time, ideally on the same day as the passing,[26] so that the body reaches its eternal rest as expeditiously as possible. The honor of caring for the dead is traditionally reserved for the most respected members of the community,[27] who are expected to maintain the highest levels of decorum, privacy, and respect throughout the entire process.

According to traditional Jewish sources, the merit of facilitating the proper burial of a Jewish corpse is immeasurable. Even the High Priest, who was even prohibited from attending the funerals of his next of kin, was *required* to preoccupy himself and personally bury a *met mitzvah,* an abandoned Jewish body that had no one to attend to its proper burial.[28]

No lengthy explanation is necessary to conclude that there can be no greater violation of our legal and moral responsibilities to the body's Owner than to cremate.

Delving Deeper into Our Relationship with Our Bodies

When the body becomes the soul's vehicle to do good deeds ("mitzvot") it—the body—is invested with permanent value and sanctity. The body is seen as sacred, as the temple of the soul, and the medium by which we do goodness in this world. According to Jewish law, an object which facilitated the fulfillment of a mitzvah must be accorded respect, and cannot be casually discarded. Examples: papers upon which are inscribed words of Torah, *tzitzit* fringes, or leather *tefillin* straps. Such articles must be buried with due respect. How much more does this idea apply to a body. In the words of the Talmud,[29] "even the wicked among [the Jewish people] are full of mitzvot"! Or, to quote the prophet Isaiah:[30] "And your nation are *all* righteous people."

On a deeper level, as Jews, we believe there is purpose to life, purpose to this world, purpose to the act of creation.

There are other belief systems that view the body and all the other physical trappings of this world, and the temptations they present, only as strategic challenges set in the soul's path, in order to overcome these challenges en route to a heavenly paradise. As such, the body has no intrinsic worth of its own, and once its function has been fully served, it retains no value whatsoever.

Jewish belief also recognizes the importance of the soul's reward earned through its life-journey,[31] but sees the refinement of the body and this physical world as the paramount objective.[32] The soul was dispatched from its heavenly abode to infuse these otherwise mundane entities with holiness and purpose. While, the soul, too, is elevated to previously unimaginable heights through fulfilling its worldly mission,[33] it is the sanctification of the physical—both the body and the world at large—that constitutes the very reason for Creation.

The Penultimate Bodily Experience

Two of the most fundamental tenets of the Jewish faith are the belief in the ultimate redemption of the Jewish people—and of all of mankind—through a righteous messiah,[34] and the concept of the resurrection of the dead, an awaited time when all souls will return to their bodies.[35] These beliefs are so central to the Jewish worldview that Maimonides considers them to be two of the thirteen principles of the Jewish faith.[36]

The Messianic Era will be ushered in by a righteous scion of King David,[37] and will be characterized by world peace and harmony. "They shall beat their swords into plowshares and their spears into pruning hooks; nations shall not lift the sword against nation; neither shall they learn war anymore."[38] The Jewish people will be gathered from all corners of the earth and will be returned to the Promised Land,[39] where the Holy Temple will be rebuilt in Jerusalem.[40]

This era will be the culmination of G-d's master plan for Creation.[41] We will then be able to enjoy the fruits of our labor; we will then see the end-product of our millennia-long labor of permeating Creation with holiness and purpose. The curtain will be ripped aside, and the flesh, our very own bodies, will perceive G-d: "And the glory of the L-rd shall be revealed, and all flesh together shall see that the mouth of the L-rd spoke.[42]

These beliefs have sustained our nation throughout a 2,000-year exile fraught with pogroms, expulsions, and persecution. Just one generation ago countless Jews entered the gas chambers whilst singing "*Ani Ma'amin*" ("I believe . . .")—expressing their firm belief in a better time to come and their trust that they would be resurrected to witness that awaited day.

Cremation is an implied statement of rejection of the concept of resurrection. It is in effect a declaration that once the soul has departed the body, the lifeless body has served its purpose and now has no further value.[43]

Our Sages teach that those who deny the notion of the resurrection will not merit to be resurrected[44] within their own bodies, rather their souls will be enclothed in different bodies when that awaited day arrives.[45] Based on this idea, many authorities conclude that a person who opts for cremation is subject to this consequence as well.[46]

(However, this applies only to such instances where the cremation was done at the behest of the deceased; only in such instances can it be said that the person rejected the notion of the resurrection, etc. Not too long ago six million of our people were denied proper burial, most of them cremated. Without a doubt these holy martyrs will be at the forefront of those who will return during the Messianic Redemption.)

Additional Prohibition and Concepts

A. We are commanded in the Torah[47] not to follow the practices of the non-Jews. Cremating the dead was (and, in fact, still is) a ritual observed by many pagan cultures, and thus is also a violation of this biblical prohibition.[48]

B. According to Kabbalah (Jewish mysticism), the soul does not depart the body immediately after death.[49] Such an abrupt departure would be intensely painful for the soul. The gradual decomposition of the body allows the soul the time to slowly depart the body and acclimate itself to its new heavenly abode.[50] The instant destruction of the body caused by cremation deprives the soul of this much-needed adjustment period.

C. Throughout our history, a traditional Jewish burial, known as *Kever Yisrael,* was always considered a highest priority. During times when many of their non-Jewish co-citizens regularly cremated their dead, the Jews were distinguishable by their commitment to bury their dead with dignity. This fact was already noted by Tacitus, the famed 1st century Roman historian.[51] Understanding the great importance of this mitzvah, the Israeli army is known to take great risks, venturing behind enemy lines to bring back to Israel the bodies of their fallen comrades.

It is safe to assume that the deceased's soul is certain to evoke heavenly mercy and blessings upon those individuals who ensured that its body was accorded its final proper respects.

To sum up:

Cremation

- is a transgression of a Biblical law to bury our dead,
- demonstrates a rejection of G-d's supreme "ownership" over all of Creation,
- violates our legal responsibility to return what was loaned to us (our bodies) in as wholesome a state as possible,
- constitutes a rejection of the Jewish belief of *tzelem Elokim* (created in G-d's image),
- constitutes a rejection of the Jewish belief in resurrection of the dead,
- (if done voluntarily, knowing fully the responsibilities) will cause the body not to be included among the Jewish People when the time of resurrection arrives,
- violates the biblical prohibition of following heathen practices,
- upends the soul's natural separation and acclimation process, thus causing it additional untold pain,
- deviates from Jewish history and our forebears' and contemporaries' selfless and heroic efforts to properly bury our dead, and
- declares, in effect, that once the soul has departed the body, the lifeless body has no further value.

May we soon merit seeing the day when this whole discussion is rendered inapplicable, for G-d will "conceal death forever, and the L-rd G-d shall wipe the tears off every face."[52]

Reprinted with permission from Chabad.org

Endnotes

[1] Code of Jewish Law, Yorah Deah 348:3; 362:1.

[2] The rabbinic responsibility to institute ordinances to deter people from violating Biblical commands is referenced in Mishna, Avot 1:1; Talmud Yevamot 21a, based on Leviticus 18:30.

[3] Melamed L'hoil Vol 2 #114 (Responsa of Rabbi David Hoffman, 1843–1921, noted German authority on Jewish law). Whether or not there is an obligation to bury the ashes elsewhere, in order to prevent further disgrace, is the subject of dispute between halachic authorities.

[4] This is based on the principle (quoted in the Code of Jewish Law, Yoreh De'ah 345:5) that we do not mourn after individuals who have "strayed from the ways of the community" (Responsa Minchat Elazar, vol. 2 ch. 34).

[5] Chatam Sofer Responsa (by Rabbi Moses Sofer, 1762–1839, famed rabbi of Pressburg, Slovakia), vol. 3 (Even Ha'ezer 1) ch. 69.

[6] Code of Jewish Law, Yoreh Deah 348:2.

[7] E.g. Code of Jewish Law, Yoreh Deah 349:2.

[8] Code of Jewish Law, Yoreh Deah 348:3 (See Jerusalem Talmud Ketubot 11:1).

[9] Talmud Nedarim 27a; Bava Kamma 28b; Avodah Zarah 54a; deduced from Deuteronomy 22:26.

[10] Talmud Shabbat 68b; Maimonides, Laws of Mamrim 3:3.

[11] Genesis 2:7.

[12] Ibid.

[13] Genesis 3:19. This is also the reason why Jewish law advocates the use of a wooden casket, which will fully disintegrate.

[14] 21:23.

[15] Nazir 7:1.

[16] See Maimonides, Laws of Murder 1:4; Ridvaz, Laws of Sanhedrin 18; Shulchan Aruch Harav (by Rabbi Schneur Zalman of Liadi) Laws of Body Damages 4.

[17] Adapted from a letter by the Lubavitcher Rebbe, of righteous memory, dated 26 Nissan 5729 (1969).

[18] Genesis 1:27.

[19] See Genesis 9:6.

[20] Deuteronomy 14:1.

[21] Leviticus 19:28.

[22] Maimonides, Laws of Murder 11:5; Code of Jewish Law, Yoreh De'ah 427:9-10.

[23] Deduced from Deuteronomy 21:23. See Da'at Cohen, Responsa of Rabbi Abraham Isaac Kook (1864–1935, Israel's first Chief Rabbi).

[24] The Talmud (Bava Batra 115a) relates: It once happened that a person sold his deceased father's estate, and then died himself. The other family members claimed that he was a minor at the time of death and was therefore unauthorized to sell the property. The rabbis did not allow them, however, to medically examine the body to determine his age. "You are not permitted to dishonor him," Rabbi Akiba said.

From here we infer that it is forbidden to modify the body of the deceased in any manner even if it would lead to tangible results. The Talmud (Chullin 11b) also discusses the possibility of performing an autopsy on a murder victim to ascertain the state of the victim's health at the time of the murder. The result of this autopsy could have possibly affected the murderer's punishment. The Talmud objects on grounds of disrespect toward the dead and concludes that only in the theoretical event that the autopsy would actually serve to *save* the murderer (considering the premium Jewish law places on saving lives) would it be allowed.
See also Noda B'Yehudah Y.D. 210; Chatam Sofer Y.D. 336.

[25] The Lubavitcher Rebbe explains in the previously cited letter (fn 17) that in those very rare cases "where an exception was made to the rule, it was because of special reasons, which in no way diminished the sanctity and inviolability of the body, as G-d's property, but only because under special circumstances, G-d Himself has permitted certain isolated exceptions, in which case it is the Owner's will that is being carried out, namely G-d's will."

[26] Deuteronomy 21:23; Code of Jewish Law, Yoreh De'ah 357:1.

[27] Kol Bo p. 175; Hadrat Kodesh 3a.

[28] Maimonides, Laws of Mourning 3:6.

[29] End of tractate Chagigah.

[30] 60:21.

[31] Maimonides even considers the concept of the soul's reward to be a principle Jewish belief.

[32] Tanya (by Rabbi Schneur Zalman of Liadi, 1745–1812, founder of Chabad chassidic movement), ch. 36.

[33] See Likutei Torah (Rabbi Schneur Zalman of Liadi), Deuteronomy 29a.

[34] Maimonides, Laws of Kings 11:1, based on Deuteronomy 30:3-5; ibid. 19:8; Numbers 24:17-18; and, to quote Maimonides, "from the words of the Prophets it is unnecessary to bring proof, for all their books are filled with this concept."

[35] The Talmud, Sanhedrin 90b–91b, brings multiple scriptural proofs for the resurrection.

[36] Introduction to his commentary on "Chapter *Chelek*" in tractate Sanhedrin.

[37] Isaiah 11:1; Maimonides, Laws of Kings 11:1.

[38] Micah 4:3.

[39] Deuteronomy 30:3-4.

[40] Maimonides, ibid.

[41] Tanya, ch. 36.

[42] Isaiah 40:5.

[43] Achiezer Vol. 3 #72 (Responsa of Rabbi Chaim Ozer Grodzinski, early 20th century Lithuanian rabbi); Beit Yitzchok, Yoreh Deah Vol. 2 #155.

[44] Mishna, tractate Sanhedrin 10:1.

[45] See Igrot Kodesh by the Lubavitcher Rebbe, vol. 1 p. 142–153.

[46] See Minchat Elazar responsa cited above in footnote 3.

[47] Leviticus 18:3.

[48] See S'dei Chemed encyclopedia, "Mourning" entry.

[49] Zohar I 122b.

[50] Jerusalem Talmud Mo'ed Kattan 3:5.

[51] Hist. 5:5.

[52] Isaiah 25:8.

Lesson 3

THE MOURNING AFTER
GRIEF AND CONSOLATION

What is the Jewish grieving process, and what is the significance of its various traditions? This lesson provides a meaningful Jewish perspective on grief itself, as well as practical shiva etiquette both for mourners and for those who wish to comfort them.

▲ **THE CHILD AND DEATH (DETAIL)**
Edvard Munch, oil on canvas, Italy, 1899. (Kunsthalle Bremen)

I. THE GRIEF SPECTRUM

The passing of a loved one is one of the greatest tragedies a person can experience. Nevertheless, while death is inevitable, the experience of loss felt by those left behind varies greatly from one individual to the next. Many factors play into the nuances of personal response, such as the circumstances of the death and the nature of the deceased's relationship with the loved one, as well as the mourner's psychological makeup.

TEXT 1

RESILIENCE IN THE FACE OF LOSS

GEORGE A. BONANNO, PHD,
THE OTHER SIDE OF SADNESS: WHAT THE NEW SCIENCE OF BEREAVEMENT TELLS US ABOUT LIFE AFTER LOSS (BASIC BOOKS, NEW YORK: 2009), PP. 1–2

GEORGE A. BONANNO, PHD
Psychologist. Dr. Bonanno is a professor of clinical psychology at Columbia University. He is known as a pioneering researcher in the field of bereavement and trauma and is a leading expert on resilience.

Heather Lindquist was in the kitchen cleaning up after lunch when she heard a dull thud. It sounded as if it came from the hallway, and it was just a little too loud to ignore. "Boys!" she yelled. "What are you up to?" There was no answer. She found her two boys playing quietly on the couch in the living room. They giggled. "You jokers," she said with a smile. "What was that sound?" They shrugged. "Where is your father?" Without waiting for an answer, she ran toward the hallway. She cried out in fear when she found her husband, John, writhing on the floor. John had severe asthma. He was taking a new medication, and it had seemed to be working, but suddenly he had collapsed in the worst attack he'd ever had. Heather tried everything she could think of to save her husband's life. Then she called an ambulance. The rest was a blur. John died of cardiac arrest on the way to the hospital.

Heather was thirty-four years old. Her boys were five and seven. At that moment, John's death felt like the worst thing that could ever have happened to her. . . .

Heather Lindquist had lived her entire life in the same quiet suburban community in northern New Jersey. She and John had been high school sweethearts. They married and purchased a small ranch-style house. They had children. They got a dog. The schools were good and the community was stable. Heather thought that the television was on more than it should be, but other than that, everything seemed in order. Then John died and she had to rethink it all.

Now she was a single parent. She had to find new ways to earn money and also find extra time to be with her boys. And somehow she had to contain everyone's anguish. She found strength she didn't know she had. It was lonely and painful at times. But Heather found meaning and vigor and even joy in the idea that she was going to make it.

"I expected to collapse. I really did. That's what I wanted to do. That would have been the easiest thing to do," Heather explained. "But . . . I couldn't. Each day I got up and did what I had to. The days passed and somehow it was OK. The boys were great. They were upset in the beginning, of course. We all were. They hung in there. And we stayed together. I love those boys so much. John would have been proud of them."

The Torah teaches how to sustain a delicate balance between grief and consolation. In "The Limits of Grief," *Rabbi Jonathan Sacks* elaborates on this: *myJLI.com/soul*

TEXT 2

OVERWHELMED BY GRIEF

FRAN SCHUMER, "AFTER A DEATH, THE PAIN THAT DOESN'T GO AWAY," *THE NEW YORK TIMES*, SEPTEMBER 28, 2009

In 2004, Stephanie Muldberg of Short Hills, N.J., lost her son Eric, 13, to Ewing's sarcoma, a bone cancer. Four years after Eric's death, Ms. Muldberg, now 48, walked around like a zombie. "I felt guilty all the time, guilty about living," she said. "I couldn't walk into the deli because Eric couldn't go there any longer. I couldn't play golf because Eric couldn't play golf. My life was a mess.

"And I couldn't talk to my friends about it, because after a while they didn't want to hear about it. 'Stephanie, you need to get your life back,' they'd say. But how could I? On birthdays, I'd shut the door and take the phone off the hook. Eric couldn't have any more birthdays; why should I?"

QUESTIONS

Heather and Stephanie reacted differently to their respective losses. Is one response healthier than the other?

Is Heather in denial?

Is Stephanie overreacting?

Why did the two women react differently?

If you know someone who did or did not deal well with loss, what might have made that person equipped or ill-equipped to cope with their grief?

"Beyond Grief" is a fascinating interview with *Rabbi Dr. Yitzchak Breitowitz* on the topic of moving on after crushing grief: *myJLI.com/soul*

II. MOURNING

How is mourning viewed from a religious and/or philosophical perspective? Is it an ideal—or even appropriate—response to death? Or is it an expression of weakness, an indication of a lack of faith in G-d's ever-present benevolence and justice?

Most of us take for granted that mourning the passing of a loved one is both natural and wise, but there have been incredibly wise people who disagreed with this assumption.

This chapter will explore Judaism's unique position on grief and mourning: Why does Judaism consider such a response appropriate? To what degree does it embrace mourning? What exactly is the Jewish mourning process?

TEXT 3

A PHILOSO-PHER'S DEATH WISH

JOWETT, B. (TRANSLATOR), *THE DIALOGUES OF PLATO*, THIRD EDITION (LONDON: OXFORD: UNIVERSITY PRESS, 1892), VOL. II, *PHAEDO*, PP. 157–265

PLATO
5TH CENTURY BCE

Philosopher. Plato was a student of Socrates and a teacher of Aristotle. His writings explored justice, beauty, and equality and also contained discussions on aesthetics, political philosophy, theology, cosmology, epistemology, and the philosophy of language. Plato founded the Academy in Athens, one of the first institutions of higher learning in the Western world.

[Socrates instructed:]

"Cebes, please relate the following message to Evenus, and bid him be of good cheer;
say that I would have him come after me [by immediately leaving this world] if he be a wise man, and not tarry; and that today I am likely to be going, for the Athenians say that I must."

Simmias said: "What a message for such a man! Having been a frequent companion of his I should say that, as far as I know him, he will never take your advice unless he is obliged."

"Why," said Socrates, "is not Evenus a philosopher?"

"I think that he is," said Simmias.

TEXT 3 CONTINUED

"Then he, or any man who has the spirit of philosophy, will be willing to die; but he will not take his own life, for that is held to be unlawful. . . . The day may come when you will understand . . . why, [though] a man is better dead, he is not permitted to be his own benefactor, but must wait for the hand of another."

TEXT 4

MANDATORY GRIEVING

MAIMONIDES, *MISHNEH TORAH*, LAWS OF MOURNING 1:1

מִצְוַת עֲשֵׂה לְהִתְאַבֵּל עַל הַקְרוֹבִים.

We are biblically commanded to mourn the [deaths of our] next of kin.

RABBI MOSHE BEN MAIMON (MAIMONIDES, RAMBAM) 1135–1204

Halachist, philosopher, author, and physician. Maimonides was born in Córdoba, Spain. After the conquest of Córdoba by the Almohads, he fled Spain and eventually settled in Cairo, Egypt. There, he became the leader of the Jewish community and served as court physician to the vizier of Egypt. He is most noted for authoring the *Mishneh Torah,* an encyclopedic arrangement of Jewish law; and for his philosophical work, *Guide for the Perplexed.* His rulings on Jewish law are integral to the formation of halachic consensus.

TEXT 5A

WE CAN'T OUTLAW NATURE

NACHMANIDES,
DEUTERONOMY 14:1–2

**RABBI MOSHE BEN NACHMAN
(NACHMANIDES, RAMBAN) 1194–1270**

Scholar, philosopher, author, and
physician. Nachmanides was born
in Spain and served as leader of
Iberian Jewry. In 1263, he was
summoned by King James of
Aragon to a public disputation with
Pablo Cristiani, a Jewish apostate.
Though Nachmanides was the
clear victor of the debate, he had to
flee Spain because of the resulting
persecution. He moved to Israel and
helped reestablish communal life
in Jerusalem. He authored a classic
commentary on the Pentateuch and
a commentary on the Talmud.

וְלֹא יֶאֱסֹר הַכָּתוּב הַבְּכִי,
כִּי הַטֶּבַע יִתְעוֹרֵר לִבְכּוֹת בְּפֵירוּד הָאוֹהֲבִים וְנִדוּדָם,
אַף בַּחַיִּים.

The Torah does not forbid us to weep
[in response to a death],
because it is human nature to be moved to tears
when separating from loved ones
and at their journeying away,
even if they are alive.

In "Usher in the Dawn: From Pain to
Purpose," *Sherri Mandell* describes
her heartrending journey from tragic
loss to finding comfort in purpose:
myJLI.com/soul

INHERITANCE (DETAIL) ▶
Edvard Munch, painting,
1897–1899. (The Munch
Museum, Oslo)

TEXT 5B

CATHARTIC CRYING

MAIMONIDES, *GUIDE FOR THE PERPLEXED* 3:41

כִּי לְבַעֲלֵי הָאֵבֶל, מְנוּחָה בִּבְכִיָּה וְעוֹרְרָם אֶבְלָם,
עַד שֶׁיֶּחֱלְשׁוּ כֹּחוֹת הַגּוּפָנִים מִסְּבוֹל הַמִּקְרֶה הַהוּא הַנַּפְשִׁי,
כְּמוֹ שֶׁלְּבַעֲלֵי הַשִּׂמְחָה מְנוּחָה בְּמִינֵי הַשְּׂחוֹק.

Mourners find comfort in crying
and in arousing their sorrow
until their bodies are too weak to handle
the intensity of their internal turmoil—
just as happy individuals find contentment
in various forms of lighthearted activities.

TEXT 5C

GOOD REASON TO CRY

RABBI DAVID IBN ZIMRA, *RESPONSA*, 3:555

שְׁאֵלָה: עַל אֶחָד מִגְּדוֹלֵי הַדּוֹר שֶׁמֵּת לוֹ בֵּן וְלֹא הוֹרִיד
עָלָיו דִּמְעָה אַחַת, אִם זוֹ מִדָּה טוֹבָה אוֹ לֹא?

תְּשׁוּבָה: זוֹ מִדָּה רָעָה, מוֹרֶה עַל קוֹשִׁי הַלֵּב וְעַל רוֹעַ תְּכוּנַת
הַנֶּפֶשׁ, וְהִיא מִדַּת אַכְזָרִיּוּת, וְהוּא דֶּרֶךְ הַפִילוֹסוֹפִים הָאוֹמְרִים
כִּי זֶה הָעוֹלָם הַכֹּל הוּא מַעֲשֶׂה תַּעְתּוּעִים...

אֲבָל אֲנַחְנוּ מְקַבְּלֵי הַתּוֹרָה יֵשׁ לָנוּ לְהַאֲמִין וְלָדַעַת כִּי הָעוֹלָם
הַזֶּה עִנְיָן נִכְבָּד מְאֹד לַמִּסְתַּפְּקִים מִמֶּנּוּ כָּרָאוּי וְלַמִּתְנַהֲגִים
בּוֹ כַּשּׁוּרָה, וּבוֹ יַשִּׂיג הָאָדָם חַיֵּי הָעוֹלָם הַבָּא...

וְהַבּוֹכֶה וּמִתְאַבֵּל וּמוֹרִיד דְּמָעוֹת עַל קְרוֹבִים, וְכָל שֶׁכֵּן עַל אָדָם כָּשֵׁר, מִדַּת
חֲסִידִים וּנְבִיאִים וְאַנְשֵׁי מַעֲשֶׂה הִיא... וְלֹא לְחִנָּם אָמְרוּ רַזַ"ל, "שְׁלֹשָׁה לַבְּכִי,
ז' לַהֶסְפֵּד, שְׁלֹשִׁים לְגִיהוּץ וְתִסְפֹּרֶת", וְאִם הָיָה הַדָּבָר בִּלְתִּי נָאוֹת לֹא הָיוּ
מְתַקְּנִין לוֹ ג' יָמִים. וְכֵן אַבְרָהָם אָבִינוּ עָלָיו הַשָּׁלוֹם כְּתִיב בֵּיהּ, "לִסְפֹּד לְשָׂרָה
וְלִבְכֹּתָהּ" (בְּרֵאשִׁית כג, ב), וְכֵן יַעֲקֹב, וְכֵן דָּוִד הַמֶּלֶךְ, וְרַבִּים כָּאֵלֶּה אֵין מִסְפָּר.

RABBI DAVID IBN ZIMRA (RADVAZ), 1479–1573

Noted halachist. Radvaz was born in Spain and immigrated to Safed, Israel, upon the expulsion of the Jews from Spain in 1492. In 1513, he moved to Egypt and served as rabbi, judge, and head of the yeshiva in Cairo. He also ran many successful business ventures and was independently wealthy. In 1553, he returned to Safed where he would later be buried. He authored what would later become a classic commentary to Maimonides's code of law and wrote many halachic responsa, of which more than 10,000 are still extant.

Question:

One of this generation's greatest personalities failed to shed a single tear upon losing a son. Is this a praiseworthy reaction?

Answer:

Such behavior is offensive and objectionable; it demonstrates heartlessness, distasteful character, and cruelty. This is the way of the philosophers who maintained that this world is without purpose. . . .

By contrast, we who have received the Torah are expected to believe and to realize that this world is of great value for those who properly utilize their time here and behave appropriately. It is through our actions in this world that we merit the World to Come. . . .

Crying, mourning, and shedding tears over the passing of a relative, and especially for an honorable individual, is the way of the pious, the prophets, and individuals renowned for their good deeds. . . . It is not for naught that our sages instruct us to observe "three days for weeping, seven for eulogies, and thirty for restrictions on wearing new clothing and getting haircuts [etc.]." If weeping were improper, the sages would not have instituted a three-day weeping period. In fact, the Torah emphasizes that our forefather Abraham came to "eulogize Sarah and weep for her" (GENESIS 23:2) and that Jacob, King David, and countless individuals of similar caliber acted likewise.

FIGURE 3.1

DEFINING KIN

The Torah rules of mourning are limited to the following next of kin:

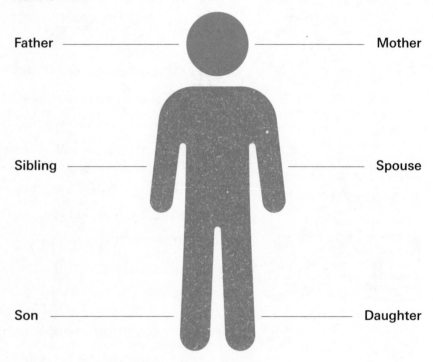

Father ——————— Mother

Sibling ——————— Spouse

Son ——————— Daughter

FIGURE 3.2

KEY JEWISH MOURNING OBSERVANCES*

Time Period	Associated Laws and Traditions
1 **Aninut** *From the moment of passing until the interment*	This is the most intense phase of mourning. At this point, no attempt is even made to comfort or console the mourners. During this period, the next of kin are absolved from all "positive" *mitzvot* (i.e., obligations to do something, such as pray or don *tefilin*). Nothing should detract or distract from the mourners' pain and their full attention to interment arrangements. Sometime during the *aninut* stage, the mourners tear their outer garment as a sign of mourning.
7 **Shiva** *A seven-day mourning period, commencing with interment*	See below, Figure 3.5 (p. 110).
30 **Sheloshim** *A thirty-day mourning period, commencing with interment*	After "getting up" from shiva and resuming the everyday routines of life, certain mourning practices are continued until thirty days from the time of burial. These include refraining from wearing new clothes, getting a haircut or shaving, and participating in festive events.
12 **Twelve months** *A twelve-month mourning period, commencing with interment*	After the passing of a parent, some of the *sheloshim* mourning practices (such as not participating in festive events) are continued by the children until twelve months have passed. It is customary for the mourners to keep a candle burning for the entire twelve-month period.
Yahrtzeit *Anniversary of the passing*	The anniversary of the death (*yahrtzeit*) is observed with the recitation of the Kaddish, additional Torah study, and other good deeds in the memory of and to bring merit to the deceased.

* Important notes:

1) The following is but a brief overview of some of the primary mourning practices (*aveilut*) mandated by Torah law. It should not be taken as practical guidance for *aveilut*, as the actual laws are quite detailed, and they do not all apply equally to each situation.

2) Almost all mourning practices are suspended on Shabbat and biblical holidays.

III. PROCESSING THE PAIN

The *mitzvot* and laws of the Torah are multifaceted and cannot be reduced to psychological benefits they may engender. At the same time, living a moral, holy, and G-dly life is beneficial in numerous ways, including for one's mental and emotional well-being.

FIGURE 3.3

THE TWO-TRACK MODEL OF BEREAVEMENT

BY SIMON SHIMSHON RUBIN, PHD, UNIVERSITY OF HAIFA

TABLE CREATED FROM CONCEPTS FROM S. S. RUBIN, ET AL., *WORKING WITH THE BEREAVED: MULTIPLE LENSES ON LOSS AND MOURNING* (NEW YORK: ROUTLEDGE, 2013), FIGURE 3.1, TABLE 3.1, TABLE 3.2, TABLE 3.3

ANXIETY
Thoughts and feelings: What are the degree and frequency of these; what triggers and what mitigates these responses?

INTERPERSONAL RELATIONSHIPS
How are the current relationships with friends, colleagues, neighbors, etc.? What has changed for the positive or negative?

HOW IS THE MOURNER'S BIOPSYCHOSOCIAL FUNCTION?

WHERE ARE STRENGTHS AND DIFFICULTIES?

DEPRESSION
Thoughts and feelings: What are the degree and frequency of these; what triggers and what mitigates these responses?

TRACK I: FUNCTION

TRACK II: RELATIONSHIP TO THE DECEASED

WHAT IS THE NATURE OF THE RELATIONSHIP WITH THE DECEASED?

WHAT ARE THE MOURNER'S ADAPTIVE STRENGTHS AND WEAKNESSES REGARDING THE DECEASED AND THE DEATH?

IMAGERY AND MEMORY
What is the degree, content, and nature of what is remembered of the deceased and the relationship with the deceased?

RECONNECTION
What is the nature, character, and strength of the wish to reconnect with the person who died?

NEGATIVE PERCEPTIONS/AFFECT
What negative perceptions and affect are present when thinking about the person who died? What stimulated negative feelings?

SELF-ESTEEM
Is there a sense of self as helpless, unimportant, worthless, alone; OR as competent, unshaken, and stimulated to grow?

MEANING STRUCTURE
How have values, worldview, spirituality, religion, or existential understanding changed?

SOMATIC CONCERNS
What is the current state of physical processes such as appetite, sleep, sexual drive, and general health concerns?

WORK
Is it possible to adequately (or more adequately) meet demands at work?

TRAUMATIC RESPONSES
What is the degree and duration of trauma symptoms? Could there be PTSD or Acute Stress Disorder?

INVESTMENT IN LIFE TASKS
Is there energy/motivation for tasks beyond just existing? Has there been any growth?

FAMILIAL RELATIONSHIPS
How are the current relationships with spouse, parent, children, siblings, and extended family? What has changed for the positive or negative?

EMOTIONAL CLOSENESS
What degree of emotional closeness involvement is experienced and communicated about the person who died and the relationship with that person?

THE LOSS TRAJECTORY
Is there a reconfigured understanding of "stages of loss" as dimensions of the response to loss?

CONFLICT
To what degree is the person who died remembered as someone with whom there was a problematic relationship?

POSITIVE PERCEPTIONS/ AFFECTS
What positive perceptions and affects are present when thinking about the person who died? What stimulates positive feelings?

UPSETTING IMPACT ON SELF-SYSTEM
Have there been feelings of lower self-esteem, such as feelings of guilt or lower self-worth?

PREOCCUPATION WITH THE LOSS
What is the degree of time invested in thinking about the loss/lost person? What precipitates or mitigates the preoccupation?

MEMORIALIZATION AND TRANSFORMATION
Have there been meaningful ways found to memorialize the person who died?

FIGURE 3.4

JEWISH MOURNING OBSERVANCES AND PSYCHOLOGY

	Track 1 Function		**Track 2** Relationship to the Deceased
	Only minimal function is expected.	**ANINUT**	At this time, *all* one's actions are aimed at furthering the respect and honor of the deceased.
	a. A time of limited function; usual duties and routines are suspended. b. Despite continuous awareness of the loss, there's a need to function and receive visitors.	**SHIVA**	a. Sharing memories of the deceased sharpens the relationship to the deceased and deepens the awareness of what was lost. b. Numerous religious rituals provide merit to the deceased in the next world.
	Outside responsibilities resume, with the exception of several requirements designed to mark one's mourning.	**SHELOSHIM**	Less time is allocated to focus on the loss, although the griever continues to contemplate the loss and engages in numerous religious activities—especially the recitation of Kaddish—to give merit to the deceased.
	Same as above with continued progress in function	**TWELVE MONTHS**	Same as above with reduced emphasis
	Continued awareness of the loss, but with function at a stable level and grief fluctuations relatively confined	**YAHRTZEIT**	Actions and prayers mark the loss. Space on the calendar is provided for additional strengthening of the relationship and the continuing bonds.

TEXT 6

TEARING GARMENTS AS AN EXPRESSION OF GRIEF

GENESIS 37:31–34

וַיִּקְחוּ אֶת כְּתֹנֶת יוֹסֵף וַיִּשְׁחֲטוּ שְׂעִיר עִזִּים וַיִּטְבְּלוּ אֶת הַכֻּתֹּנֶת בַּדָּם.
וַיְשַׁלְּחוּ אֶת כְּתֹנֶת הַפַּסִּים וַיָּבִיאוּ אֶל אֲבִיהֶם וַיֹּאמְרוּ,
"זֹאת מָצָאנוּ. הַכֶּר נָא הַכְּתֹנֶת בִּנְךָ הִוא אִם לֹא".

וַיַּכִּירָהּ, וַיֹּאמֶר,
"כְּתֹנֶת בְּנִי. חַיָּה רָעָה אֲכָלָתְהוּ. טָרֹף טֹרַף יוֹסֵף".

וַיִּקְרַע יַעֲקֹב שִׂמְלֹתָיו וַיָּשֶׂם שַׂק בְּמָתְנָיו
וַיִּתְאַבֵּל עַל בְּנוֹ יָמִים רַבִּים.

The [brothers] slaughtered a goat
and dipped Joseph's tunic in its blood.
They sent the colored tunic [home],
and [the couriers] brought it to their father and said,
"We have found this;
please identify whether or not it is your son's tunic."

Jacob recognized it and exclaimed,
"It is my son's tunic!
A wild beast has devoured him!
Joseph has been torn to pieces!"

Jacob rent his garments,
placed sackcloth on his loins,
and mourned his son for many days.

Dr. Lisa Aiken talks about shiva and
"Coping with Loss": *myJLI.com/soul*

TEXT 7

TRIGGERING THE GRIEF PROCESS

RABBI YEHUDAH AYASH,
RESPONSA BEIT YEHUDAH,
YOREH DE'AH 26

RABBI YEHUDAH AYASH
C. 1700–1760

Rabbi and halachic authority. Rabbi Yehudah Ayash was raised in Algiers, where his father, Rabbi Yitschak, served as rabbi. While still a young man, Rabbi Yehudah was appointed Chief Rabbi of Algiers, and he became one of the most prominent halachic authorities in North Africa. In 1756 he moved to Jerusalem, where he headed a yeshiva until his passing. Rabbi Ayash wrote commentaries on the Torah and Jewish law, and he is best known for his collection of responsa, *Beit Yehudah.*

בְּעִנְיַן הַקְּרִיעָה כָּתַב הָרַב בַּהֲלָכוֹת קְטַנּוֹת סִימָן קי״ו, יְעוּיָּין שָׁם, בְּטַעַם הַקְּרִיעָה הוּא כְּדֵי שֶׁלֹּא תִּיטָרֵף דַּעְתּוֹ עָלָיו. לַעֲנִיּוּת דַּעְתִּי נִרְאֶה אִיפְּכָא, דְּאַדְרַבָּה כְּדֵי שֶׁיְּעוֹרֵר עַצְמוֹ בִּבְכִי וּלְהַפְלִיג צַעֲרוֹ . . . כְּדֵי שֶׁיִּצְטַעֵר עַל מֵתוֹ וְלִדְאֹג עָלָיו בְּיוֹתֵר.

Rabbi Yaakov Chagiz states [in *Halachot Ketanot,* ch. 116] that mourners are instructed to rend their garments as a method of distracting from and reducing their overwhelming grief. In my humble opinion, the opposite is true: having to rend their garments brings mourners to tears and amplifies their pain. . . . The goal is to actively encourage mourners to express their pain over the passing, and to experience their tremendous loss.

JACOB RECEIVING JOSEPH'S BLOOD-STAINED CLOAK ▶
Nicolaes Maes, pen and brown ink, brush and brown wash, over red and traces of black chalk, Amsterdam, c. 1653. (Metropolitan Museum of Art, New York, NY)

IV. FINDING COMFORT

The Jewish way of mourning is designed to induce a gradual but progressive emergence into normal society and function. At every step of the way, the mourner needs to focus their energies on processing where they are and then moving on to the next, reduced stage of mourning.

TEXT 8

RETURN IN PHASES

TALMUD, MO'ED KATAN 27B

BABYLONIAN TALMUD

A literary work of monumental proportions that draws upon the legal, spiritual, intellectual, ethical, and historical traditions of Judaism. The 37 tractates of the Babylonian Talmud contain the teachings of the Jewish sages from the period after the destruction of the 2nd Temple through the 5th century CE. It has served as the primary vehicle for the transmission of the Oral Law and the education of Jews over the centuries; it is the entry point for all subsequent legal, ethical, and theological Jewish scholarship.

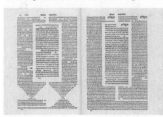

"אַל תִּבְכּוּ לְמֵת וְאַל תָּנֻדוּ לוֹ" (יִרְמְיָהוּ כב, י).

"אַל תִּבְכּוּ לְמֵת" יוֹתֵר מִדַּאי, "וְאַל תָּנֻדוּ לוֹ" יוֹתֵר מִכַּשִּׁיעוּר.

הָא כֵּיצַד? שְׁלֹשָׁה יָמִים לִבְכִי,

וְשִׁבְעָה לְהֶסְפֵּד, וּשְׁלֹשִׁים לַגִּיהוּץ וְלַתִּסְפֹּרֶת.

מִכָּאן וְאֵילָךְ אָמַר הַקָּדוֹשׁ בָּרוּךְ הוּא, "אִי אַתֶּם רַחְמָנִים בּוֹ יוֹתֵר מִמֶּנִּי".

"Neither cry for the dead nor bemoan him" (JEREMIAH 22:10).
"Neither cry for the dead" more than necessary, "nor bemoan him" more than what is prescribed.

How are we expected to act?
Three days for weeping, seven days for eulogies, and thirty days for [restrictions on] new clothing and haircuts.

Once these have elapsed, G-d declares:
"You are not more compassionate than I."

QUESTION

Take a moment to recall some of the insights you've learned in this course. Can you identify concepts that might serve as consolation to a mourner?

TEXT 9A

CONSOLATION SCRIPT

TRADITIONAL ASHKENAZIC TEXT
FOR COMFORTING MOURNERS

▼ **SIEGE AND DESTRUCTION OF JERUSALEM**
David Roberts, oil on canvas, c.1850. (Williamson Art Gallery and Museum, U.K.)

הַמָּקוֹם יְנַחֵם אֶתְכֶם
בְּתוֹךְ שְׁאָר אֲבֵלֵי צִיּוֹן וִירוּשָׁלָיִם.

May the Omnipresent G-d console you
along with the other mourners of Zion and Jerusalem.

TEXT 9B

THE INDESTRUCTIBIL-ITY OF SPIRIT

THE REBBE, RABBI MENACHEM MENDEL SCHNEERSON, *IGROT KODESH* 25, P. 5

RABBI MENACHEM MENDEL SCHNEERSON 1902–1994

The towering Jewish leader of the 20th century, known as "the Lubavitcher Rebbe," or simply as "the Rebbe." Born in southern Ukraine, the Rebbe escaped Nazi-occupied Europe, arriving in the U.S. in June 1941. The Rebbe inspired and guided the revival of traditional Judaism after the European devastation, impacting virtually every Jewish community the world over. The Rebbe often emphasized that the performance of just one additional good deed could usher in the era of Mashiach. The Rebbe's scholarly talks and writings have been printed in more than 200 volumes.

כְּמוֹ שֶׁבְּנוֹגֵעַ לְצִיּוֹן וִירוּשָׁלַיִם שָׁלְטָה יַד הָרוֹמִים, וְקוֹדֶם לָכֵן יַד הַבַּבְלִים, רַק בְּבֵית הַמִּקְדָּשׁ הַבָּנוּי מֵעֵצִים וַאֲבָנִים כֶּסֶף וְזָהָב, אֲבָל בֵּית הַמִּקְדָּשׁ הַפְּנִימִי שֶׁבְּלֵב כָּל אֶחָד וְאַחַת שֶׁל יִשְׂרָאֵל אֵין יַד הָאוּמוֹת יְכוֹלָה לִשְׁלוֹט בּוֹ וְנִצְחִי הוּא, כַּךְ הוּא גַּם בְּנוֹגֵעַ לְאֵבֶל הַיָּחִיד, אֲשֶׁר יַד הַמָּוֶת שׁוֹלֶטֶת אַךְ וְרַק בְּהַגּוּף וְעִנְיָנָיו, אֲבָל הַנְּשָׁמָה נִצְחִית, הִיא רַק שֶׁעָלְתָה לְעוֹלָם הָאֱמֶת.

In regard to Zion and Jerusalem, the Romans—and before them, the Babylonians—were given dominion only over the wood and stone, silver and gold of the Temple's physical manifestation, but not over its inner spiritual essence, contained within the heart of each and every Jew. Over this, the nations have no dominion, and it stands eternally. So too, regarding the mourning of the individual, death dominates only the physical body and concerns of the deceased person. The soul, however, is eternal; it has merely ascended to the World of Truth.

TEXT 10

GARMENT: A METAPHOR FOR THE BODY

RABBI ARON MOSS, "WHY DO WE TEAR OUR CLOTHES AFTER A DEATH?" WWW.CHABAD.ORG

RABBI ARON MOSS

Rabbi and author. Rabbi Moss is a teacher of kabbalah, Talmud, and practical Judaism in Sydney, Australia. He serves as rabbi of the Nefesh Synagogue and authors a popular weekly syndicated article on modern Jewish thought.

Often, within [their] pain, the mourners have an underlying belief that "it isn't true"—that their loved one hasn't really gone. This is not just denial; in a way they are right. Death is not an absolute reality. Our souls existed before we were born, and they continue to exist after we die. The souls that have passed on are still with us. We can't see them, but we sense they are there. We can't hear them, but we know that they hear us. On the surface, we are apart. Beyond the surface, nothing can separate us.

So we tear our garments. This has a dual symbolism. We are recognizing the loss, that our hearts are torn. But ultimately, the body is also only a garment that the soul wears. Death is when we strip off one uniform and take on another. The garment may be torn, but the essence of the person within it is still intact.

From our worldly perspective, death is indeed a tragedy, and the sorrow experienced by the mourners is real. But as they tear their garments, we hope that within their pain they can sense a glimmer of a deeper truth: that souls never die.

Are we to mourn a death or celebrate the life lived? *Rabbi Yosef Y. Jacobson's* "To Mourn or to Celebrate" offers insight: *myJLI.com/soul*

V. HEALING TRUTHS

Loss is a deeply personal experience. It is natural for individuals to react dissimilarly. In some cases, a mourner will be struck particularly deeply and find it incredibly difficult to emerge from their shell of grief. Some of the Torah insights that can be of help in such instances are presented in the following texts.

TEXT 11

FIVE STUDENTS ATTEMPT TO CONSOLE THEIR MASTER

AVOT DERABBI NATAN 14:6

AVOT DERABBI NATAN

A commentary on, and an elaboration of, the Mishnaic tractate Avot, bearing the name of Rabbi Natan, one of the sages of the Mishnah. The work exists in two very different versions, one of which appears in many editions of the Talmud.

כְּשֶׁמֵּת בְּנוֹ שֶׁל רַבָּן יוֹחָנָן בֶּן זַכַּאי, נִכְנְסוּ תַּלְמִידָיו לְנַחֲמוֹ.

נִכְנַס רַבִּי אֱלִיעֶזֶר וְיָשַׁב לְפָנָיו. וְאָמַר לוֹ, "רַבִּי, רְצוֹנְךָ, אוֹמֵר דָּבָר אֶחָד לְפָנֶיךָ". אָמַר לוֹ, "אֱמוֹר".

אָמַר לוֹ, "אָדָם הָרִאשׁוֹן הָיָה לוֹ בֵּן וָמֵת וְקִבֵּל עָלָיו תַּנְחוּמִין. וּמִנַּיִין שֶׁקִּבֵּל עָלָיו תַּנְחוּמִין? שֶׁנֶּאֱמַר (בְּרֵאשִׁית ד, א), 'וַיֵּדַע אָדָם עוֹד אֶת אִשְׁתּוֹ'. אַף אַתָּה קַבֵּל תַּנְחוּמִין".

אָמַר לוֹ, "לֹא דַי לִי שֶׁאֲנִי מִצְטַעֵר בְּעַצְמִי, אֶלָּא שֶׁהִזְכַּרְתָּ לִי צַעֲרוֹ שֶׁל אָדָם הָרִאשׁוֹן".

נִכְנַס רַבִּי יְהוֹשֻׁעַ וְאָמַר לוֹ, "רְצוֹנְךָ, אוֹמֵר דָּבָר אֶחָד לְפָנֶיךָ". אָמַר לוֹ, "אֱמוֹר".

אָמַר לוֹ, "אִיּוֹב הָיוּ לוֹ בָּנִים וּבָנוֹת, וּמֵתוּ כֻּלָּם בְּיוֹם אֶחָד, וְקִבֵּל עֲלֵיהֶם תַּנְחוּמִין. אַף אַתָּה קַבֵּל תַּנְחוּמִין. וּמִנַּיִין שֶׁקִּבֵּל אִיּוֹב תַּנְחוּמִין? שֶׁנֶּאֱמַר (אִיּוֹב א, כא), 'ה' נָתַן וַה' לָקַח, יְהִי שֵׁם ה' מְבֹרָךְ'".

אָמַר לוֹ, "לֹא דַי לִי שֶׁאֲנִי מִצְטַעֵר בְּעַצְמִי, אֶלָּא שֶׁהִזְכַּרְתָּ לִי צַעֲרוֹ שֶׁל אִיּוֹב".

נִכְנַס רַבִּי יוֹסֵי וְיָשַׁב לְפָנָיו. אָמַר לוֹ, "רַבִּי, רְצוֹנְךָ אוֹמֵר דָּבָר אֶחָד לְפָנֶיךָ". אָמַר לוֹ, "אֱמוֹר".

אָמַר לוֹ, "אַהֲרֹן הָיוּ לוֹ שְׁנֵי בָּנִים גְּדוֹלִים, וּמֵתוּ שְׁנֵיהֶם בְּיוֹם אֶחָד, וְקִבֵּל עֲלֵיהֶם תַּנְחוּמִין. שֶׁנֶּאֱמַר (וַיִּקְרָא י, ג), 'וַיִּדֹּם אַהֲרֹן'. אֵין שְׁתִיקָה אֶלָּא תַּנְחוּמִין. וְאַף אַתָּה קַבֵּל תַּנְחוּמִין".

אָמַר לוֹ, "לֹא דַי לִי שֶׁאֲנִי מִצְטַעֵר בְּעַצְמִי, אֶלָּא שֶׁהִזְכַּרְתַּנִי צַעֲרוֹ שֶׁל אַהֲרֹן".

נִכְנַס רַבִּי שִׁמְעוֹן וְאָמַר לוֹ, "רַבִּי, רְצוֹנְךָ אוֹמֵר דָּבָר אֶחָד לְפָנֶיךָ". אָמַר לוֹ, "אֱמוֹר".

TEXT 11 CONTINUED

אָמַר לוֹ, "דָּוִד הַמֶּלֶךְ הָיָה לוֹ בֵּן וָמֵת, וְקִבֵּל עָלָיו תַּנְחוּמִין. וְאַף אַתָּה קַבֵּל תַּנְחוּמִין. וּמִנַּיִן שֶׁקִּבֵּל דָּוִד תַּנְחוּמִין? שֶׁנֶּאֱמַר (שְׁמוּאֵל ב, יב, כד), 'וַיְנַחֵם דָּוִד אֵת בַּת שֶׁבַע אִשְׁתּוֹ וַיָּבֹא אֵלֶיהָ וַיִּשְׁכַּב עִמָּהּ וַתֵּלֶד בֵּן וַיִּקְרָא אֶת שְׁמוֹ שְׁלֹמֹה'. אַף אַתָּה רַבִּי קַבֵּל תַּנְחוּמִין".

אָמַר לוֹ, "לֹא דַי שֶׁאֲנִי מִצְטַעֵר בְּעַצְמִי, אֶלָּא שֶׁהִזְכַּרְתַּנִי צַעֲרוֹ שֶׁל דָּוִד הַמֶּלֶךְ".

נִכְנַס רַבִּי אֶלְעָזָר בֶּן עֲרָךְ. כֵּיוָן שֶׁרָאָהוּ, אָמַר לְשַׁמָּשׁוֹ, "טוֹל לְפָנַי כֵּלַי, וְלֵךְ אַחֲרַי לְבֵית הַמֶּרְחָץ, לְפִי שֶׁאָדָם גָּדוֹל הוּא וְאֵינִי יָכוֹל לַעֲמוֹד בּוֹ".

נִכְנַס וְיָשַׁב לְפָנָיו וְאָמַר לוֹ, "אֶמְשׁוֹל לְךָ מָשָׁל. לְמָה הַדָּבָר דּוֹמֶה? לְאָדָם שֶׁהִפְקִיד אֶצְלוֹ הַמֶּלֶךְ פִּקָּדוֹן. בְּכָל יוֹם וָיוֹם הָיָה בּוֹכֶה וְצוֹעֵק וְאוֹמֵר, 'אוֹי לִי, אֵימָתַי אֵצֵא מִן הַפִּקָּדוֹן הַזֶּה בְּשָׁלוֹם?'

"אַף אַתָּה רַבִּי, הָיָה לְךָ בֵּן. קָרָא תוֹרָה מִקְרָא נְבִיאִים וּכְתוּבִים מִשְׁנָה הֲלָכוֹת וְאַגָּדוֹת, וְנִפְטַר מִן הָעוֹלָם בְּלֹא חֵטְא. וְיֵשׁ לְךָ לְקַבֵּל עָלֶיךָ תַּנְחוּמִים כְּשֶׁהֶחֱזַרְתָּ פִּקְדוֹנֶךָ שָׁלֵם".

אָמַר לוֹ, "רַבִּי אֶלְעָזָר בְּנִי, נִחַמְתָּנִי כְּדֶרֶךְ שֶׁבְּנֵי אָדָם מְנַחֲמִין".

When the son of Rabbi Yochanan ben Zakai passed away, his students arrived to console him.

Rabbi Eliezer entered and sat before him. "Master!" he said. "Would you like me to share a thought?"

"Speak," he responded.

Rabbi Eliezer said, "Adam had a son who died, and he allowed himself to be consoled. How do we know that he accepted consolation? For it is stated (GENESIS 4:1), 'Adam was again intimate with his wife.' So you should also allow yourself to be consoled."

Rabbi Yochanan retorted, "Is it not enough that I am grieving my own loss, that you have to make me feel pained for Adam as well?"

Rabbi Yehoshua entered, and asked, "Would you like me to share a thought?"

"Speak," he responded.

Rabbi Yehoshua said, "Job had sons and daughters, and they all died in a single day, yet he allowed himself to be consoled. So you should also accept consolation. How do we know that Job was consoled? For he declared, 'G-d has given and G-d has taken; may G-d's name be blessed' (JOB 1:21)."

Rabbi Yochanan retorted, "Is it not enough that I am grieving my own loss, that you have to make me feel pained for Job as well?"

Rabbi Yosei entered and sat before him. "Master!" he said. "Would you like me to share a thought?"

"Speak," he responded.

Rabbi Yosei said, "Aaron had two illustrious sons, but they both died in a single day. And yet, he allowed himself to be consoled, as it is stated, 'Aaron kept silent' (LEVITICUS 10:3)—his silence implied that he [was without grievance and] accepted consolation. So you should also allow yourself to be consoled."

Rabbi Yochanan retorted, "Is it not enough that I am grieving my own loss, that you have to make me feel pained for Aaron as well?"

TEXT 11 CONTINUED

Rabbi Shimon entered. "Master!" he said. "Would you like me to share a thought?"

"Speak," he responded.

Rabbi Shimon said, "King David had a son who died, and he allowed himself to be consoled. And you should allow yourself to be consoled as well. How do we know that King David was consoled? For it is stated (II SAMUEL 12:24), 'David comforted Bathsheba his wife, and he was intimate with her and she bore a son, and he called his name Solomon.' So should you, Master, allow yourself to be consoled."

Rabbi Yochanan retorted, "Is it not enough that I am grieving my own loss, that you have to make me feel pained for King David as well?"

Rabbi Elazar ben Arach entered. When Rabbi Yochanan saw him, he told his attendant, "Grab a set of clothing for me and be prepared to follow me to the bathhouse, for Rabbi Elazar is a great person and I will not be able to hold out [in the face of his comforting words]."

Rabbi Elazar entered, sat before Rabbi Yochanan, and told him, "Let me share a parable: Your situation is similar to that of an individual to whom the king entrusted an article for safekeeping. Each day, the man would weep and wail [in fear], 'Woe is to me! When will I emerge unharmed from this safekeeping role?'

Yehoshua November's heartbreaking poem "Long Prayer" is a tribute to his cousin who died in the prime of his life: *myJLI.com/soul*

"You, Master, also had a son. He was fluent in the Torah, the Prophets, and Scriptures; in the Mishnah, the halachah, and the exegetical teachings; and he passed from this world without sin. You should certainly accept consolation, for you have returned your deposit in perfect condition."

Rabbi Yochanan responded, "Rabbi Elazar, my son! You have comforted me in a most humane fashion."

QUESTIONS

1. Why did Rabbi Yochanan fail to find comfort in the words of his four earlier visitors?

2. Why was he consoled by the message of Rabbi Elazar ben Arach?

▶ DANS LA SERRE (IN THE CONSERVATORY)
Édouard Manet, oil on canvas,
Berlin, Germany, c. 1877–1879.
(Alte Nationalgalerie, Staatliche
Museen zu Berlin)

TEXT 12

REGARDS, A LETTER, AND A PARCEL

RABBI AHARON OF KARLIN (CITED BY RABBI GAVRIEL ZINNER, *NITEI GAVRIEL*, LAWS OF MOURNING 2, P. 291)

RABBI AHARON OF KARLIN
1736–1772

Chasidic rebbe. Rabbi Aharon was a disciple of Rabbi Dov Ber of Mezeritch. He was known as Rabbi Aharon the Great, and was one of the pioneers of Chasidism in Lithuania. He is known for his ecstatic and unrestrained fervor during his prayers and for his caring for the needy. He is the composer of the Shabbat hymn *Kah echsof*.

כְּשֶׁהַבֵּן אוֹמֵר קַדִּישׁ עַל אָבִיו אוֹ אִמּוֹ הֲרֵי זֶה כְּמוֹ שֶׁשָּׁלַח לָהֶם פְּרִיסַת שָׁלוֹם,
כְּשֶׁלּוֹמֵד פֶּרֶק מִשְׁנָיוֹת בַּעֲדָם הֲרֵי זֶה כְּמוֹ שֶׁשָּׁלַח לָהֶם אִגֶּרֶת,
וּכְשֶׁמְּקַיֵּים מִצְווֹת וּמַעֲשִׂים טוֹבִים לְטוֹבַת נִשְׁמָתָם
הֲרֵי זֶה כְּמוֹ שֶׁשָּׁלַח לָהֶם חֲבִילָה שְׁלֵימָה.

When children say Kaddish for their parents,
it is like sending them regards.
When they learn a chapter of Mishnah on their behalf,
it is like sending them a letter.
And when they fulfill *mitzvot* and good deeds for the benefit of their souls,
it is like sending them an entire parcel.

VI. THE SHIVA HOUSE

Recognizing the need to productively process the trauma of burying a loved one, Judaism insists that after the funeral, the mourners spend the next (approximately) seven days grieving their loss in the context of the rite of shiva ("seven [days]").

The residence at which they observe this mourning period is colloquially referred to as their "shiva house." During this time, the mourners are supported by friends and community members who come to offer empathy and comfort, and to help facilitate an atmosphere of balanced reflection.

▼ **TISHAH BE'AV (LAMENTATION)**
Maurycy Minkowski, watercolor on paper, London, U.K., 1927. (Ben Uri Gallery, London)

FIGURE 3.5

BASIC SHIVA PROTOCOL**

Mirrors and pictures in the shiva house are to remain covered.

For the duration of shiva, the mourners observe the following conditions:

Remain in the house of mourning.

Continue wearing the garment that was torn as an act of mourning.

Sit on low chairs or stools.

Forgo the comfort of leather footwear.

Avoid listening to music.

Shun shaving and haircuts.

Abstain from work or business.

Refrain from marital intimacy.

Avoid studying Torah.

There are restrictions on bathing, showering, and wearing freshly laundered clothing. (Consult with a rabbi for direction.)

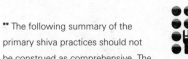

A *minyan* (prayer quorum) gathers in the house of mourning for the daily prayers. During the prayer services, the mourners recite the Kaddish.

Relatives, friends, and community members visit the mourners at their shiva house to fulfill the mitzvah of consoling the mourner and to participate in prayers, Torah study, and giving charity in the merit of the departed.

** The following summary of the primary shiva practices should not be construed as comprehensive. The actual laws and customs are quite detailed and some vary from situation to situation.

Almost all shiva practices are suspended on Shabbat and biblical holidays.

TEXT 13

THE MITZVAH TO CONSOLE MOURNERS

MAIMONIDES, *MISHNEH TORAH*,
LAWS OF MOURNING 14:1

מִצְוַת עֲשֵׂה שֶׁל דִּבְרֵיהֶם לְבַקֵּר חוֹלִים וּלְנַחֵם אֲבֵלִים . . . וְאֵלּוּ הֵן גְּמִילוּת חֲסָדִים שֶׁבְּגוּפוֹ שֶׁאֵין לָהֶם שִׁיעוּר.

אַף עַל פִּי שֶׁכָּל מִצְוֹת אֵלּוּ מִדִּבְרֵיהֶם, הֲרֵי הֵן בִּכְלָל "וְאָהַבְתָּ לְרֵעֲךָ כָּמוֹךָ" (וַיִּקְרָא יט, יח).

The sages obligated us to visit the sick and console mourners. . . . These are deeds of kindness that one carries out in person and have no limit.

Although these are rabbinic ordinances, they fall under the purview of the biblical commandment to "love your fellow as yourself" (LEVITICUS 19:18).

QUESTIONS

1. If you have ever paid a visit to someone in mourning ("sitting shiva"), did you experience discomfort or unease while doing so? If so, why might that be?

2. Have you ever said something to a mourner that, in your estimation, was either especially effective or especially ineffective?

TEXT 14

SILENT COMFORT

TALMUD, BERACHOT 6B

אַגְרָא דְּבֵי טַמְיָא שְׁתִּיקוּתָא.

The reward for visiting the home of mourning is for the silence.

TEXT 15

THE MOURNER DICTATES THE CONVERSATION

TALMUD, MO'ED KATAN 28B

אֵין מְנַחֲמִין רַשָּׁאִין לוֹמַר דָּבָר עַד שֶׁיִּפְתַּח אָבֵל.

The comforters may not say anything until the mourner opens the conversation.

TEXT 16

WHAT G-D WANTS TO HEAR

MIDRASH, *KOHELET RABAH* 12:13

סוֹף דִּיבּוּרוֹ שֶׁל אָדָם, הַכֹּל מַשְׁמִיעִין אֶת מַעֲשָׂיו,
"כָּשֵׁר הָיָה פְּלוֹנִי זֶה", "יְרֵא שָׁמַיִם הָיָה פְּלוֹנִי זֶה"...

שֶׁבְּשָׁעָה שֶׁאָדָם נִפְטַר מִן הָעוֹלָם, הַקָּדוֹשׁ בָּרוּךְ הוּא אוֹמֵר לְמַלְאֲכֵי הַשָּׁרֵת:
רְאוּ מַה הַבְּרִיּוֹת אוֹמְרוֹת עָלָיו:
כָּשֵׁר הָיָה, יְרֵא שָׁמַיִם הָיָה פְּלוֹנִי זֶה,
מִיַּד מִטָּתוֹ פּוֹרַחַת בָּאֲוִיר.

The final word regarding a person
is that of the people proclaiming his deeds,

KOHELET RABAH

A Midrashic text on the Book of Ecclesiastes. Midrash is the designation of a particular genre of rabbinic literature. The term "Midrash" is derived from the root *d-r-sh*, which means "to search," "to examine," and "to investigate." This particular Midrash provides textual exegeses and develops and illustrates moral principles. It was first published in Pesaro, Italy, in 1519, together with 4 other Midrashic works on the other 4 biblical *Megilot*.

commenting, "So-and-so was upright,"
"So-and-so was G-d-fearing." . . .

When a person departs the world,
G-d says to the ministering angels:
"See what people are saying about him."
[If they say] that he had been upright and G-d-fearing,
his soul immediately ascends to Paradise.

EXERCISE 3.1

1. This chapter included a number of powerful insights. Identify the insight that resonates with you most, and then record it in your own words.

   _____

   _____

2. If you are currently grieving the loss of a loved one, identify an idea you can focus on that will help you heal and live a fuller life.

   _____

   _____

KEY POINTS

1 Everyone reacts to and deals with grief differently. No two people are psychologically alike and no two circumstances of death and bereavement are the same.

2 It is a mitzvah to mourn the loss of a loved one. Processing a loss is critical to the healing process. This is accomplished by shiva, a mandatory period of grieving.

3 The Torah validates and encourages mourning, but only for a prescribed period of time, after which the mourner is enjoined to transition back to normal life.

4 Some ideas that give a mourner the strength to move on:

a The knowledge that the soul lives on and is not diminished by death.

b It is never too late to mend or improve our relationship with the deceased. Though our physical relationship has ended, we can still give him or her spiritual gifts.

c Life is a deposit, and G-d decides when to give it and when it must be returned.

d For this soul and its unique mission, this constituted a full life.

5 It is a mitzvah to comfort mourners. The most basic principle of comforting a mourner is simply being there. Our presence offers comfort and lessens the loneliness that often accompanies mourning.

APPENDIX A

TEXT 17

THE WAVES OF GRIEF

REDDIT.COM

Ed. Note: On May 13, 2011, someone posted on Reddit. com: "My friend just died. I don't know what to do." The following poignant response penned by "GSnow" has since gone viral.

Alright, here goes. I'm old. What that means is that I've survived (so far) and a lot of people I've known and loved did not. I've lost friends, best friends, acquaintances, co-workers, grandparents, mom, relatives, teachers, mentors, students, neighbors, and a host of other folks. I have no children, and I can't imagine the pain it must be to lose a child. But here's my two cents.

I wish I could say you get used to people dying. I never did. I don't want to. It tears a hole through me whenever somebody I love dies, no matter the circumstances. But I don't want it to "not matter." I don't want it to be something that just passes. My scars are a testament to the love and the relationship that I had for and with that person. And if the scar is deep, so was the love. So be it. Scars are a testament to life. Scars are a testament that I can love deeply and live deeply and be cut, or even gouged, and that I can heal and continue to live and continue to love. And the scar tissue is stronger than the original flesh ever was. Scars are a testament to life. Scars are only ugly to people who can't see.

As for grief, you'll find it comes in waves. When the ship is first wrecked, you're drowning, with wreckage all around you. Everything floating around you reminds you of the beauty and the magnificence of the ship that was, and is no more. And all you can do is float. You find some piece of the wreckage and you hang on for a while. Maybe it's some physical thing. Maybe it's a happy memory or a photograph. Maybe it's a person who is also floating. For a while, all you can do is float. Stay alive.

In the beginning, the waves are 100 feet tall and crash over you without mercy. They come 10 seconds apart and don't even give you time to catch your breath. All you can do is hang on and float. After a while, maybe weeks, maybe months, you'll find the waves are still 100 feet tall, but they come further apart. When they come, they still crash all over you and wipe you out. But in between, you can breathe, you can function. You never know what's going to trigger the grief. It might be a song, a picture, a street intersection, the smell of a cup of coffee. It can be just about anything . . . and the wave comes crashing. But in between waves, there is life.

Somewhere down the line, and it's different for everybody, you find that the waves are only 80 feet tall. Or 50 feet tall. And while they still come, they come further apart. You can see them coming. An anniversary, a birthday, or Christmas, or landing at O'Hare. You can see it coming, for the most part, and prepare yourself. And when it washes over you, you know that somehow you will, again, come out the other side. Soaking wet, sputtering, still hanging on to some tiny piece of the wreckage, but you'll come out.

Take it from an old guy. The waves never stop coming, and somehow you don't really want them to. But you learn that you'll survive them. And other waves will come. And you'll survive them too. If you're lucky, you'll have lots of scars from lots of loves. And lots of shipwrecks.

APPENDIX B

TEXT 18

FINDING SOLACE IN COMMUNITY

THE REBBE, RABBI MENACHEM
MENDEL SCHNEERSON, *IGROT
KODESH* 25, PP. 4–5

בְּהִתְבּוֹנְנוּת רִאשׁוֹנָה תָּמוּהַּ הַקִּשּׁוּר שֶׁבֵּין שְׁנֵי הָעִנְיָנִים. אֶלָּא שֶׁכַּאֲמוּר בָּזֶה הוּא עִקַּר הַנֶּחָמָה בְּתָכְנָהּ הַפְּנִימִי, אֲשֶׁר כְּמוֹ שֶׁאֲבֵלוּת צִיּוֹן וִירוּשָׁלַיִם הֲרֵי מִשְׁתֶּפֶת הִיא לְכָל בְּנֵי וּבְנוֹת יִשְׂרָאֵל בְּכָל מָקוֹם שֶׁהֵם, אַף כִּי נִרְגָּשׁ הַדָּבָר יוֹתֵר אֵצֶל הַיּוֹשֵׁב בִּירוּשָׁלַיִם וְרוֹאֶה כֹּתֶל הַמַּעֲרָבִי וּבֵית מִקְדָּשֵׁנוּ בְּחֻרְבָּנוּ מֵאֵלּוּ הַנִּמְצָאִים בְּרִחוּק מָקוֹם, אֲבָל גַּם אֶצְלָם גָּדוֹל הַכְּאֵב וְהַצַּעַר. וְכֵן הוּא גַם בְּאֵבֶל הַיָּחִיד וְהַמִּשְׁפָּחָה, אֲשֶׁר מֵהַנֶּחָמָה בָּזֶה הִיא שֶׁכָּל הָעָם מִשְׁתַּתֵּף בְּצַעֲרוֹ, שֶׁהֲרֵי בְּסִגְנוֹן חֲכָמֵינוּ ז"ל כָּל בְּנֵי יִשְׂרָאֵל הֵם קוֹמָה אַחַת שְׁלֵימָה.

At first glance, the connection [between the consolation offered to an individual mourning a personal loss and our national mourning for the destruction of Jerusalem] appears to be quite puzzling. In truth, however, they are connected. For the main consolation embodied by this phrase is in its inner content, namely: The grief over Zion and Jerusalem is common to all the sons and daughters of our people, Israel, wherever they may be (although it is more palpable to those who dwell in Jerusalem and actually see the Western Wall and the ruins of our Holy Temple than to those who are far away from it; nonetheless, even those who are far experience great pain and grief over the destruction). So too is the grief of a single individual Jew or Jewish family shared by the entire nation. For, as the sages have taught, all of the Jewish people comprise one integral organism.

ADDITIONAL READINGS

ARE WE DISPOSABLE?

BY JAY LITVIN

JAY LITVIN
1944–2004

Chicago-born Litvin moved to Israel in 1993 to serve as medical liaison for Chabad's Children of Chernobyl program, and he took a leading role in airlifting children from the areas contaminated by the Chernobyl nuclear disaster. He also founded and directed Chabad's Terror Victims program in Israel. He passed away in April of 2004 after a valiant 4-year battle with non-Hodgkin's lymphoma.

Not long ago, I was in a meeting with someone whose husband had passed away less than a year before. In the midst of the meeting someone cracked a joke and the woman of whom I'm speaking laughed. I was startled. "How can you laugh?" I thought. "Your spouse passed away less than a year ago!" And then an alarming thought occurred to me: "Are we all disposable and that easily replaceable? Can our loved ones laugh so quickly after we're gone?"

Right now and before writing another word, I want to clear up any misconceptions: Within seconds of thinking this I knew that that's not what I really think. My wife suggested that perhaps my own condition had something to do with my response. Being in remission from lymphoma does not mean that I believe 100% of the time that I'm out of the woods. Mainly, I'm very optimistic. But I'm not Mr. Bitachon every second of every day. And, whenever I hear of someone who passes away from some version of what I have (or, please G-d, had), it re-opens unpleasant thoughts and fears. Unfortunately, hearing about such people is all too common these days.

"It was laughter with a broken heart that will never mend in full," my wife assured me.

Are we disposable? Sounds ridiculous doesn't it? And of course we are not. But death is not the only place I find evidence to my fear that our lives are too quickly forgotten and replaced not only by laughter, but by others.

Look at divorce. People marry. People divorce. Their spouse remarries. And there is someone else who comes to take his or her place. In some cases, he or she comes to parent the children. Now you see him, now you don't. There seems to be this space—husband, father, whatever—that can be filled by a variety of candidates. Perhaps not in the same way, but still . . . filled. What is the message to our children? He was your Daddy. But *he* can be your Daddy, too.

I'm taking a risk here. I know that what I'm writing is an exaggeration, and certainly not the most rational or wisest train of thought. I'm inviting you on a journey with my darker side. My fearful side. The side that emerges when my worst nightmares and thoughts overpower my higher and better self. Can I trust you to come along without too much judgment? Will you hang in there with me a little while longer as I flesh this out?

If Daddies are replaceable, is the same true of the children? In a disposable, replaceable world, do we need ponder too long why kids sometimes wonder if their lives are worth anything? Why we sometimes wonder the same?

But, when we lose someone in our life there is a dilemma. On the one hand we are to mourn. On the other, we are to carry on with our lives. And, in today's modern world, it seems that the faster and fuller we do this, the healthier we are. Rarely, today, do we see a widow or widower whose loss is worn constantly on his sleeve. Whose grief becomes an indelible look in the eyes and tension on the face. And even though someone may have once been the "love of my life," in today's world it seems that after loss we are encouraged to pick ourselves up and begin a new life. But if one creates a new life can't one also then have a new "love of my life"? New life; new love. Disposable life; replaceable love.

I'm traveling further downward. Spinning really. Can you feel it? I've done this before, but it's different having you with me. And not even knowing who you are: faceless, unknown confidants!

Have I come to the point where I trust you all so much? Or is it just the chemo and past months of battle that have left me not even caring what you think?

Perhaps if I thought about my own parents more. Perhaps if they occupied more of my thoughts and speech? Perhaps if I didn't feel that my own life had continued on so easily after they both passed away? Were they disposable? Of course not. Were they replaceable? Impossible. And yet . . .

No, I don't want anyone to suffer after loss. Not anyone in my family. Not anyone in yours. I want for there to be laughter again. Full lives. Happiness. Joy. Song. A warm, lively Shabbos table filled with children and grandchildren, great-grandchildren. Even the ones I might never meet.

But, oh, how I don't want ever to be forgotten. For life to be as if I never was. Can you understand that? Do you ever feel that? Someone told me recently that they never think about one day not being here, yet for me, not one day passes without that thought.

They say "Jacob lived through the good deeds of his children." But that was Jacob. And look at who his children were. But what about me?

Have you never thought these thoughts? Never felt the fear? Never been caught in the spiral of your own darker self with no escape in view? Never wished you could ascend towards the point of light you know is there, somewhere . . . but where?

I'm lucky enough to have a person in my life who motivates me to reach a little higher, and helps me get there some of the time. His name is Rav (Rabbi) Gluckowsky. He's the guy in my community who is my teacher and guide. He's someone I learn from not just in a class, but from the way he lives his life.

(A lot of people call him by his first name, but I prefer to always call him "Rav Gluckowsky," even though we're pretty good friends and I'm older by a long shot. Perhaps it's because we're friends that I call him "Rav." I enjoy giving things to my friends. And, in this case, I enjoy giving respect to someone I like very much. The respect and honor I afford him in no way lessens the familiarity and comfort I feel when I'm with him. He is my Rav and we are friends.)

I never met Rav Gluckowsky's father. And yet he accompanies Rav Gluckowsky almost everywhere he goes and certainly in most every meeting I have with him. There is not a talk Rav Gluckowsky gives in which he doesn't quote his father. The other day we were speaking of our sons' singing in the choir and he mentioned what a great voice his father had. Last week I went to a birthday *farbrengen* and Rav Gluckowsky was asked to tell a story. "Let me tell you a story about the previous Rebbe that my father used to tell . . ." He not only told the story in his father's name, his father was imbedded throughout the story.

His father's picture hangs prominently in his living room. We are invited to his home several times a year to share in some event commemorating his father. And one has the feeling that Rav Gluckowsky's entire life is dedicated to his father, that he is busily and consciously being the son his father would have wanted him to be.

In shul, we all know that many of the tunes he sings during *davening* come from his father. And in our community, we all know we are the beneficiaries of the wonderful man Rav Gluckowsky's father must have been. We, too, are better off because Rav Gluckowsky's father once blessed the earth.

Would Sukkot be Sukkot without the stories of the sukkahs that Rav Gluckowsky built together with his father and brothers? How many times have we heard the one about the last minute car ride with the police chasing behind just minutes before candle lighting time? Would our boys school be the same if it was not filled with the educational adages from Rav Gluckowsky's father, an educator who taught first through eighth grades in Toronto for forty years?

And would we not all love to say to our children as Rav Gluckowsky recently said to his: How proud I would be if you grew up to be a teacher like Zaidy, a man who, through his teaching, improved the lives of so many, many people.

Funny, but when I finally saw a video of Rav Gluckowsky's father, he looked like an ordinary guy. A school teacher. Someone a lot like you and I. But someone who had risen to near mythic stature through the love, respect and devotion of his son.

Listening to Rav Gluckowsky, I, this ordinary father, could imagine one day being lifted to such heights by my own children. And such fantasies fill me with warmth and courage. They ease my fears. They impel me forward to live a life full of actions that will give my children something to talk about one day to their children and to their communities.

If Rav Gluckowsky's father is not disposable, neither am I. Neither are you. We are as irreplaceable as the love we give. Our indelible mark is invisibly carved on the hearts of our children and loved ones. Our mark is contained not only in their laughter, but in the laughter they impart to others. Laughter, as my wife says, that comes from a broken heart. But a heart filled with love breaks and then grows stronger through mending. Its strength comes from its softness, a softness made softer by the love we left behind, perhaps softer, even, through the loss our children feel after we've left.

The woman who laughed came into my office the other day. She stopped by to tell me about the event held in her community the night before to commemorate the first anniversary of her husband's passing. She described the event for a long time and then went on to tell me about the highlight of the evening.

"My daughter read a letter she had written to her Abba," she began. "In the letter she described all the family events of the past year. She described them in detail so that my husband, her father, would be able to take nachas from her piano recital, from her brother's first bike ride, from the first day mommy was able to go back to work after months of feeling too sad to even leave the house . . ."

As the woman spoke her eyes welled with tears. They never spilled over. It was as if her heart had simply filled with so much love it had to relieve itself through her eyes.

She stood in my doorway for a long time reciting all the events that her daughter had recounted in her letter to her father. She even told me how her daughter had described to her father what she knew her father's reactions would be. "You would have laughed so hard, Abba . . ." "You would have told us your famous story about the time you . . ." "Oh, Abba, how you would have enjoyed the music . . ."

I never grew tired of listening to this woman tell about this evening of remembrance. Long past the time when I should have returned to my work, I listened attentively about her children and their love for their father and for his memory.

And when she finally finished and continued down the hall, I could have continued listening even longer.

But instead I sat down and wrote this article. Perhaps one day my children will read it. Or, better yet, perhaps they'll read to their children one day.

May I live to be 120.

Chabad.org editor's note: Jay sent us this article two-and-a-half years ago, at a time when—as he writes in its opening paragraphs—he was very optimistic about his prognosis. But shortly thereafter, while we were still working on the article, a blood test result brought the news that his illness had turned once more aggressive. Indeed, such ups-and-downs often occurred during his valiant four-year battle with the disease. Because of the unfortunate turn of events, Jay felt that the subject of this article was too "close to home" to publish. Now, after the worst has occurred, Jay's family decided that the time has come to share it with our readers. —Rabbi Yanki Tauber

COMFORTING THE BEREAVED (*NICHUM AVEILIM*)

BY RABBI MAURICE LAMM

RABBI MAURICE LAMM

Congregational rabbi and noted author. Rabbi Lamm is the author of *The Jewish Way in Death and Mourning* and *The Jewish Way in Love and Marriage*. He was the rabbi of Beth Jacob of Beverly Hills from 1972–1985. He is president of the National Institute for Jewish Hospice and professor at Yeshiva University's rabbinical seminary in New York.

A sacred obligation devolves upon every Jew to comfort the mourners, whether he is related to them or not, and whether he was a close friend or a passing acquaintance. In Judaism, exercising compassion by paying a condolence call is a mitzvah, considered by some of our greatest scholars to be biblically ordained. The Bible records that G-d visited Isaac: "And it came to pass after the death of Abraham, that G-d blessed Isaac, his son" (Genesis 25:11). The sages infer from this verse that G-d Himself, as it were, was comforting the bereaved Isaac.

It is a man's duty to imitate G-d: as G-d comforts the bereaved, so man must do likewise. Consolation is considered a G-d-like action which all the children of Israel must perform. When, following the destruction of Jerusalem and the decimation of the Jewish people, Isaiah proclaimed G-d's message: "Comfort ye, comfort ye my people" (Isaiah 40:1), it indicated not merely a recommendation from on high, but a specific mandate obliging the prophet to bring consolation to his people.

The fundamental purpose of the condolence call during shiva is to relieve the mourner of the intolerable burden of intense loneliness. At no other time is a human being more in need of such comradeship. *Avelut* means withdrawal, the personal and physical retreat from social commerce and the concern for others. It is the loss that he alone

has suffered. All the traditions of mourning express this troubled loneliness in diverse ways, covering the spectrum of social life—from the excessive growing of hair in indifference to social custom, to the avoidance of greetings, the minimum social courtesy.

Recognizing this state of mind, the visitor comes to the house of mourning, silently, to join the bereaved in his loneliness, sorrowfully to sit alongside him, to think his thoughts and to linger on his loss. The warmth of such human presence is inestimable. Practiced as the tradition prescribes it, true consolation is the distillation of empathy. The sum effect of the visitation of many friends and relatives, some long forgotten, others members of a community who may rarely have paid the mourner any attention at all, is the softening of loneliness, the relief of the heavy burden of internalized despair, and the affirmation that the world at-large is not a hateful and angry place, but a warm and friendly one. It is a beckoning with open arms for the mourner to return to society. Comforting the mourners, says Maimonides, is *gemillat chasadim*, a genuine kindness to both the dead and the living.

The purpose of the condolence call is not to convince the mourner of anything at all. This is the time for accompanying him on his very own path, not for argumentation or debate. It is the time for the contemplation of disaster. While the mourner himself may wish to discuss it, it is not the prime purpose of this visit to relieve his fears for the future or his guilt for the past. It is not proper, say the sages (indeed it borders on sacrilege), to impress upon the mourner the inevitability of death, as though to doubt the true purpose and justice of a decree that G-d issued, but would change if only He were free to do so. It is not seemly, perhaps it is even entirely useless, to assure the mourner that others have suffered similar tragedies, or worse fates, as though by right he should be less despairing. "It could have been worse," is cold consolation. This is a time for subjectivity, for an intensely personal evaluation of life, and the mourners should not be deprived of even this indulgence. Some of the importuning of visitors that "life must go on," and that the mourner should be "thankful that worse did not occur," are well-meaning, but hollow and sometimes annoying expressions.

The strategy of true compassion is presence and silence, the eloquence of human closeness. Sad, muttered words are clumsy openers of the heart compared with the whisper of soft eyes. The comradeship demonstrated by the expression on the face speaks volumes that the ancient bards could not match with mere words, no matter how beautiful. It fulfills at once the mourner's desperate need for both companionship and privacy. It was, therefore, an old custom, unfortunately lost to our generations, for visitors to sit silently on the earth with, and like, the mourner. How magnificent an expression of compassion!

The first principle of comforting the mourners, found in the major codes of Jewish law, is that one should remain silent and allow the mourner to speak first. In many Jewish communities in olden days, the congregants accompanied the mourner as he walked home from synagogue on the Sabbath or holiday, and there they sat with him. How warm the mere physical presence of other human beings! How it relieves the sharp sting of tragedy! The classic mourner, Job, visited by three friends, sat with them for seven days and none uttered a sound. Ecclesiastes wisely notes that there "is a time to keep silent and a time to speak." The Midrash (Kohelet Rabbah on 3:5) records that the wife of Rabbi Mana died. His colleague, Rabbi Abin, came to pay a condolence call. Asked Rabbi Mana, "Are there any words of Torah you would like to offer us in our time of grief?" Rabbi Abin replied, "At times like this the Torah takes refuge in silence!"

It is in this spirit that Maimonides cautions visitors that they not speak overly much as, somehow, words have the tendency to generate a spirit of frivolity so contrary to the spirit of shiva. Indeed, the Talmud notes this when it remarks perceptively, "True reward comes to one who is silent in the house of mourning, and voluble in the wedding hall!"

It is true, of course, that it is exceedingly difficult to comfort with warmth and hope and compassion, while sitting relatively silent. Perhaps, that is the reason for the parting phrase of comfort, "May G-d comfort you among the other mourners of Zion and Jerusalem." For only G-d can truly comfort, even as He consoled Isaac after his father Abraham's death, and as He has comforted, through the ages, the other mourners of Zion after the tragic destruction of the ancient Temple, and has comforted the exiled, and those who suffered in pogroms and crusades. If the visitor feels uncomfortable in the tension of silence, he may of course converse with the mourner, but— little and wisely.

This excerpt from *The Jewish Way in Death and Mourning* by Rabbi Maurice Lamm, copyright 2000, is reproduced by arrangement with Jonathan David Publishers, Inc., *www.jdbooks.com*.

THE BLESSING OF A BROKEN HEART

BY SHERRI MANDELL

SHERRI MANDELL

Writer. Mandell wrote her memoir, *The Blessing of a Broken Heart*, after enduring the horrific murder of her eldest son, Koby. She later founded the Koby Mandell Foundation, which offers healing retreats for bereaved mothers and widows as well as a camp for children whose parents or siblings have been killed by terrorists.

The Shiva and the Faces of G-d

It is as if I have left my body. My husband and I have become one body, one soul, joined together in our pain, alone with our pain together. That first night we sleep a few hours, wake at 4:00 A.M. and go out to the terrace off our bedroom. The birds are singing, it is growing light, the sky is streaked with purple and pink, and we wrap our arms around each other and cry together.

My husband remembers friends of his who died young. I remember waking up with Koby when he was a baby early in the morning, nursing him. The birds sang loudly, sweeping across the sky. It was a secret, magic time, a time alone with my baby when the true beauty of the world was revealed to me.

This morning I hear the birds again. The sound is so loud, it seems like a texture, something you can touch, like a thick blanket over us. The sound is a sign telling me that the ordinary life we knew is being transformed; intangible sound has suddenly become material, tangible. We are not just one form but can be transformed; matter transmuting itself into spirit and back. Death is a permutation, a change of form. Rimbaud wrote about different senses merging in poetry. Touch and sound have merged, as synesthesia is made manifest for me.

The moon still in the sky looks like the opening of a tunnel, calling me to believe that my son is on a journey to a land I cannot yet know. I want to hold his hand, and yank him back to me. I want to say to him: Did you take a jacket? Did you take water? Did you eat? I want to take care of him.

My husband and I stand together in a kind of tenderness that we haven't felt in years, perhaps never. We are fully present for each other. Koby has given the gift of a bond that feels necessary, urgent, a life support system that will keep us alive.

Later that day, Gavi asks me: "Who is Koby's mommy, now?"

I wonder what to answer. It's true that I am still Koby's mommy, but I am no longer the one who takes care of him. I answer, "G-d is his mommy."

"Oh good," answers Gavi. "Then he can see a falling star whenever he wants."

My child believes in the goodness of the world. My child believes in magic. My child believes in G-d. . . .

During the seven days of mourning, the *shiva*, I live in the land of pain. My friends fear I won't return to myself, that I won't have the strength to go on. Seth worries about me because my eyes swing in their sockets; I can't eat. My friends beg me to eat. They rub my shoulders and my back. They try to spoon baby food into my mouth. The doctor comes and checks my tongue, my blood pressure. He tells me I must eat. But food is for people who are alive, and I am not. I get up and go downstairs and cry out in my pain. I sit on the floor and am cradled by thousands of people who reach out to me. My children join me on the floor; they are in their rooms with friends; they play upstairs, I don't know who is taking care of them but I see them eating. I see adults surrounding them. I speak to them and hold them, but they prefer to be with their friends. My pain is a flame that they can feel in my hands, see in my eyes.

Seven days of mourning. The mirrors are covered. Vanity is a luxury in the midst of such pain. One wants to forget the material world, be transformed into a spirit so that one can merge with the dead. This world seems like a world of shadow. The body is insubstantial. I don't want to perform my rituals of vanity—the quick dab of eye makeup, lipstick. I don't bathe. I wear the same ripped shirt all week. Breathing is all I can manage. Most people can't tolerate a mourner's silence, and rush to fill it, but Jewish mourning laws dictate that a person paying a *shiva* call should be silent until the mourner speaks. If the mourner says nothing, the person visiting should say nothing as well. Neither should greet each other. The first three days, when the pain is most intense, the mourner is like an egg, without a mouth, dwelling in silence. The point of the *shiva* is not to comfort a mourner for her loss but to stand with her in the time of her grief. As Rabbi Maurice Lamm notes, the main purpose of the *shiva* is to relieve the mourner of his loneliness. A person expresses compassion for the mourner through his presence and silence. Job sat with his friends for seven days and none uttered a sound. For only G-d can comfort. That is why, when departing a *shiva,* many traditional Jews state these words: "May G-d comfort you among the mourners of Zion and Jerusalem." But I am not silent. I need to talk about Koby. I cannot contain the pain of silence.

And there are people who come and offer me words that ease my loneliness. Not formulaic statements like 'he's in a better place', or 'thank G-d you have your other children', but words that tell me that they can stand with us in this place of sorrow. I need to speak. I need people to talk to me. I ask my friend to put a sign on a door—this is a house of *shiva* and all conversation should be about Koby. I refuse to listen to anything trite, anything mundane. I tell people: only Koby, only Koby.

There are many people who offer me wisdom, and I hold on to their words like a rope that I can climb. The women bend down to me, sitting on the floor, putting their faces to mine. Their faces are so beautiful—their eyes open, their voices soft and strong. Today I know that each person is created in the image of G-d, because I see and hear G-d in their faces, the faces of G-d. I know all of these women are G-d coming to comfort me, their arms wrapped around me; their eyes looking into mine. They reach into their souls and give me divine pieces of themselves; love and compassion—they feed me with their words. Israeli women are unafraid of suffering; they know death as a companion. They say:

"Your son will not be forgotten. We will not let him be forgotten . . ."

"We will be with you. You will never be alone, never . . ."

"He is our son too; we are crying with you . . ."

"He is with G-d and he is basking in G-d's love and you will bask in our love . . ."

"Your son is like a boat, a beautiful boat sailing and when it goes over the horizon you won't be able to see it, but it's still there, sailing along the open waters . . ."

And this: "My brother was killed and my mother suffered but after the terrible pain, there were gifts. My mother was a Holocaust survivor, her parents and brothers and sisters were killed in the war. She made a new life here in Israel. Then my brother was killed in a terrorist attack on a bus in 1979." I remember this. I once stayed at this woman's house for *Shabbat,* and all night, the picture of the handsome young man in the photograph looked down at me, and I felt he had died. In the morning, I asked her, and she told me that her brother had died when he was twenty-six. She says: "My mother had great blessings in her life, even with her misfortune, and so will you. G-d takes away, but he also gives. You will receive. G-d will give you *bracha*."

These words move me, and I want to believe them. But I don't understand them.

The mothers who have lost children to terrorism arrive. One, who lost her teenage son in an attack when he was hiking in Wadi Kelt, says: "You will go on. You will live." She gives me practical advice: "Don't make a shrine for your son. Pack up his things and put them away. Use his room. You don't need to keep out his pictures everywhere."

She is an attractive woman, her hair styled in a fashionable, short cut. She is wearing makeup, earrings. I look at her and realize: You can still be alive after your son is dead.

A woman who lost her nineteen-year-old son in a drive-by shooting says: "He is not gone. He will live inside of you now. We miss their physical bodies but we are still tied to them. You will never forget him."

I reach out for their hands like branches that will pull me across a raging river. One of my friends tells me: "You are all soul, you are letting us see your soul."

The politicians arrive. Israel is a small country with a history of conflict, and there is a custom of politicians attending the funeral or the *shiva* of each person killed by terror or war, each person killed by a national enemy. I tell the President, Moshe Katzav—I need a father to comfort me. He stares at me without seeing me. The chief rabbi, the ministers, the mayors . . . none of them have the right words of comfort for me.

"What do we do with the pain?" my husband asks a rabbi who, years ago, lost his eleven-year-old child in a bus accident. The rabbi answers: "You must use it to grow."

Another rabbi says that ours is a heartbreaking test, but we need to turn to G-d, that only G-d can give us comfort. Outside of the house, my friend Valerie tells me, the rabbis cry like babies.

Because no matter how much we try to intellectualize or interpret the pain, to will it away, the pain crouches on our heart like a beast who is waiting to crush us, to chew us to bits until we are nothing, dust that the wind can blow away. I wake up each morning crying and I go to sleep in tears. My body is a poor companion now. It is too material. I want to peel it away, find the soul inside and merge with my son.

I look at the women who wrap their arms around me, who give me their bodies to cry on. They are my Yemenite and Moroccan and Portuguese and American mothers. There is so much love in that *shiva,* so much love; the love lifts me up and keeps me afloat like I am a body being carried. . . .

The Broken Glass

. . . I cry and grieve, but at the same time, I have not shut down my capacity for feeling joy and awe at the world. On the contrary, it is as if my palate of emotion has expanded. Now when I feel joy it is more exquisite because I know that love needs to be held on to, gathered close, appreciated because it is so precious. Being home when my children return from school is a moment of gratitude for me.

My heart now feels like a heart of truth, a heart that yearns for eternity. It's a heart that is broken like the goblet at a Jewish wedding ceremony.

At my own wedding, I had learned the meaning of breaking the glass. I knew that it meant that even in the greatest of happiness, we need to remember our obligations to G-d—not to get too carried away in our joy. It reminds us that we are always dependent on G-d's mercy. It reminds us that we can't have complete happiness because of the destruction of the Temple, the place of G-d's dwelling, in Jerusalem. It reminds us that perfect joy is not possible in this world.

Back then, I understood the meaning of the broken glass in an abstract way. Now I have lived the broken glass. G-d himself seeks out broken vessels for use (*Leviticus Rabah* 7:2). As it says in Psalm 147, verse 3, "G-d is the healer of shattered hearts." Now I understand that there is a shattering first. Then there will be a healing. It is out of destruction that the Resurrection will come. The Messiah was born on the day that the Temple was destroyed. It is out of pain that the Messiah will be born. In this world, pain and beauty coexist. In the World-to-Come, as I understand it, the pain will be gone. We won't need answers to our suffering, because we will no longer have questions.

In the book *Made in Heaven*, Aryeh Kaplan teaches us that a human being can be likened to glass—vulnerable. But glass, when it is broken, can be re-melted and re-blown. It can be made whole again. So, too, even after a person dies, his life is not over. He too can be restored, made whole. And so, too, can our hearts. Though I will never again be that same innocent bride, and I will never again look at a wedding without pain in my heart, I have become a different person, one who is more vulnerable, more open and, I hope, has more compassion. I pray that one day I will meet my son in the World-to-Come. All of the broken fragments of the world will be mended, and I will know that as Rabbi Menachem Mendel of Kotsk, a nineteenth century Chassidic rabbi, said: There is nothing so whole as a broken heart.

The Blessing of a Broken Heart (London: Toby Press, 2009), pp. 51–56, 97–98. Reprinted with permission of the author and publisher

Lesson

4

WHERE WE GO
HEAVEN AND HELL

For centuries, human beings have been motivated by the promise of Heaven and frightened by the threat of Hell. Discover what Jews believe about where every soul goes and how Kaddish aids a soul in reaching true peace.

I. BEYOND OUR REALITY

The concepts of the afterlife, Heaven and Hell, and divine reward and punishment remain—for most people—shrouded in mystery at best, and may even trigger angst and dread. This chapter will explore these topics through the clear lens of Jewish tradition.

For the sake of contrast-induced clarity, it will prove beneficial to first investigate currently held conceptions of the afterlife— as well as current conceptions of pleasure.

EXERCISE 4.1

What (I think) I know about the Jewish view on afterlife:

1. _____

2. _____

3. _____

4. _____

5. _____

What I would like to know about the Jewish view on afterlife:

1. _____

2. _____

3. _____

4. _____

5. _____

What is unique about Judaism's view of the afterlife? Watch *Rabbi Jonathan Sacks's* explanation in "This Life": *myJLI.com/soul*

EXERCISE 4.2

What word or idea immediately enters your mind when you hear the word "Hell"?

_____

_____

▼ **BURNED OUT (HOMELESS)**
Ludwig Meidner, oil on canvas,
1912. (Jüdisches Museum der
Stadt Frankfurt am Main)

EXERCISE 4.3

Rate the following according to the degree of pleasure they would provide you (1 = least pleasurable; 10 = most pleasurable).

Happiness

① ② ③ ④ ⑤ ⑥ ⑦ ⑧ ⑨ ⑩

Hawaiian cruise

① ② ③ ④ ⑤ ⑥ ⑦ ⑧ ⑨ ⑩

Lifetime membership to an exclusive country club

① ② ③ ④ ⑤ ⑥ ⑦ ⑧ ⑨ ⑩

Lifetime of meaning

① ② ③ ④ ⑤ ⑥ ⑦ ⑧ ⑨ ⑩

Love

① ② ③ ④ ⑤ ⑥ ⑦ ⑧ ⑨ ⑩

Social status

① ② ③ ④ ⑤ ⑥ ⑦ ⑧ ⑨ ⑩

Wealth

① ② ③ ④ ⑤ ⑥ ⑦ ⑧ ⑨ ⑩

Wisdom

① ② ③ ④ ⑤ ⑥ ⑦ ⑧ ⑨ ⑩

QUESTION

Take a moment to analyze your responses to Exercise 4.3. What do your responses tell you about your conception of pleasure? What general genres of pleasure do you consider more pleasurable than others?

II. REWARD AND PUNISHMENT

Judaism regards death as the freedom of the soul from the constraints of the physical realm and its return to leading a purely spiritual existence. This post-corporeal stage in the soul's experience is colloquially known as the afterlife.

While the soul is freed from corporeal existence, it continues to be influenced by the experiences it accumulated during its stay inside a human body. In fact, the soul's experience in the afterlife is entirely shaped by its actions here in this world.

Good actions are rewarded in a state that we refer to as Heaven; wicked actions are expiated in a stage that we refer to as Hell To better understand the phenomenon of afterlife, it is imperative to explore the mechanism that shapes it: namely, the divine system of reward and punishment, as viewed in the unique—and perhaps surprising—Jewish understanding of the topic.

▼ **THE ALEPH**
Hendel Lieberman,
oil on canvas, 1965.

Rabbi Manis Friedman on how to
punish a soul, in "The Movie of Life":
myJLI.com/soul

TEXT 1A

THE REWARD AND PUNISHMENT PRINCIPLE

MAIMONIDES, *COMMENTARY ON THE MISHNAH*, SANHEDRIN, INTRODUCTION TO CH. 10 (*PEREK CHELEK*)

RABBI MOSHE BEN MAIMON (MAIMONIDES, RAMBAM) 1135–1204

Halachist, philosopher, author, and physician. Maimonides was born in Córdoba, Spain. After the conquest of Córdoba by the Almohads, he fled Spain and eventually settled in Cairo, Egypt. There, he became the leader of the Jewish community and served as court physician to the vizier of Egypt. He is most noted for authoring the *Mishneh Torah*, an encyclopedic arrangement of Jewish law; and for his philosophical work, *Guide for the Perplexed*. His rulings on Jewish law are integral to the formation of halachic consensus.

הַיְסוֹד הָאֶחָד עָשָׂר: כִּי הוּא, הַשֵּׁם יִתְבָּרֵךְ, נוֹתֵן שְׂכַר לְמִי שֶׁעוֹשֶׂה מִצְוֹת הַתּוֹרָה. וְיַעֲנִישׁ לְמִי שֶׁעוֹבֵר עַל אַזְהָרוֹתֶיהָ.

The eleventh [of the Thirteen Principles of Jewish Faith] is that G-d, blessed be He, rewards those who observe the commandments of the Torah and punishes those who transgress its prohibitions.

TWELVE STEPS TO BLISS ▶
Sheeba Khan, acrylic on canvas, Dubai, 2017.

TEXT 1B

THE ULTIMATE REWARD IS SPIRITUAL

MAIMONIDES, IBID.

וְכִי הַשָּׂכָר הַגָּדוֹל הָעוֹלָם הַבָּא, וְהָעוֹנֶשׁ הֶחָזָק הֶכָּרֵת.

The greatest reward is
[the pleasures of] the World to Come;
the strongest punishment is
to be cut off [from the World to Come].

HAVE YOU EVER WONDERED?

The Torah specifies numerous material rewards and penalties. Why is it silent on *spiritual* consequences—Heaven and Hell? A number of explanations have been suggested by scholars over the generations; see Appendix A of this lesson (p. 156) for one explanation.

EXPLORE MORE

Maimonides offers an interesting take on reward and punishment—see Text 19 in the Appendix section of this lesson (p. 158).

TEXT 2

PENALTIES OR CONSEQUENCES?

RABBI MENACHEM RECANATI,
EXODUS 29:1

RABBI MENACHEM BEN BINYAMIN RECANATI
C. 1250–1310

Italian rabbi and kabbalist of note. He authored *Pirush Al HaTorah,* a mystical commentary on the Bible; *Pirush Hatefilot,* a commentary on the siddur; and *Ta'amei Hamitzvot,* an explanation of the commandments. In addition, his halachic rulings are collected in his *Piskei Recanati.*

וְאַל יַעֲלֶה בְּדַעְתְּךָ כִּי הָעוֹנָשִׁים הַכְּתוּבִין בַּתּוֹרָה הֵם כְּמוֹ הַמַּעֲנִישׁ אֶת הָאָדָם עַל עָבְרוֹ עַל מִצְוֹת הַמֶּלֶךְ, לֹא כֵן, רַק הֵן דָּבָר טִבְעִי מַמָּשׁ, כִּי הַמְבַטֵּל מִצְוָה מִמִּצְוֹת הַתּוֹרָה, אוֹתוֹ הַטּוֹב שֶׁהָיָה נִשְׁפָּע בְּסִבַּת עֲשִׂיָּיתָהּ הוּא נִמְנָע, כְּדִמְיוֹן מִי שֶׁאֵינוֹ זוֹרֵעַ שָׂדֵהוּ שֶׁאֵינוֹ קוֹצֵר, וּכְמִי שֶׁאֵינוֹ לוֹבֵשׁ בְּגָדִים שֶׁהוּא מִתְקָרֵר וּכְמוֹ שֶׁטֶּבַע הָאֵשׁ לְחַמֵּם וְטֶבַע הַמַּיִם לְהַרְטִיב וְהַלֶּחֶם לְהַשְׂבִּיעַ, כַּךְ טֶבַע כָּל מִצְוָה וּמִצְוָה לַעֲשׂוֹת אוֹתָם הַטּוֹבוֹת שֶׁנֶּאֶמְרוּ בָּהּ, אוֹ אוֹתָם הָעוֹנָשִׁים שֶׁנֶּאֶמְרוּ.

Do not consider the punishments described in the Torah as comparable to penalties a person incurs for disobeying the decree of a [mortal] king. Not at all. Rather, they are completely natural consequences. For one who fails to observe a Torah commandment is denied the good that naturally results from its observance. It is comparable to one who fails to sow his field and therefore cannot reap a harvest or one who fails to wear clothes and is then cold. It is as natural a consequence as the warmth provided by fire, the wetness of water, and the satiation of bread. In the same way, it is the nature of each mitzvah to provide the positive consequences that are promised for its observance or the negative consequences that are stated regarding its transgression.

For more on the nature of the soul's pleasures in the next world, see *Dr. Lisa Aikin's* "The Soul's Journey": *myJLI.com/soul*

TEXT 3

INTRINSIC CONSEQUENCE

ETHICS OF THE FATHERS 4:2

ETHICS OF THE FATHERS (*PIRKEI AVOT*)

A 6-chapter work on Jewish ethics that is studied widely by Jewish communities, especially during the summer. The first 5 chapters are from the Mishnah, tractate Avot. Avot differs from the rest of the Mishnah in that it does not focus on legal subjects; it is a collection of the sages' wisdom on topics related to character development, ethics, healthy living, piety, and the study of Torah.

שֶׁשְּׂכַר מִצְוָה, מִצְוָה. וּשְׂכַר עֲבֵרָה, עֲבֵרָה.

The reward of a mitzvah is a mitzvah;
the retribution for a sin is a sin.

▼ **JEW AT WORK (SEWING TEFILIN)**
Artur Markowicz, c. 1872–1934, pastels on cardboard. (Jewish Historical Institute Museum, Krakow)

TEXT 4

CREATING FIRE AND PLEASURE

RABBI YEHUDAH ARYEH LEIB ALTER, *SEFAT EMET, LIKUTIM* 1, P. 134

RABBI YEHUDAH ARYEH LEIB ALTER (*SEFAT EMET*) 1847–1905

Chasidic master and scholar. Rabbi Yehudah Aryeh Leib Alter assumed the leadership of the Chasidic dynasty of Gur (Gora), a town near Warsaw, Poland, at the age of 23. He was the grandson and successor of Rabbi Yitschak Meir of Gur, the founder of the Gur dynasty. He is commonly referred to as the *Sefat Emet,* after the title of his commentaries on the Torah and Talmud.

"כְּגַוְונָא דְחַיָּיבַיָּא מִתְחַמְמִין בְּיֵצֶר הָרַע הָכִי אִתּוּקַד נוּרָא דְגֵיהִנֹּם כו'". לְפִי זֶה נֵימָא נַמִי, דְהַגַּן עֵדֶן מִתְרַבֶּה בְּרוֹב הִתְלַהֲבוּת הַצַּדִיקִים בַּתּוֹרָה וּמִצְוֹת ה', שֶׁמִּתְעַנְּגִין עַל ה' מַמָּשׁ, שֶׁבְּמַעֲשֵׂיהֶם מִתְרַבֶּה הָאוֹר בְּגַן עֵדֶן.

"The fires of Gehinom [Hell] are stoked in direct proportion to the degree to which the wicked fan their fiery passions" (ZOHAR, VOL. 2, P. 150B). Accordingly, we must say that Gan Eden [Paradise] is amplified by the tremendous passion that the righteous invest in their Torah study and in their performance of G-d's commandments. They take great pleasure and delight in G-d Himself, and their deeds generate a corresponding abundance of light in Gan Eden.

III. GEHINOM: SOUL CATHARSIS

According to Jewish tradition, souls who, due to their actions in this world, are not (yet) worthy of entering Paradise—referred to in traditional sources as Gan Eden, the celestial "garden of Eden"—are redirected. Their destination? A spiritual realm referred to as Gehinom, but often translated as Hell.

Forget any hellish visions of the deceased getting their "just deserts" or suffering "eternal damnation." The Jewish idea of Gehinom does not include dramatic images of leaping pyres, pitchforks, and horned devils. You could say that Gehinom is nothing like Hell. The only common denominator between Gehinom and the common conceptions of Hell is that it is indeed a painful experience for the soul.

▼ THE FIRE CAME AND
BURNT THE STICK
El Lissitzky, lithograph
on paper, Kiev, Ukraine,
1919. (The Jewish
Museum, New York)

TEXT 5

RIGHT OF ENTRY TO GEHINOM

TALMUD, CHAGIGAH 15B

BABYLONIAN TALMUD

A literary work of monumental proportions that draws upon the legal, spiritual, intellectual, ethical, and historical traditions of Judaism. The 37 tractates of the Babylonian Talmud contain the teachings of the Jewish sages from the period after the destruction of the 2nd Temple through the 5th century CE. It has served as the primary vehicle for the transmission of the Oral Law and the education of Jews over the centuries; it is the entry point for all subsequent legal, ethical, and theological Jewish scholarship.

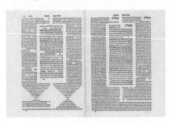

כִּי נָח נַפְשֵׁיהּ דְּאַחֵר, אָמְרִי "לֹא מִידָן לִידַיְינֵיהּ וְלֹא לְעָלְמָא דְּאָתֵי לֵיתֵי".
לֹא מִידָן לִידַיְינֵיהּ, מִשּׁוּם דְּעָסַק בְּאוֹרַיְיתָא,
וְלֹא לְעָלְמָא דְּאָתֵי לֵיתֵי, מִשּׁוּם דְּחָטָא.
אָמַר רַבִּי מֵאִיר, "מוּטָב דְּלִידַיְינֵיהּ וְלֵיתֵי לְעָלְמָא דְּאָתֵי".

[Elisha ben Abuyah was a former Mishnaic sage who turned to such public heresy and treachery that he was derogatively nicknamed Acher, "something else."]

When Acher died, the Heavenly Court declared, "We will not afflict him with judgment [in Gehinom], nor will we permit him to enter Paradise."

[Their reasoning?]
We will not afflict him with judgment because he studied much Torah, but we will not permit him to enter Paradise because he sinned [egregiously].

[Acher's former disciple] Rabbi Meir said, "Better that he indeed be judged [and punished], so that he may then enter Paradise."

"Punishment vs. Purification: The Afterlife Revisited," by *Rabbi Avrohom Bergstein: myJLI.com/soul*

TEXT 6

PURIFYING FIRES

RABBI SHNE'UR ZALMAN OF
LIADI, *TORAH OR* 49B

**RABBI SHNE'UR ZALMAN OF LIADI
(ALTER REBBE) 1745–1812**

Chasidic rebbe, halachic authority,
and founder of the Chabad
movement. The Alter Rebbe was
born in Liozna, Belarus, and was
among the principal students of the
Magid of Mezeritch. His numerous
works include the *Tanya*, an early
classic containing the fundamentals
of Chabad Chasidism; and *Shulchan
Aruch HaRav,* an expanded and
reworked code of Jewish law.

עִנְיַן הַגֵּיהִנֹּם הוּא כְּדֵי לְצָרֵף הַנֶּפֶשׁ מֵחוֹלַאַת הָרַע אֲשֶׁר בְּקִרְבָּהּ, כְּמוֹ מְצָרֵף
לַכֶּסֶף, שֶׁהַפְּסוֹלֶת וְהַסִּיגִים נִשְׂרָפִים תּוֹךְ הַכּוּר וְנִשְׁאַר הַכֶּסֶף נָקִי מִכָּל סִיג. כָּךְ,
כְּדֵי שֶׁתּוּכַל הַנֶּפֶשׁ לְקַבֵּל אוֹר עֹנֶג הָעֶלְיוֹן לִהְיוֹת נֶהֱנִים כו', צְרִיכָה לְהִתְבָּרֵר
תְּחִלָּה בְּאֵשׁ שֶׁל גֵּיהִנֹּם לְהַפְרִיד הָרַע מִן הַטוֹב.

The purpose of Gehinom is to refine the soul and rid
it of any sickness that it contracted. This is similar to
the process of smelting silver, wherein the dross and
sediment is burned away in a furnace, leaving the silver
clean and free of impurities. Similarly, for the soul to
be able to experience the light of the supernal pleasures
and bask in G-d's radiance, it must first be refined in
the [spiritual] fire of Gehinom, whereby the negative is
purged from the positive.

TEXT 7

WHAT A SHAME!

RABBI ARYEH KAPLAN, *THE
ARYEH KAPLAN READER* (NEW
YORK: MESORAH PUBLICATIONS,
1985), PP. 175FF

Then, an individual will also see himself in a new light.
Even in our mortal physical state, looking at oneself
can sometimes be pleasing and at other times very
painful. Imagine standing naked before G-d, with your
memory wide open, completely transparent, without

TEXT 7 CONTINUED

RABBI ARYEH KAPLAN
1934–1983

American rabbi, author, and physicist. Rabbi Kaplan authored more than 50 volumes on Torah, Talmud, Jewish mysticism, and philosophy, many of which have become modern-day classics. He is best known for his popular translation and elucidation of the Bible, *The Living Torah*; and his translation of the Ladino biblical commentary, *Me'am Lo'ez*.

any jamming mechanism or reducing valve to diminish its force. You will remember everything you ever did. You will see it in the light of the unshaded spirit, or, if you will, in G-d's own light that shines from one end of creation to the other.

The memory of every good deed and mitzvah will be the sublimest of pleasures. But your memory will also be open to all the things of which you are ashamed. They cannot be rationalized away or dismissed. You will be facing yourself, fully aware of the consequences of all your deeds. We all know the terrible shame and humiliation experienced when one is caught in the act of doing something wrong. Imagine being caught by one's own memory with no place to escape. . . . A number of our great teachers (R. YOSEF ALBO, *IKARIM* 4:33; R. MANASSEH BEN ISRAEL, *NISHMAT CHAIM* 1:13) write that the fire of Gehenna is actually the burning shame one experiences because of one's sins. Of course, these concepts, as used by our Sages, may also contain deeper mysteries and meanings. But a major ingredient of this "fire" may be shame. How else could one characterize the agony of unconcealed shame upon a soul?

We are taught (TALMUD, EDUYOT 2:10) that the judgment of the wicked lasts twelve months. The pain eventually subsides.

TEXT 8

MAXIMUM SENTENCE

MISHNAH, EDUYOT 2:10

מִשְׁפָּט רְשָׁעִים בְּגֵיהִנֹּם, שְׁנֵים עָשָׂר חֹדֶשׁ.

The [maximum] sentence of the wicked in Gehinom is twelve months.

TEXT 9

ALL END UP IN GAN EDEN

MISHNAH, SANHEDRIN 10:1

MISHNAH

The first authoritative work of Jewish law that was codified in writing. The Mishnah contains the oral traditions that were passed down from teacher to student; it supplements, clarifies, and systematizes the commandments of the Torah. Due to the continual persecution of the Jewish people, it became increasingly difficult to guarantee that these traditions would not be forgotten. Rabbi Yehudah Hanassi therefore redacted the Mishnah at the end of the 2nd century. It serves as the foundation for the Talmud.

כָּל יִשְׂרָאֵל יֵשׁ לָהֶם חֵלֶק לָעוֹלָם הַבָּא, שֶׁנֶּאֱמַר, "וְעַמֵּךְ כֻּלָּם צַדִּיקִים, לְעוֹלָם יִירְשׁוּ אָרֶץ. נֵצֶר מַטָּעַי, מַעֲשֵׂה יָדַי לְהִתְפָּאֵר" (יְשַׁעְיָהוּ ס, כא).

Each member of the Jewish people has a portion in the World to Come, as it is stated (ISAIAH 60:21), "Your people are all righteous; they shall inherit the land forever; they are the branch of My planting, the work of My hands, in which [I] take pride."

IV. PARADISE

The above texts clarified that the pain a soul experiences in Gehinom is well worth the suffering because it forges a bridge to the delights and pleasures that await the soul in Gan Eden. What might be the nature of these (literally) otherworldly pleasures, for which it is worth suffering?

Naturally, it is impossible for mortals, whose minds are networks of neurons, to fully fathom or appreciate the purely spiritual pleasures that await a disembodied soul. That said, we are capable of relating to spiritual pleasures even now—(refer back to Exercise 4.3)—which in itself allows us to understand that there might be even greater—infinitely superior—spiritual pleasures that we have yet to experience.

Scientific studies on coping with loss and grief have demonstrated the significant benefits that spring from an understanding that the departed soul is now in a better place—a place devoid of the pain and struggles that characterize life in this world; instead, the departed souls now inhabit a realm of indescribable spiritual delights and soul-pleasures.

TEXT 10

TO IMAGINE THE UNIMAGINABLE

RABBI DON YITSCHAK
ABARBANEL, LEVITICUS 26:3–46

RABBI DON YITSCHAK ABARBANEL
1437–1508

Biblical exegete and statesman.
Abarbanel was born in Lisbon,
Portugal, and served as a minister
in the court of King Alfonso V of
Portugal. After intrigues at court
led to accusations against him, he
fled to Spain, where he once again
served as a counselor to royalty. It is
claimed that Abarbanel offered King
Ferdinand and Queen Isabella large
sums of money for the revocation of
their Edict of Expulsion of 1492, but
to no avail. After the expulsion, he
eventually settled in Italy, where he
wrote a commentary on Scripture,
as well as other venerated works.

שֶׁהַגְּמוּל הָרוּחָנִי הוּא דָּבָר עָמוֹק וְקָשֶׁה עַל הַשֵּׂכֶל הָאֱנוֹשִׁי לְצַיְּרוֹ וּלְהַשִּׂיגוֹ בִּהְיוֹתוֹ מְחוּבָּר לַגּוּף. כִּי כְּמוֹ שֶׁלֹּא יַשִּׂיג הַסּוּמָא עִנְיַן הַמַּרְאִים, כֵּן הַנְּפָשׁוֹת בִּהְיוֹתָם עִם הַגְּשָׁמִים לֹא יַשִּׂיגוּ הַדְּבָרִים הָרוּחָנִיִּים.

Spiritual reward is abstruse and difficult for mortal intellect to visualize and grasp as long as the intellect remains attached to a corporeal body. Just as one who is blind cannot grasp the concept of colors, so the spirit that is engaged with corporeality cannot grasp purely spiritual matters.

HAGGADAH
ELIYAHU HANAVI
[PROPHET ELIJAH] ▶
Zalman Kleinman,
watercolor on
paper, New York.

TEXT 11

A UTOPIAN EXPERIENCE

TALMUD, BERACHOT 17A

הָעוֹלָם הַבָּא אֵין בּוֹ לֹא אֲכִילָה, וְלֹא שְׁתִיָּה, וְלֹא פְּרִיָּה וּרְבִיָּה, וְלֹא מַשָּׂא וּמַתָּן, וְלֹא קִנְאָה, וְלֹא שִׂנְאָה, וְלֹא תַּחֲרוּת. אֶלָּא צַדִּיקִים יוֹשְׁבִין וְעַטְרוֹתֵיהֶם בְּרָאשֵׁיהֶם וְנֶהֱנִים מִזִּיו הַשְּׁכִינָה.

In the hereafter,

there is no eating, drinking, procreation,

commerce, jealousy, hatred, or competition.

Rather, the righteous sit,

their heads adorned with crowns,

and they delight in the radiance of the Divine Presence.

FIGURE 4.1

EFFECTS OF SPIRITUAL AND RELIGIOUS BELIEFS ON BEREAVEMENT

BECKER, G., ET AL. "DO RELIGIOUS OR SPIRITUAL BELIEFS INFLUENCE BEREAVEMENT? A SYSTEMATIC REVIEW," *PALLIATIVE MEDICINE*, MAY 2007, 21 (3), PP. 207–217.

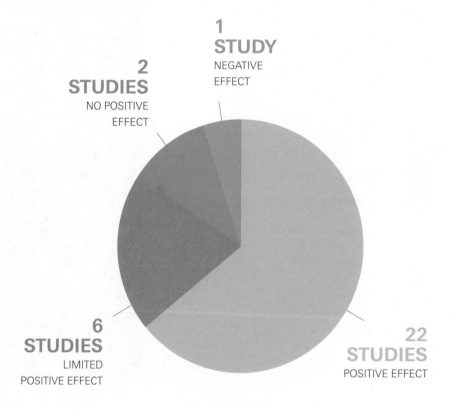

1 STUDY NEGATIVE EFFECT

2 STUDIES NO POSITIVE EFFECT

6 STUDIES LIMITED POSITIVE EFFECT

22 STUDIES POSITIVE EFFECT

V. OUR CONTRIBUTION

Paradise is not the conclusion of the journey; it is not a celestial albeit luxurious retirement destination for accomplished souls. Rather, it is filled with infinite opportunities that enable the continuation of the soul's journey. Entry to Paradise marks the start of a fresh and exciting course of advance.

The fuel that drives that advance is mostly determined by a soul's actions while it was in this world. A soul cannot generate fresh reserves after it has left its body. However, the deceased's loved ones that remain behind in this world are fully capable, and therefore duty bound, of engaging in activities that positively impact the soul's status in Heaven, propelling it further into even brighter realms, increasing its merit and reward.

It is especially significant to a departed soul, due to the enormous impact in Heaven, that the Kaddish be recited in its merit for eleven months following the passing; that good deeds be done for its merit (along with the recital of Kaddish) on its *yahrtzeit* (the anniversary of passing on the Jewish calendar); and that Yizkor is recited, along with a pledge to donate money to charity in its memory four times a year.

▼ **TORAH CURTAIN**
silk appliqué, embroidered with freshwater pearls and Bohemian garnets, Prague, 1592 (renovated 1767). (Acquired by the Jewish Museum in Prague in 1942-45 from the "Maisel Synagogue" collection in Prague)

TEXT 12

OUR MERITS CREDITED TO THE DECEASED

RABBI SHLOMO BEN ADERET,
RESPONSA 5:49

**RABBI SHLOMO BEN ADERET
(RASHBA) 1235–1310**

Medieval halachist, Talmudist, and philosopher. Rashba was born in Barcelona, Spain, and was a student of Nachmanides and Rabbi Yonah of Gerona. He was known as *El Rab d'España* ("the Rabbi of Spain") because of his fame as a rabbinical authority. More than 3,000 of his responsa are extant, dealing with varied questions on halachah and religious philosophy, addressed to him from Spain, Portugal, Italy, France, Germany, and even from Asia Minor. Among his numerous students were the Ritva, Rabbeinu Bechaye, and the Re'ah.

כְּשֶׁהוּא מוֹלִיד בֵּן צַדִּיק עוֹבֵד אֱלֹקִים, נִרְאֶה כְּאִילוּ מְסִיבּוֹ
הוּא עוֹבֵד אֱלֹקִים, שֶׁהוּא הֱבִיאוֹ לָעוֹלָם לִהְיוֹת צַדִּיק...
וְעַל כֵּן רָאוּי בֶּאֱמֶת שֶׁיִּזְכֶּה הָאָב בִּזְכוּת הַבֵּן...

אָמְנָם, מִי שֶׁעוֹשֶׂה צְדָקָה אוֹ תְּפִלָּה בְּעַד מִי שֶׁכְּבָר מֵת, מוֹעִיל לַמֵּת...
וְזֶהוּ מָה שֶׁנָּהֲגוּ יִשְׂרָאֵל בִּצְדָקוֹת, וְנִיחוֹת נֶפֶשׁ.

When individuals act righteously and are outstanding in the service of their Creator, they generate tremendous merit for the souls of their parents. This merit is simply by virtue of their parents having served as the instruments of their births; it is the parents who enabled their soul to be born into this world, which in turn enabled the many righteous deeds that they perform. The parents therefore have a share in their meritorious acts.

However, anyone's charity or prayers on behalf of a departed person are beneficial for the soul of the deceased. . . . It is therefore a Jewish custom to give charity and [do other good deeds on behalf of the deceased in order to cause] satisfaction to the soul.

FIGURE 4.2

A PARTIAL LIST OF SUGGESTED *MITZVOT* TO BENEFIT THE SOULS OF THE DEPARTED

 Donate to charity. Especially in the first year after the passing, donate daily (even if only a small amount). Particularly opportune times to give charity are before praying and before lighting Shabbat candles.

 Attend Yizkor services and pledge to give charity in memory of the deceased.

 Study Torah.

 Provide financial support to Torah students and scholars or institutions of Torah study and education.

 Sponsor a Torah class.

 Sponsor or donate books on Torah and Jewish practices to a synagogue or library.

 Write (or donate) a Torah scroll in the deceased's honor.

FIGURE 4.3

YAHRTZEIT CUSTOMS

Any mitzvah done in the merit of the deceased is beneficial for the soul. Especially beneficial are good deeds whose observance the deceased encouraged in his or her will, or those in which the deceased excelled.

Light a 24-hour *yahrtzeit* candle.

Recite the Kaddish during all the day's prayers. If possible, lead the congregational prayers.

Visit the grave and recite chapters of Psalms.

Donate to charity.

Study Torah, especially Mishnah.

Receive an *aliyah* to the Torah on the Shabbat preceding the *yahrtzeit*.

Sponsor a Kiddush for your congregation; the blessings recited there serve as a merit for the soul.

Convene a gathering of relatives and friends to commemorate the deceased, and discuss and learn from the deceased's good deeds.

TEXT 13

TEXT OF THE MOURNER'S KADDISH

SIDDUR, KADDISH
(NUSACH HA'ARIZAL)

SIDDUR

The siddur is the Jewish prayer book. It was originally developed by the sages of the Great Assembly in the 4th century BCE, and later reconstructed by Rabban Gamliel after the destruction of the Second Temple. Various authorities continued to add prayers, from then until contemporary times. It includes praise of G-d, requests for personal and national needs, selections of the Bible, and much else. Various Jewish communities have slightly different versions of the siddur.

יִתְגַּדַּל וְיִתְקַדַּשׁ שְׁמֵהּ רַבָּא.

בְּעָלְמָא דִי בְרָא כִרְעוּתֵהּ, וְיַמְלִיךְ מַלְכוּתֵהּ וְיַצְמַח פֻּרְקָנֵהּ וִיקָרֵב מְשִׁיחֵהּ.

בְּחַיֵּיכוֹן וּבְיוֹמֵיכוֹן וּבְחַיֵּי דְכָל בֵּית יִשְׂרָאֵל, בַּעֲגָלָא וּבִזְמַן קָרִיב. וְאִמְרוּ אָמֵן.

יְהֵא שְׁמֵהּ רַבָּא מְבָרַךְ לְעָלַם וּלְעָלְמֵי עָלְמַיָּא.

יִתְבָּרֵךְ וְיִשְׁתַּבַּח וְיִתְפָּאֵר וְיִתְרוֹמַם וְיִתְנַשֵּׂא, וְיִתְהַדָּר וְיִתְעַלֶּה וְיִתְהַלָּל שְׁמֵהּ דְּקֻדְשָׁא בְּרִיךְ הוּא.

לְעֵלָּא מִן כָּל בִּרְכָתָא וְשִׁירָתָא, תֻּשְׁבְּחָתָא וְנֶחֱמָתָא, דַּאֲמִירָן בְּעָלְמָא. וְאִמְרוּ אָמֵן.

יְהֵא שְׁלָמָא רַבָּא מִן שְׁמַיָּא וְחַיִּים טוֹבִים עָלֵינוּ וְעַל כָּל יִשְׂרָאֵל. וְאִמְרוּ אָמֵן.

עוֹשֶׂה שָׁלוֹם בִּמְרוֹמָיו הוּא יַעֲשֶׂה שָׁלוֹם עָלֵינוּ וְעַל כָּל יִשְׂרָאֵל. וְאִמְרוּ אָמֵן.

Exalted and hallowed be His great Name
(congregation: *Amen.*)
throughout the world
which He has created according to His will.

May He establish His kingship,
bring forth His redemption,
and hasten the coming of His Messiah
(*Amen.*)
in your lifetime and in your days,
and in the lifetime of the entire House of Israel,
speedily and soon, and say, Amen.

May His great Name be blessed
forever and to all eternity.

TEXT 13 CONTINUED

Blessed and praised, glorified, exalted and extolled, honored, adored and lauded be the Name of the Holy One, blessed be He, (*Amen.*)
beyond all the blessings, hymns, praises and consolations that are uttered in the world;
and say, Amen. (*Amen.*)

May there be abundant peace from heaven, and a good life for us and for all Israel;
and say, Amen. (*Amen.*)

He Who makes peace in His heavens, may He make peace for us and for all Israel;
and say, Amen. (*Amen.*)

THERE'S MORE...

For a fascinating tale from the Talmud regarding the experience of the great sage, Rabbi Akiva, that demonstrates the power of Kaddish, refer to Text 20 in the Appendix to this lesson (p. 160).

MACHZOR (PRAYER BOOK FOR THE HIGH HOLY DAYS) ▶
parchment, France, 13th–14th centuries. (Braginsky Collection)

TEXT 14

THE SIGNIFICANCE OF THE KADDISH

RABBI ADIN EVEN-ISRAEL
(STEINSALTZ), *HASIDDUR
VEHATEFILAH* 1, P. 295

**RABBI ADIN EVEN-ISRAEL (STEINSALTZ)
1937–2020**

Talmudist, author, and philosopher.
Rabbi Even-Israel (Steinsaltz) is
considered one of the foremost
Jewish thinkers of the 20th century.
Praised by *Time* magazine as a
"once-in-a-millennium scholar,"
he was awarded the Israel Prize
for his contributions to Jewish
study. He lived in Jerusalem and
founded the Israel Institute for
Talmudic Publications, a society
dedicated to the translation and
elucidation of the Talmud.

כָּל אָדָם בְּיִשְׂרָאֵל הוּא בְּמוּבָן מְסֻיָּם אֶחָד מֵאֵלֶּה הַנּוֹשְׂאִים וּמְקַיְּמִים אֶת מַלְכוּת ה' בָּעוֹלָם, וּכְדִבְרֵי הַכָּתוּב "אַתֶּם עֵדַי נְאֻם ה'" (יְשַׁעְיָהוּ מג, י). מִשּׁוּם כָּךְ, חֶסְרוֹנוֹ שֶׁל כָּל אֶחָד מִיִּשְׂרָאֵל יוֹצֵר כִּבְיָכוֹל חָלָל וְחֶסֶר בְּמַלְכוּת ה' בָּעוֹלָם. וּכְדֵי לְהַשְׁלִים הַחִסָּרוֹן, אֶת פְּגַם הַמְּצִיאוּת, צְרִיכִים הָאֲחֵרִים לְהִתְגַּבֵּר בְּיֶתֶר שְׂאֵת, וּלְהַכְרִיז שׁוּב בְּשֵׁם עַצְמָם וּבְשֵׁם הַנִּפְטָרִים, "יִתְגַּדַּל וְיִתְקַדַּשׁ".

וְכָאן הוּא גַם מָקוֹר הַהַכָּרָה כִּי אֲמִירַת הַקַּדִּישׁ הִיא עִלּוּי לְנִשְׁמַת הַמֵּת. חֶשְׁבּוֹן מַעֲשָׂיו וּפְעֻלּוֹתָו שֶׁל אָדָם הֵם בְּעִיקָּר הַתַּמְצִית שֶׁל חַיָּיו, שֶׁל מַה שֶׁהִצְלִיחַ לַעֲשׂוֹת בִּזְמַן הֱיוֹתוֹ עַל הָאֲדָמָה. אוּלָם, חֶשְׁבּוֹן זֶה אֵינוֹ נִגְמָר תָּמִיד עִם הַמָּוֶת. הָהַעֲרָכָה הַשְּׁלֵמָה שֶׁל אָדָם קְשׁוּרָה לֹא רַק בְּמַה שֶׁהוּא עַצְמוֹ עָשָׂה, אֶלָּא גַם בִּדְבָרִים שֶׁנּוֹצְרוּ וְצָמְחוּ מִכּוֹחוֹ וְעַל יָדוֹ. וּמִשּׁוּם כָּךְ, כַּאֲשֶׁר הַמַּמְשִׁיכִים הַחַיִּים (וּבְיֶתֶר שְׂאֵת - הַבָּנִים וְהַצֶּאֱצָאִים, שֶׁעֶצֶם קִיּוּמָם הָיָה תָּלוּי בְּהוֹרֵיהֶם) עוֹשִׂים מַעֲשִׂים טוֹבִים - הֲרֵי הֵם מַשְׁלִימִים אֶת הַהַעֲרָכָה עַל הָאָדָם, שֶׁאַף שֶׁאֵינוֹ פּוֹעֵל יוֹתֵר בְּעַצְמוֹ בָּעוֹלָם, מַמְשִׁיכִים דְּבָרִים וְנַעֲשִׂים מִכּוֹחוֹ.

וּמִשּׁוּם כָּךְ, אֲמִירַת הַקַּדִּישׁ הִיא עִלּוּי לְנִשְׁמַת הַנִּפְטָר, שֶׁהֲרֵי בִּגְלָלוֹ וְלִשְׁמוֹ מַמְשִׁיכִים וּמוֹסִיפִים לִפְעוֹל בְּתוֹךְ הַמְּצִיאוּת.

Every member of the community of Israel is, in a sense, among those who establish and proclaim G-d's sovereignty in this world. As the verse states, "You [Israel] are My witnesses, G-d declares" (ISAIAH 43:10). Therefore, the absence of any individual creates a void, as it were, in G-d's sovereignty in the world. In order to fill this void, others need to intensify their work and to proclaim on their own behalf as well as on behalf of the deceased—"Exalted and hallowed be His great name!"

With this perspective, we can understand why reciting the Kaddish elevates the soul of the deceased. The

TEXT 14 CONTINUED

aggregate of a person's actions and accomplishments in this world define his or her life. However, the tally of a person's achievements does not necessarily conclude at the moment of death. A complete evaluation of a person's accomplishments must also include all that is accomplished as a result of the person's inspiration and actions. Therefore, when those who remain alive (and especially the person's children and descendants, whose very existence is a credit to their forebears) do good deeds, they contribute to the deceased's balance of accomplishments. For although the deceased is no longer active in this world, his or her actions continue to inspire positive deeds and actions.

That is why the recitation of Kaddish elevates the soul: because G-d is being exalted in this world as a result of and in the name of the deceased.

NER NESHAMAH ▼
Baruch Nachshon, acrylic on canvas, Chevron, 1997. (nachshonart.com)

The afterlife's implications on this world are explained by *Rivkah Slonim* in "Radiology of the Soul": *myJLI.com/soul*

VI. PROPER PRIORITIES

This chapter and its predecessors focus heavily on matters that lie beyond our view: an exploration of the afterlife, Gan Eden, and Gehinom. It is critical, however, to remain focused on matters of ultimate importance to our souls; not the next world, but our current universe of tangible materiality.

TEXT 15

GREATER THAN HEAVEN

RABBI ELIYAHU OF VILNA,
COMMENTARY ON SONG
OF SONGS 1:3

**RABBI ELIYAHU OF VILNA
(VILNA GA'ON, GRA) 1720–1797**

Talmudist, halachist, and kabbalist. The Vilna Ga'on was one of the greatest scholars of his day. In addition to Talmud, he excelled in all aspects of Torah study, including kabbalah, and was proficient in secular subjects as well. He left a tremendous legacy, both from his vast writings on the Tanach, Talmud, and Shulchan Aruch, and from the many students that he inspired to Torah and scholarship.

כִּי עִיקַר עוֹלָם הַבָּא הוּא לְהָשִׁיב הַנְּשָׁמָה לִמְקוֹרָהּ
לִידָבֵק בַּשְּׁכִינָה, וּבְוַדַּאי יוֹתֵר טוֹב מִזֶּה כְּשֶׁהַשְּׁכִינָה דְּבֵקָה לְמַטָּה
כַּאֲשֶׁר הָיְתָה כַּוָּנַת הַבְּרִיאָה.

The primary reward in the hereafter
is the soul returning to its Source
and uniting with G-d.
Certainly, however, it is even greater
when the soul connects with G-d
here *in this world* [through the study of Torah
and the performance of *mitzvot*],
for that is the purpose of Creation.

TEXT 16

I ONLY WANT YOU

RABBI MENACHEM MENDEL
OF LUBAVITCH, *DERECH
MITSVOTECHA* 138A

**RABBI MENACHEM MENDEL
OF LUBAVITCH
(*TSEMACH TSEDEK*) 1789–1866**

Chasidic rebbe and noted
author. The *Tsemach Tsedek* was
the third leader of the Chabad
Chasidic movement and a noted
authority on Jewish law. His
numerous works include halachic
responsa, Chasidic discourses,
and kabbalistic writings. Active in
the communal affairs of Russian
Jewry, he worked to alleviate the
plight of the cantonists, Jewish
children kidnapped to serve
in the Czar's army. He passed
away in Lubavitch, leaving seven
sons and two daughters.

וְכָךְ הָיָה נִשְׁמַע הַלָּשׁוֹן מִמּוֹרֵינוּ וְרַבֵּינוּ נִשְׁמָתוֹ עֵדֶן
בִּדְבֵיקוּתוֹ, שֶׁהָיָה אוֹמֵר בְּזֶה הַלָּשׁוֹן:

אִיךְ וְוִיל זַע גָאָר נִיסְט. אִיךְ וְוִיל נִיט דַאיֵין גַן עֵדֶן. אִיךְ וְוִיל נִיט
דַאיֵין עוֹלָם הַבָּא כו'. אִיךְ וְוִיל מֶער נִיט אַז דִיךְ אַלֵיין.

When our master and teacher
[Rabbi Shne'ur Zalman of Liadi]
would enter a state of spiritual ecstasy,
he would be heard exclaiming:

"I want nothing at all!
I don't want Your Paradise,
I don't want Your World to Come.
I want nothing but You alone."

EXERCISE 4.4

1. Record the point from today's lesson that resonated
   with you most.

   _____

   _____

2. Identify a good deed you can do in memory of a
   deceased loved one.

   _____

   _____

KEY POINTS

1 G-d's rewards and punishments are natural consequences of our actions.

2 When we do *mitzvot*, we forge an intimate relationship with G-d. In the afterlife, our souls experience the effects of our actions: our relationship with G-d. This is the greatest possible pleasure—and it is also known as Paradise (Gan Eden).

3 At times, a soul cannot enter Paradise immediately, for its inappropriate actions in this world diminished its capacity to experience spiritual pleasures. Gehinom—a painful yet cleansing process—is temporary; every soul ultimately reaches Paradise.

4 In Gan Eden, the soul constantly ascends to higher levels. Good deeds performed in a person's memory—including the recital of Kaddish—elevate the soul to higher levels that it cannot attain on its own.

5 What we do in the here and now is more important than the pleasure (or pain) of the afterlife. Living in order to receive rewards in the next world (or to avoid Heavenly punishment) distracts our focus from where it belongs—increasing goodness and G-dliness in this world.

APPENDIX A

TEXT 17

THE PROMISE OF REWARD

LEVITICUS 26:3–6

אִם בְּחֻקֹּתַי תֵּלֵכוּ וְאֶת מִצְוֹתַי תִּשְׁמְרוּ וַעֲשִׂיתֶם אֹתָם.

וְנָתַתִּי גִשְׁמֵיכֶם בְּעִתָּם, וְנָתְנָה הָאָרֶץ יְבוּלָהּ, וְעֵץ הַשָּׂדֶה יִתֵּן פִּרְיוֹ.

וְהִשִּׂיג לָכֶם דַּיִשׁ אֶת בָּצִיר וּבָצִיר יַשִּׂיג אֶת זָרַע, וַאֲכַלְתֶּם לַחְמְכֶם לָשֹׂבַע, וִישַׁבְתֶּם לָבֶטַח בְּאַרְצְכֶם.

וְנָתַתִּי שָׁלוֹם בָּאָרֶץ וּשְׁכַבְתֶּם וְאֵין מַחֲרִיד, וְהִשְׁבַּתִּי חַיָּה רָעָה מִן הָאָרֶץ, וְחֶרֶב לֹא תַעֲבֹר בְּאַרְצְכֶם.

If you follow My laws and observe My commandments and perform them:

I will give your rains in their time, the land will yield its produce, and the tree of the field will give forth its fruit.

Your threshing will last until the vintage, and the vintage will last until the sowing; you will eat your food to satiety, and you will live in security in your land.

I will grant peace in the land, and you will rest with no one to frighten [you]; I will remove wild beasts from the land, and no army will pass through your land.

TEXT 18

WHY ONLY MATERIAL INCENTIVES?

RABBI DON YITSCHAK
ABARBANEL, LEVITICUS 26:3–46

שֶׁהַגְּמוּל הָרוּחָנִי הוּא דָּבָר עָמוֹק וְקָשֶׁה עַל הַשֵּׂכֶל הָאֱנוּשִׁי לְצַיְּירוֹ וּלְהַשִּׂיגוֹ
בִּהְיוֹתוֹ מְחוּבָּר לַגּוּף. כִּי כְּמוֹ שֶׁלֹּא יַשִּׂיג הַסּוּמָא עִנְיַן הַמַּרְאִים, כֵּן הַנְּפָשׁוֹת
בִּהְיוֹתָם עִם הַגְּשָׁמִים לֹא יַשִּׂיגוּ הַדְּבָרִים הָרוּחָנִיִּים.

וְהִנֵּה, הַתּוֹרָה הָאֱלֹקִית לֹא נִיתְּנָה לַחֲכָמִים לְבַד, כִּי אִם לְכָל הָעָם מִקָּצֶה,
הַקְּטַנִּים עִם הַגְּדוֹלִים. וְלָכֵן . . . הוּצְרְכָה לְיַעֲדָם בִּגְמוּלִים גַּשְׁמִיִּים שֶׁיְּצַיְּירֵם
כָּל אָדָם.

Spiritual reward is abstruse and difficult
for mortal intellect to visualize and grasp
as long as the intellect remains
attached to a corporeal body.
Just as one who is blind
cannot grasp the concept of colors,
so the spirit that is engaged with corporeality
cannot grasp purely spiritual matters.

Now, the divine Torah was not given
exclusively to the wise,
but to the entire nation,
small and great alike.
Therefore . . . the Torah promises
physical incentive
that can be envisioned by all.

APPENDIX B

TEXT 19

THE BENEFIT OF ULTERIOR MOTIVES

MAIMONIDES, *COMMENTARY ON THE MISHNAH*, SANHEDRIN, INTRODUCTION TO CH. 10 (*PEREK CHELEK*)

שִׂים בְּדַעְתְּךָ כִּי נַעַר קָטָן הֱבִיאוּהוּ אֵצֶל הַמְלַמֵּד לְלַמְּדוֹ תּוֹרָה. וְזֶהוּ הַטּוֹב הַגָּדוֹל לוֹ . . . אֶלָּא שֶׁהוּא, לְמִיעוּט שְׁנוֹתָיו וְחוּלְשַׁת שִׂכְלוֹ, אֵינוֹ מֵבִין מַעֲלַת אוֹתוֹ הַטּוֹב . . . וּלְפִיכָךְ בְּהֶכְרֵחַ יִצְטָרֵךְ הַמְלַמֵּד . . . שֶׁיְזָרֵז אוֹתוֹ עַל הַלִּמּוּד בִּדְבָרִים שֶׁהֵם אֲהוּבִים אֶצְלוֹ לְקַטְנוּת שְׁנוֹתָיו. וְיֹאמַר לוֹ: "קְרָא וְאֶתֵּן לְךָ אֱגוֹזִים אוֹ תְאֵנִים, וְאֶתֵּן לְךָ מְעַט דְּבַשׁ" . . .

וּכְשֶׁיַּגְדִּיל וְיֶחֱזַק שִׂכְלוֹ וְיֵקַל בְּעֵינָיו אוֹתוֹ הַדָּבָר שֶׁהָיָה אֶצְלוֹ נִכְבָּד מִלְּפָנִים, וְחָזַר לֶאֱהוֹב זוּלָתוֹ . . . יֹאמַר לוֹ מְלַמְּדוֹ: "קְרָא וְאֶקַּח לְךָ מִנְעָלִים יָפִים אוֹ בְּגָדִים חֲמוּדִים" . . . וּכְשֶׁיִּהְיֶה דַעְתּוֹ שְׁלֵמָה . . . יֹאמַר לוֹ רַבּוֹ: "לְמוֹד כְּדֵי שֶׁתִּהְיֶה רֹאשׁ וְדַיָּן, וִיכַבְּדוּךָ בְּנֵי אָדָם וְיָקוּמוּ מִפָּנֶיךָ" . . .

וְכָל זֶה מְגוּנֶּה . . . שֶׁאֵין לָשׁוּם תַּכְלִית הַחָכְמָה לֹא לְקַבֵּל כָּבוֹד מִבְּנֵי אָדָם וְלֹא לְהַרְוִיחַ מָמוֹן . . . וְלֹא תִהְיֶה אֶצְלוֹ תַּכְלִית לִמּוּד הַחָכְמָה אֶלָּא לָדַעַת אוֹתָהּ בִּלְבַד . . . וְאוּלָם זֶה טוֹב לָהֶם, עַד שֶׁיִּהְיֶה לָהֶם כֹּחַ וְהֶרְגֵּל וְהַשְׁתַּדְּלוּת בַּעֲשִׂיַּית הַתּוֹרָה, וּמִזֶּה יִתְעוֹרְרוּ לָדַעַת הָאֱמֶת וְיַחְזְרוּ עוֹבְדִים מֵאַהֲבָה.

וְזֶה הוּא מַה שֶּׁאָמְרוּ ז"ל (פְּסָחִים נ, ב) "לְעוֹלָם יַעֲסוֹק אָדָם בַּתּוֹרָה וַאֲפִילוּ שֶׁלֹּא לִשְׁמָהּ, שֶׁמִּתּוֹךְ שֶׁלֹּא לִשְׁמָהּ בָּא לִשְׁמָהּ".

Imagine young children brought to a teacher to learn Torah, which is for the children's greatest good . . . but due to the children's tender age and mental immaturity, they do not appreciate the tremendous goodness in this development. . . . The teacher must therefore . . . motivate the children with age-appropriate incentives. The teacher should tell them, "Read your lesson, and I will give you nuts or figs, or a little honey." . . .

As the children mature and their minds develop, the incentives they once found highly attractive now appear pathetic; they are now interested in other things. . . . The teacher should encourage them, "Read your lesson, and I will buy you nice shoes" or "attractive clothes." . . . When the students' minds reach full maturity . . . the teacher should say, "Study, and you will become a leader and scholar. People will respect you, and they will rise in your honor." . . .

In truth, however, all this is shameful. . . . For the purpose of wisdom is not for any specific gain—not to receive honor from others nor to bring monetary profit. . . . We should study wisdom for no purpose other than to know it. . . . Yet the above approach is for the children's own good, motivating them to regularly study and exert themselves in observing the Torah, from which they will [eventually] be inspired to know the truth [for its own sake] and to start serving [G-d] out of love.

Our sages therefore stated (TALMUD, PESACHIM 50B): "We should always study and observe the Torah, even with ulterior motives, because we will eventually come to do it for its own sake."

APPENDIX C

TEXT 20

THE TAX COLLECTOR'S RECTIFICATION

RABBI YITSCHAK BEN MOSHE
OF VIENNA, *OR ZARU'A*, VOL. 2,
SHABBAT 50

RABBI YITSCHAK BEN MOSHE OF VIENNA
C. 1180–1250

Student of the German tosafists.
His fame stems primarily from
his influential halachic work and
commentary to the Talmud, *Or
Zaru'a*, which was subsequently
quoted by many halachic
authorities. His son Rabbi Chaim
wrote a compendium of his father's
work, which for many generations
was the only widely used version of
the *Or Zaru'a*. In the 19th century,
the original work was found and
published. Among his students
was the Maharam of Rothenburg.

מַעֲשֶׂה בְּרַבִּי עֲקִיבָה, שֶׁרָאָה אָדָם אֶחָד שֶׁהָיָה עָרוֹם וְשָׁחוֹר כְּפֶחָם,
וְהָיָה טוֹעֵן עַל רֹאשׁוֹ כְּטַעַן עֲשָׂרָה טְעוּנִין וְהָיָה רָץ כִּמְרוּצַת הַסּוּס.
גָּזַר עָלָיו רַבִּי עֲקִיבָה, וְהֶעֱמִידוֹ. וְאָמַר לְאוֹתוֹ הָאִישׁ, "לָמָּה אַתָּה
עוֹשֶׂה עֲבוֹדָה קָשָׁה כָּזֹאת? אִם עֶבֶד אַתָּה וַאֲדוֹנְךָ עוֹשֶׂה לְךָ כָּךְ,
אֲנִי אֶפְדֶּה אוֹתְךָ מִיָּדוֹ. וְאִם עָנִי אַתָּה, אֲנִי מַעֲשִׁיר אוֹתְךָ".

אָמַר לוֹ, "בְּבַקָּשָׁה מִמְּךָ, אַל תְּעַכְּבֵנִי, שֶׁמָּא יִרְגְּזוּ עָלַי הַמְמוּנִים עָלַי".

אָמַר לוֹ, "מַה זֶּה וּמַה מַעֲשֶׂיךָ?"

אָמַר לוֹ, "אוֹתוֹ הָאִישׁ מֵת הוּא. וּבְכָל יוֹם וָיוֹם שׁוֹלְחִים
אוֹתִי לַחְטוֹב עֵצִים וְשׂוֹרְפִין אוֹתִי בָּהֶם".

וְאָמַר לוֹ, "בְּנִי, מֶה הָיְתָה מְלַאכְתְּךָ בָּעוֹלָם שֶׁבָּאתָ מִמֶּנּוּ?"

אָמַר לוֹ, "גַּבַּאי הַמַּס הָיִיתִי וְהָיִיתִי מֵרָאשֵׁי הָעָם,
וְנוֹשֵׂא פָנִים לַעֲשִׁירִים וְהוֹרֵג עֲנִיִּים".

אָמַר לוֹ, "כְּלוּם שָׁמַעְתָּ מִן הַמְמוּנִים עָלֶיךָ אִם יֵשׁ לְךָ תַּקָּנָה?"

אָמַר לוֹ, "בְּבַקָּשָׁה מִמְּךָ אַל תְּעַכְּבֵנִי, שֶׁמָּא יִרְגְּזוּ עָלַי בַּעֲלֵי פּוּרְעָנוּת,
שֶׁאוֹתוֹ הָאִישׁ אֵין לוֹ תַּקָּנָה. אֶלָּא שָׁמַעְתִּי מֵהֶם דָּבָר שֶׁאֵינוֹ יָכוֹל לִהְיוֹת,
שֶׁאִילְמָלֵי הָיָה לוֹ לְזֶה הֶעָנִי בֵּן שֶׁהוּא עוֹמֵד בַּקָּהָל וְאוֹמֵר 'בָּרְכוּ אֶת ה'
הַמְבוֹרָךְ' וְעוֹנִין אַחֲרָיו 'בָּרוּךְ ה' הַמְבוֹרָךְ לְעוֹלָם וָעֶד', אוֹ יֹאמַר 'יִתְגַּדַּל'
וְעוֹנִין אַחֲרָיו 'יְהֵא שְׁמֵיהּ רַבָּא מְבָרַךְ', מִיַּד מַתִּירִין אוֹתוֹ הָאִישׁ מִן
הַפּוּרְעָנוּת. וְאוֹתוֹ אִישׁ לֹא הִנִּיחַ בֵּן בָּעוֹלָם, וְעָזַב אִשְׁתּוֹ מְעוּבֶּרֶת וְאֵינוֹ
יוֹדֵעַ אִם תֵּלֵד זָכָר, מִי מְלַמְּדוֹ? שֶׁאֵין לְאוֹתוֹ הָאִישׁ אָהוּב בָּעוֹלָם".

בְּאוֹתָהּ שָׁעָה קִיבֵּל עָלָיו רַבִּי עֲקִיבָה לֵילֵךְ וּלְחַפֵּשׂ אִם הוֹלִיד בֵּן כְּדֵי שֶׁיְּלַמְּדוֹ
תּוֹרָה וְיַעֲמִידוֹ לִפְנֵי הַצִּבּוּר. אָמַר לוֹ, "מַה שְּׁמֶךָ?" אָמַר לוֹ "עֲקִיבָה".

"וְשׁוּם אִנְתְּתָךְ?" אָמַר לוֹ, "שׁוֹשְׁנִיבָא".

"וְשׁוּם קַרְתָּךְ?" אָמַר לוֹ, "לוֹדְקַיָּא".

מִיַּד נִצְטַעֵר רַבִּי עֲקִיבָה צַעַר גָּדוֹל וְהָלַךְ וְשָׁאַל עָלָיו. כֵּיוָן שֶׁבָּא
לְאוֹתוֹ מָקוֹם שָׁאַל עָלָיו. אָמְרוּ לוֹ, "יִשְׁתַּחֲקוּ עַצְמוֹתָיו שֶׁל אוֹתוֹ

הָרָשָׁע". שָׁאַל עַל אִשְׁתּוֹ, אָמְרוּ לוֹ, "יִמָּחֶה זִכְרָהּ מִן הָעוֹלָם". שָׁאַל
עַל הַבֵּן, אָמְרוּ, "הֲרֵי עָרֵל הוּא, אֲפִילוּ מִצְוַת מִילָה לֹא עָסַקְנוּ".

מִיָּד נְטָלוֹ רַבִּי עֲקִיבָא וּמִלּוֹ וְהוֹשִׁיבוֹ לְפָנָיו, וְלֹא הָיָה מְקַבֵּל תּוֹרָה עַד
שֶׁיָּשַׁב עָלָיו מ' יוֹם בְּתַעֲנִית. יָצְתָה בַּת קוֹל וְאָמְרָה לוֹ, "רַבִּי עֲקִיבָא,
לֵךְ וְלַמֵּד לוֹ". הָלַךְ וְלִמְּדוֹ תּוֹרָה, וּקְרִיאַת שְׁמַע, וי"ח בְּרָכוֹת, וּבִרְכַּת
הַמָּזוֹן, וְהֶעֱמִידוֹ לִפְנֵי הַקָּהָל וְאָמַר, "בָּרְכוּ אֶת ה' הַמְבוֹרָךְ!" וְעָנוּ הַקָּהָל,
"בָּרוּךְ ה' הַמְבוֹרָךְ לְעוֹלָם וָעֶד!" "יִתְגַּדַּל", "יְהֵא שְׁמֵיהּ רַבָּא".

בְּאוֹתָהּ שָׁעָה, מִיָּד הִתִּירוּ הַמֵּת מִן הַפֻּרְעָנִיּוֹת. מִיָּד בָּא לְרַבִּי עֲקִיבָא בַּחֲלוֹם
וְאָמַר, "יְהִי רָצוֹן מֵה' שֶׁתָּנוּחַ דַּעְתְּךָ בְּגַן עֵדֶן, שֶׁהִצַּלְתָּ אוֹתִי מִדִּינָהּ שֶׁל גֵּיהִנֹּם".

Rabbi Akiva once saw a man, naked and darkened by coal dust, carrying an extremely heavy load of firewood on his head and running at a rapid pace. Rabbi Akiva commanded the man to stop. Rabbi Akiva said to him, "Why are you running with such a heavy load? If you are a slave, I shall free you! If you are poor and must exert yourself to such an inhuman extent, let me give you money and make you wealthy!"

"Please," the man entreated Rabbi Akiva, "Let me continue my work, lest my overseers become angry with me!"

Rabbi Akiva asked, "And what is your work?"

The man replied, "I am a dead man. Each day, I am sent to collect wood for a giant fire into which I am then cast."

Rabbi Akiva asked, "What was your occupation in this world?"

TEXT 20 CONTINUED

The man answered, "I was a tax collector. I accepted bribes from the rich, and I executed the poor."

Rabbi Akiva inquired, "My son, have you not heard in the other worlds that something might be done to help you and alleviate your suffering?"

"Please," he cried, "Allow me to resume my work. My taskmasters will be angry with me and punish me further. They say that I have no way of being redeemed. Had I had a child who would stand up in public and cause others to praise G-d through prayers or Kaddish, then they could release me from this punishment. But I left behind a wife who was pregnant, and I'm not sure if she gave birth to a child. And even if she did, there is no one who would teach my child Torah, for I have no friend left in the world."

At that moment, Rabbi Akiva resolved to seek out and teach this man's child and teach him Torah and stand him before the congregation. "What is your name?" he asked.

"My name is Akiva, my wife's name is Shoshniba, and I am from the town of Ludkiya," said the man.

Rabbi Akiva felt extremely pained because of this soul. He traveled until he came to that town and inquired about him.

"May his bones be ground to dust in Hell!" the villagers answered.

"Where is this man's wife?"

The villagers answered, "May her memory be blotted out from this world!"

"Where is this man's child?"

"He is uncircumcised, and no one will circumcise him!"

Rabbi Akiva took the man's son, circumcised him, and began to teach him Torah. But the boy was unable to understand. Rabbi Akiva fasted for forty days on his behalf until a Heavenly voice proclaimed, "Rabbi Akiva, you may now teach him."

Rabbi Akiva taught him Torah, how to recite the *Shema,* silent prayer, and the Grace after Meals. He placed the child before the congregation, and he led them in prayers and in the reciting of Kaddish.

The soul was then spared from his punishment. He came to Rabbi Akiva in a dream and said, "May G-d grant you a peaceful portion in Heaven because you have spared me from the punishments of Hell."

ADDITIONAL READINGS

THRIVING AFTER TRAUMA:

THE EXPERIENCE OF PARENTS OF MURDERED CHILDREN

JOSE PARAPPULLY, ROBERT ROSENBAUM, LELAND VAN DEN DAELE, ESTHER NZEWI

Excerpted from the complete study. View the complete study and endnotes online at myJLI.com/JOTS4_AR

JOSE PARAPPULLY

Psychologist. Parappully is the director of Bosco Psychological Services in New Delhi, India. The focus of his work is on the integration of psychological practices and spiritual traditions in the healing and transformation of individuals, groups, and organizations.

Psychological literature on trauma usually focuses on pathology that results from trauma and pays little attention to positive outcomes. This article presents a phenomenological inquiry into the experiences of a profoundly traumatized group of people—parents whose son or daughter has been murdered—to assess if they were able to experience a positive outcome resulting from their trauma and to identify associated processes and resources. Of 65 parents who volunteered, 16 were selected to complete a questionnaire and were given in-depth, semi-structured interviews. The interview data, analyzed qualitatively, affirm positive outcomes for these parents. Four processes—acceptance, finding meaning, personal decision making, and reaching out to others in compassion—and six resources—personal qualities, spirituality, continuing bond with the victim, social support, previous coping experience, and self-care—facilitate a positive outcome.

Trauma is at times a "horrendous experience" that debilitates and even fragments a person irreparably. However, horrendous as trauma is, it can become the initiatory gate and pathway to wholeness. Life stories of highly generative individuals show that decidedly bad events are reworked to result in good outcomes. As Shabad and Dietrich observed, "Out of the ashes, at times literal ashes of loss and death, . . . a phoenix-like process of internal restructuring may be set in motion which can have a liberating, regenerative effect upon the survivor."

When people undertake the journey into what van der Kolk and McFarlane described as "The Black Hole of Trauma," what enables some of them to rise phoenix-like from the ashes of their tragic experience? The present study provides some answers to this important question.

Previous research has shown that victims of trauma cope with tragedy through social support; reliance on G-d and religious faith; cognitive reframing by downward comparison; positive illusions; self-blame; belief systems and principles they live by; reconstruction of shattered assumptions through a reappraisal of fundamental schemas about the self and the world; rebuilding basic trust in the benevolence and meaningfulness of the world and in their own worthiness; and finding some meaning in the experience; disclosure of feelings; psychotherapy; empowerment and the creation of new connections; and finding a positive benefit in the traumatic experience.

Victims of trauma are able sometimes not only to cope but also to grow and thrive. Adversity can sometimes yield benefits to the person who experiences it. Recent research increasingly supports the claim that traumatic experiences can lead to growth. The person who experiences adversity may not only return to the previous level of functioning but also surpass it. Thriving "represents something more than a return to equilibrium" following tragedy; the notion of thriving suggests "growth and greater well-being." Carver described thriving as "the better-off-afterward experience." One who experiences thriving comes to function at a continuing higher level than was the case before the adverse event.

Recent research has shown that there are certain resources and processes that promote such thriving. Among these are certain personal qualities, cognitive reframing, finding a positive benefit in the traumatic experience, social status, social support, religious beliefs and spirituality, and psychotherapy.

One of the severest forms of psychological trauma is that suffered by parents whose son or daughter has been murdered. Some authors have pointed out that there is relatively little research on the trauma of these parents. Most of the available psychological literature on homicide focuses on the character profile and motives of the murderer and on the situational determinants of criminal activity. The few studies on surviving relatives of homicide victims do not specifically inquire whether these survivors, particularly the parents, had been able to find a positive outcome from the trauma. For these reasons, the present study focused on the transformative experience of parents whose son or daughter had been murdered. It sought to find out by listening to their stories, first, if some of these parents had been able to experience thriving in response to their traumatic experience, and second, if they had, to discover the process and resources that facilitated this thriving.

THRIVING AFTER TRAUMA

The basic premise of the present study is that some parents whose son or daughter was murdered become transformed in positive ways through their struggle to recover from their horrendous experience. The question arises: Do the data support this premise?

Trauma

In the days, months and, in some cases, years following the murder of their son or daughter, the surviving parents who participated in the present study manifested several of the themes of traumatic sequelae frequently cited in clinical literature, such as intense fear, helplessness, anxiety, rage at the source of the trauma, sadness over loss, marked loss of interest in significant activities, psychic numbness, intrusive thoughts and affects, discomfort over aggressive impulses, hypervigilance, disintegration of beliefs, loss of meaning, disruption of personal relationships, feelings of isolation, guilt over presumed responsibility, and psychosomatic disturbances. Trauma refers to these and other negative consequences of murder experienced by these parents.

Thriving

Participants in the present study identified numerous positive outcomes that followed the tragedy, both for themselves and for society as a whole. *Thriving*, in the present study, refers to this "better-off-afterward experience," particularly "growth and greater well-being" experienced by the participants and the wider community.

Positive Impact on Society

It is incredible, the goodness that has come out of this. And you cannot deny that. You cannot deny it. . . . Unfortunately, I have to say yes to that. If I say no, I am lying. I don't want to say yes. But I have to. My head would like to say no. And my heart says, Darlene, you have to be an honest person. So many wonderful things have happened to heal people, and deep inside themselves at a soul level, because of Mat's murder. I cannot deny it. (Darlene)

It wasn't a mindless tragedy. If it were a mindless tragedy, it wouldn't have made a difference. You know what I am saying? It wouldn't have made a difference. . . . But it did. It touched so many people. . . . I feel that their death has helped people. I feel fortunate enough to be put in places to help others that have lost kids. (Julia)

The consequences of these murders, tragic as they were, appear to have had a positive impact on society in many ways. The survivor parents have made and continue to make a difference in the communities in which the murders occurred. Many survivor parents have become vocal and proactive on social issues. Survivors have dedicated their lives to working with young delinquents and prisoners to turn their lives around. Support groups established by survivors are helping other victims move toward healing and transformation. Actions taken following these murders have helped to solve other crimes and prevented further loss of lives.

> *The murder rechanneled my energies into working with victims' issues and into crime and punishment, into working with victims and trying to help them understand the system. . . . Through these organizations it is my goal that change can and will happen and hopefully not everyone will have to endure what my family and myself has felt. (Anne)*

The metaphor of a streetlight, which one participant used, is an apt illustration of the positive outcome that can result from a tragic event. She said:

> *Something good did happen. . . . Unfortunately, it is like the street light. We need a street light at the corner. But until someone dies. . . . they are not going to do anything. That is what I meant by saying it is like the street light. . . . Something good did come from his death. . . . Unfortunately, from a real tragedy some good did come. (Agnes)*

Transformation of Self

We have grown tremendously from it. We are not done growing yet. In that sense good has come from it, you know. (John)

I think I became stronger, really stronger. (Maria)

Something good has come from it. I became involved in trying to help other people, those who went through what I went through. . . . I have now a lot of feeling for other people. (Diane)

I started reading things, and so I started looking at myself in a different way and I think my spiritual awakening grew. (Jay)

My first reaction was anger at G-d. . . . It wasn't until months later, months later . . . we did go to Church. . . . I think this whole affair, the whole experience from start to now, has in the end, strengthened my faith. . . . It brought me close to G-d. (Nora)

Each parent's struggle to recover from the horrendous effects of the murder of their son or daughter served as a catalyst for emotional growth. It began a process that made the parents more self-confident and self-reliant. The tragedy in their lives brought out strengths in them that these survivors never imagined they had. It helped them reframe their previous traumatic experiences and find meaning and value in them. It led to a greater awareness of the preciousness and precariousness of life and to a greater appreciation for it.

Their struggle led to a deeper awareness of the importance of relationships, and deepened and strengthened relationships, particularly marital relationships. In some cases, the impact of the murder severely strained the marital relationship in the beginning. However, the couples were able eventually to come out stronger and more committed to each other.

Initially, the tragedy severely tested the religious faith of some participants, but ultimately it deepened and strengthened it. Their suffering made them more compassionate and caring. It changed their beliefs and attitudes in a positive direction.

> *One way to kind of put it all under one heading . . . is that his death provided an opportunity to each of us that paid attention to his death, to grow suddenly and dramatically toward a positive direction as a human being, to become more spiritual, to become more love oriented. (Darlene)*

It is important to point out here that all these parents observed that they would gladly trade all the growth and transformation they had experienced if they could have their murdered son or daughter still with them. But, they could not deny that they had experienced a positive transformation because of the tragedy in their lives.

What is it that helped the participants in this study to experience this transformation? The next sections seek to provide some clues.

PROCESSES INVOLVED IN THE TRANSFORMATION OF TRAUMA

Cognitive-Emotional Processes

The transformation these parents experienced was mediated primarily through cognitive-emotional processes. Every one of the participants (100%) engaged in some form of cognitive-emotional processing to cope with and transform his or her trauma. The processes can be subsumed under three main categories: (a) accepting the tragedy as a reality that could not be undone, (b) finding a meaning in the tragedy, and (c) making a personal decision not to allow the tragedy to ruin the survivors' lives. These three processes influenced one another.

Resources That Facilitated Transformation

Accepting, finding meaning, personal decision making, and reaching out to others were helped by six major resources: personal qualities, spirituality, continuing affective bond with the victim, social support, previous coping experience, and self-care.

Personal Qualities

The ability to cope with tragedy and, especially, to create something positive and constructive out of it appeared to be influenced by personal qualities and skills the parents possessed. All 16 participants mentioned personal qualities that were influential. These personal qualities fell into three main categories. First, there was strength of character, which was manifested in independence, determination, self-confidence, self-reliance, and optimism. Second, there was a goodness, a largeness of heart, which evoked deep

compassion in them and which enabled them to reach out to others. Third, there was a group of personal qualities, which can be collectively described as their spirituality. Because of its significant contribution to the transformative process, it will be considered as a separate resource.

Spirituality

Spirituality, "deep feelings about soul and eternity," was a very powerful resource, which helped all the participants transform their trauma and experience growth. Most of the participants had a spirituality that was shaped by the religious traditions they follow. However, they took care to point out that spirituality was different from and went beyond an institutional allegiance to any particular religious tradition. They understood spirituality more as an attitude of mind and heart that nourished their spirit and emotions and influenced their behavior. Faith in G-d, belief in a life after death, being thankful, and engaging in prayers and rituals were important components of this spirituality.

Faith in G-d and Religious Belief

All the participants professed faith in G-d. They believed that a loving and benign G-d was in control of their lives and would be there to see them through their tragedies. Faith in G-d and religious beliefs were powerful resources that helped survivors to make sense of the tragedy, to accept it, to find strength and comfort, and to transform it.

I was absolutely devastated. . . . It was a horrible, horrible night. And I can remember . . . I had gone to bed and all I did was to cry and cry and cry and cry and cry and then . . . there weren't simply any more tears to cry. I had reached a depth of pain within me that . . . there weren't any tears left. And I got out of bed, and it was in the middle of the night . . . and I was standing in front of my closet and on the closet was hanging a religious calendar, with a Bible quote for each day. And I looked up at the date for that day, and the Bible quote was: "Those who sow in tears shall reap rejoicing." And I just felt it was . . .

a word from G-d to say, you know, if you hang on, I will get you through this and then we will bring a gift of life from this terrible, terrible death. And it was the beacon of hope that I needed to grab onto, and . . . which is not to say that all the pain was gone. It wasn't. But it was a point at which I knew I could live through this. And my life would go on. (Andrea)

Belief in Life After Death

Belief in life after death was an important component of the spirituality of these survivors, although a skeptic might label such belief as "denial." Thirteen (81.25%) participants specifically mentioned it as a significant factor. That belief provided the survivors comfort and hope. The hope of reunion with their loved one helped them accept the tragedy and sustained them as they sought to rebuild their lives.

I know we will see our son again. I know that for a fact. . . . Knowing that we have something to look forward to, that is the main thing—seeing our son again. . . . Just knowing, believing what is going to happen when we die, and it is a better place for Tommy, that he is happy there, with family and friends that have died. (Maggie)

Thankfulness

Of the survivors, 10 (62.5%) specifically mentioned the importance of thankfulness. These survivors, despite the tragedy in their lives, were grateful people. They were appreciative of the gifts and blessings in their lives. Thankfulness enabled these survivors to move away from bitterness and self-pity toward growth and personal transformation. What they were most grateful for were the years they had with their son or daughter. Julia, whose two daughters were murdered together, stated

I am so fortunate that . . . that it just amazes me, you know. . . . I am lucky. I am so fortunate. . . . I could not have had them. What they brought into my life is so wonderful and precious, that I really am blessed. And lucky to have had them in my life. And I am lucky to have those memories now. They

are still in my life. Those bullets didn't take those away. . . . And I have tons of gifts in my life. You know, in the balance of my life, yeah, there is a lot of tragedy, but look at the happiness I've got, look at the neat things that there are in my life.

Prayer and Rituals

Prayer and religious rituals were valuable support in moments of grief and anguish. They provided solace, support, strength, inspiration, and guidance. Survivors filled the void left by the murder with prayers, rituals, and scripture readings. Eleven participants (68.75%) specifically mentioned that prayers and rituals were powerful resources.

I spent a lot of time in prayer. I spent a lot of time just asking G-d to hold me, and to heal me. . . . I really believe that there is . . . there is . . . —I don't know what is the word I want to use—existential or spiritual, there is a reality to the power of prayer. And . . . I benefited from the prayers of other people. . . . There were a lot of people praying for me. Loving me and praying me through that. . . . I am sure that I am standing today strong and straight because lots of people prayed me through that. (Andrea)

Several survivors wondered how one could cope with a tragedy like murder without spirituality. In response to the question, "What is the advice you have for survivors who are still struggling to come to terms with their trauma?" some participants emphasized the importance of spirituality and suggested that these survivors give spirituality a try.

Whereas for some participants their spirituality acted as a buffer providing solace and support from the beginning, for most participants the support came only after they had gone through . . . the experience of the total absence of the G-d who had seen them through many difficult moments earlier in their lives and rage and anger against a G-d who could permit such a tragedy. However, beneath such disillusionment, rage, and horror, there was in these survivors a bedrock of faith that the tragedy shook but could not destroy.

Continuing Bond with the Victim

One important resource that played a significant role in the transformation of the tragedy was a continuing affective bond parents had with their son or daughter. This continuing bond was experienced in many ways: through the awareness of the victim's continued presence, by focusing attention on the love for the victim rather than on the murderer, by filling the void in their lives with happy memories, through an awareness of what the victim would want for the survivor, and through mementos and linking objects such as journals, photo albums, and things that belonged to the victim. Dreams and paranormal experiences also served to maintain the continuing bond. All the participants reported some form of continuing bond with the victim that brought them joy and satisfaction and motivated them to transform their trauma into a gift.

> *Jennifer is a part of me now. She walks with me. . . . I keep a part of her alive within me. And now I can go on. (Terri)*

> *I don't look at Jim's death that it is an end in some way. . . . The spiritual side of our relationship is ongoing and gaining momentum all the time. . . . I have an ongoing connection with him. I still talk with him, I ask him questions, I ask for his advice. (Katherina)*

The awareness of the victim's presence was enhanced through the efforts of the survivors to keep alive the memory of their murdered son or daughter. The organizations, foundations, and groups they founded were part of this effort. These provided them with a continuing link with their memories of their son or daughter. The good accomplished by these groups and organizations strengthened their belief that in this sense their son or daughter continued to be alive and active in the world.

Social Support

All the participants were helped to cope with the tragedy in their lives and to transform it through the support they received from those around them. Such support came from friends, members of the family, the clergy, professional helpers like psychotherapists and grief counselors, the groups of which they were members, and their community. Almost all the participants had one particular individual who was there for him or her whenever needed.

Successful Coping with Previous Difficulties and Crises

Successful coping with previous difficulties and challenges in their lives was a major factor in the survivors' ability to cope with and grow from the trauma of their son's or daughter's murder. All the participants had faced challenges and difficulties earlier in their lives and negotiated them successfully. The awareness that they had coped successfully earlier gave them hope and confidence. They were able to call on the skills and processes they had employed in successfully negotiating past crises and challenges. Those crises and challenges shaped their attitudes and contributed to build up their resilience. The difficulties and challenges they had faced earlier in their lives included dysfunctional family situations; physical, emotional, and sexual abuse; divorce; accidents; serious illness; deaths and suicides in the family; financial reverses; or, as in the case of one participant, nervous breakdown and suicide attempt.

CONCLUSION

Data from this phenomenological study of 16 parents whose son or daughter had been murdered demonstrate that these parents were able to experience a positive transformation as they struggled to recover from the consequences of that horrendous event. Their efforts to come to terms with the murders have also had some positive impact on the society around them.

The general profile of the transformed survivor that emerged from this study is that of a resilient, competent, compassionate, and caring individual, characterized by a benevolent, benign, and thankful attitude toward life; shaped by belief systems; strengthened by successful coping with previous tragic experiences; supported by spirituality, friends, family, community, and a strong affective bond with the victim; and nourished through self-care.

The processes that facilitated the transformation were accepting the tragedy, finding meaning in it, making the personal decision to leave the tragedy behind and move on with their lives, and, in a very special way, reaching out in compassion to others. The resources that helped most in this transformation were personal qualities, spirituality, having a continuing bond with the victim, social support, previous coping experiences, and self-care.

Author's Note: This article is based on *Finding the Plentifulness in the Darkness: Transforming Trauma into Gift*, a dissertation submitted by the first author in partial fulfillment of the degree of doctor of philosophy in clinical psychology at the California Institute of Integral Studies in San Francisco, California.

Journal of Humanistic Psychology 42:1 (winter 2002), pp. 33–70.

Reprinted with permission of Sage Publications

THE FAMILY'S CONNECTION WITH THE SOUL

FROM THE CORRESPONDENCE OF THE LUBAVITCHER REBBE

RABBI MENACHEM MENDEL SCHNEERSON
1902–1994

The towering Jewish leader of the 20th century, known as "the Lubavitcher Rebbe," or simply as "the Rebbe." Born in southern Ukraine, the Rebbe escaped Nazi-occupied Europe, arriving in the U.S. in June 1941. The Rebbe inspired and guided the revival of traditional Judaism after the European devastation, impacting virtually every Jewish community the world over. The Rebbe often emphasized that the performance of just one additional good deed could usher in the era of Mashiach. The Rebbe's scholarly talks and writings have been printed in more than 200 volumes.

By the Grace of G-d
5 Tammuz 5743
Brooklyn, NY

Blessing and Greeting:
I have just received your letter of 3 Tammuz.

To begin with a blessing, may G-d grant that henceforth you and all your family should have only goodness and benevolence—in the kind of good that is revealed and evident.

At the same time, you must make every effort to regain the proper state of mind, despite the pain.

You should remember the teaching and instruction of the Torah which is called Toras Chayim, Guide in Life, and Toras Emes, the Torah of Truth, meaning that what it teaches is not just to ease the mind, but the actual truth. Thus, the Torah, taking into account human nature/feelings in a case of bereavement, and the need to provide an outlet for the natural feelings of sorrow and grief, prescribes a set of regulations and period of mourning.

At the same time the Torah sets limits in terms of the duration of the periods of mourning and the appropriate expression, such as shiva (the first seven days), shloshim (thirty days), etc. If one extends the intensity of mourning which is appropriate for shiva into shloshim, it is not proper, for although shloshim is part of the overall mourning period, it is so in a lesser degree. And since the Torah says that it is not proper to overdo it, it does no good for

the neshama [soul] of the dearly departed. On the contrary, it is painful for the neshama to see that it is the cause for the conduct that is not in keeping with the instructions of the Torah.

A second point to bear in mind is that a human being cannot possibly understand the ways of G-d. By way of a simple illustration: An infant cannot possibly understand the thinking and ways of a great scholar or scientist—even though both are human beings, and the difference between them is only relative, in terms of age, education and maturity. Moreover, it is quite possible that the infant may someday surpass the scientist, who also started life as an infant. But the difference between a created human being and his Creator is absolute.

Therefore, our Sages declare that a human being must accept everything that happens, both those that are obviously good and those that are incomprehensible, with the same positive attitude that "all that G-d does is for the good," even though it is beyond human truths that the neshama is part of G-dliness and is immortal. When the time comes for it to return to Heaven, it leaves the body and continues its eternal life in the spiritual World of Truth.

It is also a matter of common sense that whatever the direct cause of the separation of the soul from the body (whether a fatal accident, or a fatal illness, etc.), it could affect only any of the vital organs of the physical body, but could in no way affect the spiritual soul.

A further point, which is also understandable, is that during the soul's lifetime on earth in partnership with the body, the soul is necessarily "handicapped"—in certain respects—by the requirements of the body (such as eating and drinking, etc.). Even a tzaddik [holy man], whose entire life is consecrated to Hashem, cannot escape the restraints of life in a material and physical environment. Consequently, when the time comes for the soul to return "home," it is essentially a release for it, as it makes its ascent to a higher world, no longer restrained by a physical body and physical environment. Henceforth the soul is free to enjoy the spiritual bliss of being near to Hashem in the fullest measure. This is surely a comforting thought!

It may be asked: if it is a "release" for the soul, why has the Torah prescribed periods of mourning, etc. But there is really no contradiction. The Torah recognizes the natural feeling of grief that is felt by the loss of a near and dear one, whose passing leaves a void in the family, and the physical presence and contact of the beloved one will be sorely missed. So the Torah has prescribed the proper periods of mourning to give vent to these feelings and to make it easier to regain the proper equilibrium and adjustment.

However, to allow oneself to be carried away by these feelings beyond the limits set by the Torah—in addition to its being a disservice to one's self and all around, as well as to the neshama, as mentioned above—would mean that one is more concerned with one's own feelings than with the feelings of the dear neshama that has risen to new spiritual heights of eternal happiness. Thus, paradoxically, the overextended feeling of grief, which is due to the great love of the departed one, actually causes pain to the loved one, since the neshama continues to take an interest in the dear one left behind, sees what is going on

(even better than before), rejoices with them in their joys, etc.

One thing the departed soul can no longer do, and that is, the actual fulfillment of the mitzvoth, which can be carried out only jointly by the soul and body together in this material world. But this, too, can at least partly be overcome when those left behind do a little more mitzvoth and good deeds in honor and for the benefit of the dear neshama.

More could be said on the subject, but I trust the above will suffice to help you discover within you the strength that G-d has given you, not only to overcome this crisis, but also to go from strength to strength in your everyday life and activities in full accord with the Torah.

In your case, there is an added G-d-given capacity, having been blessed with lovely children, long may they live, with a strong feeling of motherly responsibility to raise each and all of them to a life of Torah, chuppah [marriage], and good deeds, with even greater attention and care than before, and in this, as in all good things, there is always room for improvement.

Now to conclude with a blessing, may G-d grant you much Yiddishe nachas [Jewish happiness] from each and all your children, raising them to Torah, chuppah, and good deeds in good health and peace of mind, and in comfortable circumstances.

With blessing,
[Signature]

P.S. I do not know if you were aware of it when writing your letter on 3 Tammuz. But it is significant that you wrote the letter on the anniversary of the beginning of the geula [redemption] of my father-in-law of saintly memory—an auspicious time for geula from all distractions and anxieties, to serve Hashem wholeheartedly and with joy.

Lesson

WHERE
WE GO *AGAIN*
UNDERSTANDING
REINCARNATION

*Reincarnation: more than a
fascinating topic, Judaism provides
a practical way to imagine this
mystical process and explains why
it is important both to departed
souls and to our lives today.*

▲ **MEMORY**
Elihu Vedder, oil on mahogany panel, United States,
1870. (Los Angeles County Museum of Art)

I. HAVE I BEEN HERE BEFORE?

This chapter will explore a concept that fascinated the ancients just as it remains highly intriguing today: reincarnation, or in Hebrew, *gilgul*. Simply put, it is the mystical concept that a soul that once lived in a body can be returned to this world to inhabit a second body and live a second lifetime.

Not surprisingly for such an ethereal (and for some, spooky) subject, the idea of reincarnation has itself been reincarnated repeatedly, through multiple religions and superstitions. What is the unique Jewish mystical tradition on reincarnation? Can we come back? Must we come back? Why? How?

For the sake of clarity, it is necessary to first examine currently held ideas or intuitions about soul reincarnation:

QUESTIONS

How do you feel about the concept of soul reincarnation?

Are you fascinated with—perhaps even charmed by—the idea? Or does it disturb you?

EXERCISE 5.1

Circle **T** or **F** to indicate whether you consider each of the following statements regarding reincarnation to be true or false:

T **F**   1. Belief in reincarnation is basic to Judaism.

T **F**   2. In the Jewish view, reincarnation means that a soul that inhabited one body returns to inhabit another.

T **F**   3. A human soul can be reincarnated in a nonhuman entity, such as an animal or plant.

T **F**   4. A reincarnated soul does not have its own identity but shares its identity with someone who lived in a previous lifetime.

T **F**   5. The purpose of doing good in one's current lifetime is to be reincarnated as a person of higher status.

T **F**   6. A soul is reincarnated as a penalty for sins committed in a prior life.

T **F**   7. Most souls today are reincarnations.

TEXT 1

FORGIVING OFFENSES COMMITTED IN PREVIOUS INCARNATIONS

SIDDUR TEHILLAT HASHEM, PRAYER BEFORE RETIRING AT NIGHT

SIDDUR

The siddur is the Jewish prayer book. It was originally developed by the sages of the Great Assembly in the 4th century BCE, and later reconstructed by Rabban Gamliel after the destruction of the Second Temple. Various authorities continued to add prayers, from then until contemporary times. It includes praise of G-d, requests for personal and national needs, selections of the Bible, and much else. Various Jewish communities have slightly different versions of the siddur.

רִבּוֹנוֹ שֶׁל עוֹלָם, הֲרֵינִי מוֹחֵל לְכָל מִי שֶׁהִכְעִיס וְהִקְנִיט אוֹתִי אוֹ שֶׁחָטָא כְּנֶגְדִּי בֵּין בְּגוּפִי בֵּין בְּמָמוֹנִי בֵּין בִּכְבוֹדִי בֵּין בְּכָל אֲשֶׁר לִי, בֵּין בְּאוֹנֶס בֵּין בְּרָצוֹן בֵּין בְּשׁוֹגֵג בֵּין בְּמֵזִיד בֵּין בְּדִבּוּר בֵּין בְּמַעֲשֶׂה בֵּין בְּגִלְגּוּל זֶה בֵּין בְּגִלְגּוּל אַחֵר . . .

Master of the Universe!

I hereby forgive anyone who has angered or vexed me,

or sinned against me,

either physically or financially,

against my honor or anything else that is mine,

whether accidentally or intentionally,

inadvertently or deliberately,

by speech or by deed,

in this incarnation or in any other. . . .

EIN JUDE ▶
Jankel Adler, etching, 1926.
(Ben Uri Gallery, London)

II. THE MANY LIVES OF A SOUL

Anyone hoping to shed light on the genuine Jewish perspective of the purpose and function of reincarnation must first turn to the teachings of the sixteenth-century master kabbalist, Rabbi Yitschak Luria, universally accepted as the preeminent authority on the matter (his teachings were transcribed by his student, Rabbi Chaim Vital).

The first step of this journey is to explore the fascinating evolution of souls and their universal mission:

TEXT 2

BRANCHES OF A SOUL

RABBI CHAIM VITAL, *SHAAR HAGILGULIM*, INTRODUCTION 11

RABBI CHAIM VITAL
C. 1542–1620

Lurianic kabbalist. Rabbi Vital was born in Israel, lived in Safed and Jerusalem, and later lived in Damascus. He was authorized by his teacher, Rabbi Yitschak Luria, the Arizal, to record his teachings. Acting on this mandate, Vital began arranging his master's teachings in written form, and his many works constitute the foundation of the Lurianic school of Jewish mysticism. His most famous work is *Ets Chaim*.

כִּי תְּחִלָּה יֵשׁ נְשָׁמָה אַחַת אָב לְכֻלָּם, וְהוּא אָדָם הָרִאשׁוֹן כּוֹלֵל כֻּלָּם.
וְאַחַר כָּךְ נִכְלָלוֹת כֻּלָּם בְּג' אָבוֹת: אַבְרָהָם, יִצְחָק, וְיַעֲקֹב.
וְאַחַר כָּךְ נִכְלָלוֹת כֻּלָּם לִשְׁנֵים עָשָׂר שְׁבָטִים, וְאַחַר כָּךְ נֶחְלָקִים לְע' נֶפֶשׁ.
וְאַחַר כָּךְ אֵלּוּ הָע' נֶפֶשׁ נֶחְלָקִים עַד ס' רִבּוֹא נִצוֹצוֹת גְּדוֹלִים.

It all began with one master soul:
the soul of Adam, which included all future souls.
Subsequently, this master soul passed on
to Abraham, Isaac, and Jacob
and was then divided among the twelve tribes.
Afterward, the soul was further partitioned
among the seventy souls [the descendants of Jacob that
accompanied him to Egypt]
and, eventually, among the 600,000 [souls who
left Egypt].

TEXT 3

MULTITASKERS

RABBI CHAIM VITAL, IBID.,
INTRODUCTION 16

עוֹד צָרִיךְ שֶׁתֵּדַע, כִּי הָאָדָם צָרִיךְ לְקַיֵּים כָּל הַתַּרְיַ"ג מִצְוֹת,
בְּמַעֲשֶׂה, וּבְדִבּוּר, וּבְמַחְשָׁבָה . . .
וְאִם לֹא קִיֵּים כָּל הַתַּרְיַ"ג בִּשְׁלָשָׁה בְּחִינוֹת הַנִּזְכָּר,
מְחוּיָיב לְהִתְגַּלְגֵּל עַד שֶׁיַּשְׁלִים אוֹתָם.

Furthermore, you must know that every person
must fulfill all of the 613 *mitzvot*. . . .
If a soul does not fulfill all 613 *mitzvot*
—in action, speech, and thought—
it must be reincarnated until it completes them all.

TEXT 4

MASTERING THE "ORCHARD"

RABBI CHAIM VITAL, IBID.

עוֹד דַּע, כִּי הָאָדָם מְחוּיָיב לַעֲסוֹק בַּתּוֹרָה בְּד' מַדְרֵגוֹת,
שֶׁסִּימָנָם פַּרְדֵּ"ס, וְהֵם, פְּשָׁט, רֶמֶז, דְּרוּשׁ, סוֹד.
וְצָרִיךְ שֶׁיִּתְגַּלְגֵּל עַד שֶׁיַּשְׁלִים אוֹתָם.

You should also realize that each individual
must study all four of the Torah's layers
(which are referred to by their acronym
pardes, "orchard").
These are: *peshat*, *remez*, *derush*, and *sod*
—literal, allusion, exegetic, and mystical.
It is necessary for a soul to be reincarnated repeatedly
until it completes them all.

TEXT 5A

PRAYING FOR OUR PORTION

ETHICS OF THE FATHERS 5:20

ETHICS OF THE FATHERS (*PIRKEI AVOT*)

A 6-chapter work on Jewish ethics that is studied widely by Jewish communities, especially during the summer. The first 5 chapters are from the Mishnah, tractate Avot. Avot differs from the rest of the Mishnah in that it does not focus on legal subjects; it is a collection of the sages' wisdom on topics related to character development, ethics, healthy living, piety, and the study of Torah.

MISHNEH TORAH, SEFER AVODAH (BOOK OF SERVICE) ▶
Manuscript illustration, tempera and gold leaf on parchment, ca. 1457, Northern Italy. (Jointly owned by The Israel Museum, Jerusalem and The Metropolitan Museum of Art, New York).

In this short read, *Rabbi Aron Moss* explains the connection between reincarnation and your wireless plan: *myJLI.com/soul*

יְהִי רָצוֹן מִלְפָנֶיךָ, ה' אֱלֹקֵנוּ וֵאלֹקֵי אֲבוֹתֵינוּ,
שֶׁיִּבָּנֶה בֵּית הַמִּקְדָּשׁ בִּמְהֵרָה בְיָמֵינוּ,
וְתֵן חֶלְקֵנוּ בְּתוֹרָתֶךָ.

May it be Your will,
our G-d and G-d of our fathers,
that the Holy Temple be rebuilt speedily in our days;
and grant us our portion in Your Torah.

TEXT 5B

THE UNIVERSE IS WAITING FOR YOU

THE REBBE, RABBI MENACHEM
MENDEL SCHNEERSON, *TORAT
MENACHEM* 5746:1, P. 363

**RABBI MENACHEM MENDEL SCHNEERSON
1902–1994**

The towering Jewish leader of
the 20th century, known as "the
Lubavitcher Rebbe," or simply as "the
Rebbe." Born in southern Ukraine,
the Rebbe escaped Nazi-occupied
Europe, arriving in the U.S. in June
1941. The Rebbe inspired and guided
the revival of traditional Judaism
after the European devastation,
impacting virtually every Jewish
community the world over. The
Rebbe often emphasized that the
performance of just one additional
good deed could usher in the era
of Mashiach. The Rebbe's scholarly
talks and writings have been printed
in more than 200 volumes.

מְבוֹאָר בְּכַמָּה מְקוֹמוֹת שֶׁכָּל אֶחָד מִיִּשְׂרָאֵל יֵשׁ לוֹ חֵלֶק בַּתּוֹרָה הַשַּׁיָּיךְ
אֵלָיו, וְזֶהוּ גַם בִּיאוּר לָשׁוֹן רַזַ"ל "וְתֵן חֶלְקֵנוּ בְּתוֹרָתֶךָ", חֶלְקֵנוּ פֵּירוּשׁ
שֶׁיֵּשׁ לְכָל אֶחָד חֶלְקוֹ בַּתּוֹרָה. דְּזֶהוּ מַה שֶׁאָמְרוּ רַזַ"ל שֶׁיֵּשׁ דְּבָרִים
שֶׁ"תַּלְמִיד וָתִיק עָתִיד לְחַדֵּשׁ". הַיְינוּ שֶׁכָּל הָעוֹלָם כֻּלּוֹ מְחַכֶּה עַד שֶׁיָּוָלֵד
הַתַּלְמִיד וָתִיק וִיחַדֵּשׁ וִיגַלֶּה עִנְיָן זֶה בַּתּוֹרָה, כִּי זֶהוּ חֶלְקוֹ בַּתּוֹרָה.

As explained in numerous sources, the soul of
each Jew has a specific segment of the Torah with
which it is particularly associated. This explains
the phrasing of our sages' statement, "Grant us our
portion in Your Torah"—*our portion* implies that
each of us has a unique portion within the Torah.
This concept is further expressed in our sages'
statement that there are novel Torah concepts that
"an accomplished student of the Torah is destined
to introduce" (TALMUD, MEGILAH 19B). In other
words, the entire universe anticipates the birth of
this particular diligent student, awaiting the moment
that the student innovates—meaning, uncovers—
this specific concept within the Torah. For this
concept is *this student's* portion in the Torah.

FIGURE 5.1

In order to fulfill its mission and gain rectification, each of the 600,000 root souls must:

 fulfill all 613 *mitzvot*

 study the Torah, using all four different ways of interpretation

 reveal its own unique part of the Torah

▶ **JEWISH WOMAN PRAYING** Maurycy Minkowski (1881–1930), oil on canvas.

"The Riddle of Reincarnation" is an enlightening lecture by *Rabbi Avrohom Plotkin: myJLI.com/soul*

III. MECHANISM OF REINCARNATION

The *purpose* of reincarnation is now a lot clearer, but how does it actually work? What is the *mechanism* of recycling souls?

It is important to note that there are relatively standard forms of reincarnation—for the above stated purposes—but there are also several variations of reincarnation, including "partial reincarnation," known as *ibur* ("impregnation"), and even nonhuman reincarnation.

TEXT 6

SOULS ARE NOT RECYCLED

RABBI CHAIM VITAL, *SHAAR HAGILGULIM*, INTRODUCTION 14

דַּע, כִּי אַף עַל פִּי שֶׁתִּמְצָא כָּתוּב אֶצְלֵינוּ בִּמְקוֹמוֹת רַבִּים כִּי פְּלוֹנִי נִתְגַּלְגֵּל בִּפְלוֹנִי, וְאַחַר כָּךְ בִּפְלוֹנִי וְכוּ', אַל תִּטְעֶה לוֹמַר כִּי הַנְּשָׁמָה הָרִאשׁוֹנָה עַצְמָהּ הִיא הַמִּתְגַּלְגֶּלֶת תָּמִיד. אֲבָל הָעִנְיָן הוּא, כִּי הִנֵּה כַּמָּה שָׁרָשִׁים לְאֵין קֵץ נִתְחַלְקוּ נִשְׁמוֹת בְּנֵי אָדָם, וּבְשֹׁרֶשׁ אֶחָד מֵהֶם יֵשׁ כַּמָּה נִצוֹצוֹת נְשָׁמוֹת לְאֵין קֵץ, וּבְכָל גִּלְגּוּל וְגִלְגּוּל נִתְקָנִים קְצָת נִצוֹצוֹת מֵהֶם, וְאוֹתָם נִצוֹצוֹת שֶׁלֹּא נַתַּקְנוּ, חוֹזְרִים לְהִתְגַּלְגֵּל לְהִתַּקֵּן. וְאוֹתָם שֶׁכְּבָר נִתַּקְנוּ, אֵינָם מִתְגַּלְגְּלִים, אָמְנָם עוֹלִים וְעוֹמְדִים בְּמַדְרֵגָה הָרְאוּיָה לָהֶם.

Although we've stated in numerous passages [of this treatise] that a specific individual's soul was reincarnated in a particular person, and it was subsequently re-reincarnated in another specific individual, and so on, do not misread this as implying that the original soul itself is reincarnated repeatedly. Rather, each human soul branches out into innumerable roots. Every root contains an infinite quantity of soul-sparks. With each subsequent reincarnation, a number of these sparks are rectified and they ascend [to enjoy the rewards of Heaven and] dwell in the particular strata [of Gan Eden that are] appropriate for them. However, those soul-sparks that were *not* rectified are reincarnated to provide further opportunity for rectification.

TEXT 7A

SOUL IMPREGNATION

RABBI CHAIM VITAL, *SEFER HAGILGULIM*, CH. 5

הִנֵּה עִנְיַן גִּלְגּוּל הוּא, שֶׁבְּצֵאת הַוָּלָד מִמְּעֵי אִמּוֹ נִכְנֶסֶת הַנְּשָׁמָה הַמְגוּלְגֶּלֶת בְּגוּף הַוָּלָד, וְאֵין בִּרְשׁוּתָהּ לָצֵאת מִמֶּנּוּ עַד יוֹם מוֹתוֹ... וְעִנְיַן הָעִבּוּר הוּא שֶׁבִּהְיוֹת הָאָדָם גָּדוֹל... הִנֵּה מִלְּבַד נְשָׁמָה הָעִיקָרִית שֶׁנִּכְנְסָה בּוֹ בְּצֵאתוֹ מֵרֶחֶם אִמּוֹ, מִתְעַבֶּרֶת בּוֹ נְשָׁמָה אַחֶרֶת זוּלָתָהּ. וְדוֹמֶה לְאִשָּׁה עוּבָּרָה שֶׁיֵּשׁ לָהּ וָלָד בְּתוֹךְ מֵעֶיהָ.

The concept of *gilgul*, reincarnation, is that a soul [requiring further rectification] enters the body of a child as it emerges from its mother's womb, to serve as the newborn's soul. It has no permission to leave that individual until the person's destined day of death. By contrast, the concept of *ibur*, soul-impregnation, is that a soul enters an *adult* body that is already inhabited by a soul—the person's primary soul received at birth. In this case, the individual is merely impregnated with a guest soul in addition to harboring a primary soul; the individual then carries the extra soul much as a woman carries a child in her womb.

TEXT 7B

PURPOSES OF SOUL IMPREGNATION

RABBI CHAIM VITAL, IBID.

וְעִנְיַן הָעִבּוּר נֶחֱלָק לִב' חֲלָקִים:

א) שֶׁהַנְּשָׁמָה בָּאָה לְהִתְעַבֵּר בָּאָדָם לְצוֹרֶךְ עַצְמָהּ, לְפִי שֶׁחָסֵר לָהּ אֵיזֶה מִצְוָה שֶׁלֹּא קִיְּמָהּ בְּגִלְגּוּל הַקּוֹדֵם, וְהִיא מִן הַמִּצְוֹת שֶׁלֹּא בָּאוּ לְיָדָהּ - כְּגוֹן מִצְוַת יִבּוּם וַחֲלִיצָה וְכַיּוֹצֵא בָּהֶם - לָכֵן לֹא נִתְחַיְּיבָה בְּגִלְגּוּל כַּנַּ"ל בְּפֶרֶק ד' וְדַי לָהּ בְּעִבּוּר.

ב) שֶׁהַנְּשָׁמָה בָּאָה לְהִתְעַבֵּר בָּאָדָם לְסַיְּיעוֹ וּלְזַכּוֹתוֹ וּלְהַדְרִיךְ אוֹתוֹ בַּתּוֹרָה וּבְמִצְוֹת, וְאֵינָהּ חֲסֵרָה דָּבָר לְצֹרֶךְ עַצְמָהּ.

A soul experiences *ibur* for one of two reasons:

(a) The impregnated soul comes to an individual for its own sake. In its previous life, it failed to perform a particular mitzvah and was therefore left lacking. This was the kind of mitzvah that was impossible to perform under the conditions of that lifetime, such as the mitzvah of *yibum, chalitsah*, and the like. It is therefore not obligated to engage in a full-scale incarnation (described earlier in this treatise), for soul-impregnation is sufficient.

(b) The impregnated soul comes solely to assist an individual, to bring a person additional merit, or to guide an individual in matters of Torah and *mitzvot*. In this case, the impregnated soul lacks nothing for itself.

"A Fascinating Voyage into Our Souls." Reincarnation expounded upon by modern-day kabbalist *Rabbi DovBer Pinson*: *myJLI.com/soul*

TEXT 8

MULTIPLE CHANCES FOR RECTIFICATION

RABBI CHAIM VITAL, *SHAAR HAGILGULIM,* INTRODUCTION 4

כַּאֲשֶׁר נֶפֶשׁ הָאָדָם, אַחַר שֶׁבָּא מֵחָדָשׁ בְּפַעַם א', וְחָטָא וּפָגַם בָּהּ,
הִנֵּה אַחַר כָּךְ מִתְגַּלְגֶּלֶת בְּגוּף אֶחָד לְהִתַּקֵּן, וְזֶה נִקְרָא גִלְגּוּל א'.
וְאִם לֹא נִתְקְנָה אָז, חוֹזֶרֶת בְּגִלְגּוּל שֵׁנִי.
וְאִם לֹא נִתְקְנָה אָז, חוֹזֶרֶת בְּגִלְגּוּל שְׁלִישִׁי.
וּמִשָּׁם וְאֵילָךְ, אֵין לָהּ עוֹד תַּקָּנָה בְּגִלְגּוּל.

When a human soul comes to the world
and becomes soiled by sin in the process,
it reincarnates in another body to rectify itself.
That second life is its first reincarnation.
If it fails to rectify itself during that lifetime,
it may return in a second reincarnation.
If it again fails to find rectification,
it may endure a third reincarnation.
After that, however, it is no longer provided
opportunities for rectification via reincarnation.

▶ **MAN IN A TALLIT**
Jozef Israëls (1824–1911), watercolor,
pen, and ink on paper; Netherlands.

TEXT 9

INANIMATE, VEGETATIVE, OR ANIMAL REINCARNATION

RABBI NAFTALI HERTS
BACHARACH, *EMEK
HAMELECH, SHAAR TIKUNEI
HATESHUVAH*, CH. 1

**RABBI NAFTALI HERTS BACHARACH
17TH CENTURY**

Born in Frankfurt am Main, Germany, he was a rabbi and kabbalist and the author of *Emek Hamelech*, which he described as an explanation of passages and teachings from Lurianic kabbalah. The book had a major impact on later kabbalah.

[הֶן כָּל אֵלֶּה יִפְעַל אֵ-ל פַּעֲמַיִם שָׁלוֹשׁ עִם גָּבֶר (אִיּוֹב לג, כט).]

"עִם גָּבֶר" דַּיְקָא. שֶׁלֹּא יָבֹא עוֹד בְּגִלְגּוּל בְּנֵי אָדָם עַד שֶׁיֵּלֵךְ נָע וָנָד בָּאָרֶץ,
וְאָז יִתְגַּלְגֵּל בְּדוֹמֵם צוֹמֵחַ חַי . . . וְיֵשׁ תִּקְוָה לְאַחֲרִיתוֹ אַחַר שֶׁקִּבֵּל עָנְשׁוֹ,
כִּי לֹא כָלוּ רַחֲמָיו עַל כָּל בְּרִיּוֹתָיו.

"Behold, G-d does all these, twice or thrice with man" (JOB 33:29).

The limitation of twice or thrice applies "with man," meaning that a human soul is not subsequently reincarnated in a *human* body.

Rather it is forced to wander the planet until it is reincarnated in an inanimate, vegetative, or animal entity. . . .

Then, after it has done its penance, there is hope for its future, for G-d's endless mercies extend to all of His creations.

▼ BIRDS' HEAD HAGGADAH
block calligraphy, Southern Germany, c. 1300. (Israel Museum, Jerusalem)

In "The Wonder Horse," *Rabbi Yerachmiel Tilles* tells the tale of a horse sale with an interesting ending:
myJLI.com/soul

IV. WHO WAS I?

Is there a way to discover our identities in previous reincarnations? And perhaps more critical for the mission-minded, is there a way to discover the purpose—the unique task and individual mission—for which our soul was compelled to return to this world?

TEXT 10

WHO WAS I? WHAT IS MY MISSION?

RABBI MOSHE CORDOVERO, *SHI'UR KOMAH* 84

RABBI MOSHE CORDOVERO (RAMAK), 1522–1570

Prominent kabbalist. Ramak belonged to the circle of Jewish mystical thinkers who flourished in 16th-century Safed. The name Cordovero indicates that his family originated in Córdoba, Spain. His most famous kabbalistic work is *Pardes Rimonim*.

אֵין מִי שֶׁיֵּדַע מִצַּד מְצִיאוּת עַצְמוּתוֹ אוֹ יַרְגִּישׁ בְּעַצְמוֹ שֶׁהוּא מְגוּלְגָּל אוֹ בִּלְתִּי מְגוּלְגָּל אֶלָּא מִי שֶׁנִּמְסַר לָהֶם עַל צַד הַקַּבָּלָה . . .

וְאִם תֹּאמַר, בַּמֶּה יֵדַע הָאָדָם אֶת הַדָּבָר שֶׁעַל אוֹתוֹ דָּבָר בָּא, אִם מִצְוָה אוֹ עֲבֵירָה, כְּדֵי שֶׁיַּזְהִיר עַצְמוֹ אוֹ יְתַקֵּן עַצְמוֹ? הָעִנְיָן הַזֶּה הוּא מוּטְבָּע בְּסְגֻלָּה בָּאָדָם בְּסוֹד רְדִיפַת הַנְּשָׁמָה וְחֶשְׁקָהּ בְּעִנְיַן הַמִּצְוָה אוֹ יִצְרוֹ מְפַתֵּהוּ עַל אוֹתָהּ עֲבֵירָה שֶׁהִכְשִׁילוֹ קוֹדֶם.

It is impossible to deduce or intuit whether one possesses a reincarnated soul or not, unless one is the recipient of a mystical communication in this regard. . . .

You may wonder: How then will we know the purpose for which we entered this world, which mitzvah we must scrupulously perform or which transgression we must especially avoid? The answers are naturally ingrained in us: We experience natural affinity and longing to perform a certain mitzvah [when that mitzvah is critical to our present incarnation]. Or,

TEXT 10 CONTINUED

our inclination strives especially hard to entice us to commit a particular sin, for it is the very same sin in which we blundered during our previous life.

TEXT 11

YOUR MISSION WILL CHALLENGE YOU

THE REBBE, RABBI MENACHEM MENDEL SCHNEERSON, *IGROT KODESH* 5, P. 39

בְּמַעֲנֶה עַל מִכְתָּבוֹ מִי"ב מַר-חֶשְׁוָן בּוֹ מוֹדִיעַ אֲשֶׁר קִבֵּל עָלָיו וּמְקַיֵּים הַהוֹרָאוֹת בְּעִנְיַן הַשִּׁיעוּרִים וּנְתִינַת הַצְּדָקָה, אֲבָל בְּנוֹגֵעַ לְשָׁלוֹם בַּיִת הֲרֵי בְּחִיצוֹנִיּוּת הוּטַב אֲבָל בִּפְנִימִיּוּת עֲדַיִין אֵינוֹ כִּדְבָעֵי.

כְּבָר כָּתַבְתִּי לוֹ בְּמִכְתָּבִי הַקּוֹדֵם עַל דְּבַר זֶה שֶׁבְּוַדַּאי יִהְיוּ הָעֲלָמוֹת וְהֶסְתֵּרִים בְּיִחוּד עַל עִנְיַן הַשָּׁלוֹם בַּיִת, וְדַוְקָא בָּזֶה נְחוּצָה הִתְאַמְּצוּת בְּיוֹתֵר, כִּי מֵרַבּוּי הָעֲלָמוֹת וְהֶסְתֵּרִים מוּכָח אֲשֶׁר זֶהוּ דַוְקָא מֵעִיקַר הַבֵּירוּרִים שֶׁלּוֹ.

וּכְמוּבָן מִכִּתְבֵי הָאֲרִיזַ"ל וּמְבוֹאָר בְּדַא"ח . . . אֲשֶׁר לְבַד יְחִידִים הֲרֵי הַנְּשָׁמוֹת דְּדוֹרוֹתֵינוּ אֵלֶּה הָיוּ כְּבָר בָּעוֹלָם, וּבָאִים עַתָּה בְּגִלְגּוּל וְעִיקַר בִּיאָתָם הוּא לְתַקֵּן אֶת מַה שֶּׁחָסְרוּ בְּקִיּוּם הַתַּרְיַ"ג מִצְוֹת בְּגִלְגּוּלִים הַקּוֹדְמִים, וּבְכָל זֹאת כַּמּוּבָן גַּם הֵם מְחוּיָּבִים בְּקִיּוּם כָּל הַתַּרְיַ"ג מִצְוֹת אַף אֵלּוּ שֶׁלֹּא חָסְרוּ בְּגִלְגּוּלָם הַקּוֹדֵם, וְהַחִילוּק הוּא אֲשֶׁר בְּאֵלּוּ הַמִּצְוֹת שֶׁלֹּא חָסְרוּ בְּפַעַם הַקּוֹדֶמֶת הֲרֵי הַיֵּצֶר הָרַע אֵין מְנַגֵּד עַל זֶה בְּיוֹתֵר, כִּי אִם רַק כְּדֵי שֶׁיִּשָּׁאֵר הָעִנְיָן דִּבְחִירָה חָפְשִׁית, כִּי בְּעִנְיָנִים אֵלּוּ כְּבָר הוּבְרַר בְּפְעָמִים הַקּוֹדְמוֹת, מַה שֶּׁאֵין כֵּן בְּהָעִנְיָנִים שֶׁחָסְרוּ בְּפְעָמִים הַקּוֹדְמוֹת הַיְינוּ שֶׁלֹּא הוּבְרַר חֶלְקָם בָּעוֹלָם [הַ]זֶה וְחֶלְקָם בַּנֶּפֶשׁ הַשַּׁיָּיךְ לְעִנְיָנִים אֵלּוּ, הֲרֵי הַהִתְנַגְּדוּת שֶׁל הַיֵּצֶר הָרַע הִיא בְּכָל תּוֹקֶף, וְאֵין לְהַאֲרִיךְ בְּדָבָר הַמְבוֹאָר וְכוּ'.

וּבְנוֹגֵעַ אֵלָיו לַעֲשִׂיָּה בְּפוֹעַל שֶׁזֶּהוּ הָעִיקָר, הֲרֵי עוֹד הַפַּעַם אֲעוֹרֵר אוֹתוֹ וַאֲזָרְזוֹ בְּעִנְיַן הַשְׁתַּדְּלוּת בְּהַשָּׁלוֹם בַּיִת בְּיוֹתֵר, אַף שֶׁנִּדְרָשׁ לָזֶה וִיתּוּרִים (מִכֵּיוָן שֶׁהַוִיתּוּרִים אֵינָם בְּעִנְיְנֵי תּוֹרָה וּמִצְוָה).

I am replying to your letter in which you inform me that you accepted and are implementing my directives regarding Torah study classes and giving charity, but as far as the situation at home is concerned, your marital

"Biblical Personalities and their Reincarnation History" with *Rabbi Chaim Miller*: myJLI.com/soul

harmony appears only superficially to have improved, while the underlying reality remains unsatisfactory.

I already told you in my previous letters that it would be challenging. You are *meant* to find it difficult—for the success of your life's mission hinges upon your sincere efforts toward marital harmony.

Our mystical teachings reveal that rare individuals are born with original souls; the rest of us are reincarnations. We return to complete the fulfillment of the *mitzvot* that we missed in previous lifetimes. Certainly, we are obligated in *all* of the *mitzvot* in *every* lifetime, but the specific *mitzvot* we omitted in earlier incarnations are critical to the rectification of our souls (and the rectification of this world).

Using the evil inclination as a guide, we can identify the *mitzvot* that determine the outcome of our life's mission: Our inclination opposes the *mitzvot* that we finalized in previous lifetimes—but only to the degree necessary to create free choice between good and evil. By contrast, it unleashes a fierce storm of opposition, with countless hurdles and challenges, when we approach a mitzvah that we failed to fulfill in previous incarnations. Therefore, your many hurdles to marital harmony reveal its indispensability to your rectification. Do whatever it takes to achieve harmony.

TEXT 12

LED BY G-D'S PLAN

RABBI SHALOM DOVBER
SCHNEERSOHN, CITED IN *HAYOM YOM*, 1 CHESHVAN

RABBI SHALOM DOVBER SCHNEERSOHN (RASHAB), 1860–1920

Chasidic rebbe. Rabbi Shalom Dovber became the 5th leader of the Chabad movement upon the passing of his father, Rabbi Shmuel Schneersohn. He established the Lubavitch network of *yeshivot* called Tomchei Temimim. He authored many volumes of Chasidic discourses and is renowned for his lucid and thorough explanations of kabbalistic concepts.

מֵאָז שֶׁאָמַר הַקָּדוֹשׁ בָּרוּךְ הוּא לְאַבְרָהָם אָבִינוּ עָלָיו הַשָּׁלוֹם, "לֶךְ לְךָ מֵאַרְצְךָ גוֹ'" (בְּרֵאשִׁית יב, א), וּכְתִיב, "וַיִּסַּע אַבְרָם הָלוֹךְ וְנָסוֹעַ הַנֶּגְבָּה" (שָׁם ט), הֻתְחַל סוֹד הַבֵּירוּרִים. וְעַל פִּי גְזֵרַת הַהַשְׁגָּחָה הָעֶלְיוֹנָה, הָאָדָם הוֹלֵךְ לְמַסָּעָיו בַּמָּקוֹם אֲשֶׁר הַנִּיצוֹצוֹת הַצְּרִיכִים לְהִתְבָּרֵר עַל יָדוֹ מְחַכִּים לִגְאוּלָתָם.

הַצַּדִּיקִים שֶׁהֵם בַּעֲלֵי רְאִיָּה רוֹאִים הֵם בְּאֵיזֶה מָקוֹם הַבֵּירוּרִים שֶׁלָּהֶם מְחַכִּים לָהֶם וְהוֹלְכִים שָׁמָּה בְּעַצְמָם, וְעַמָּא דְבַר, הִנֵּה עִילַת כָּל הָעִילוֹת וְסִיבַּת כָּל הַסִּיבּוֹת מְסַבֵּב כַּמָּה עִילוֹת וְסִיבּוֹת שֶׁיָּבוֹאוּ לַמָּקוֹם הַהוּא אֲשֶׁר שָׁם הֻטְלָה עֲלֵיהֶם הָעֲבוֹדָה בַּעֲבוֹדַת הַבֵּירוּרִים.

From the moment that G-d instructed our forefather Abraham, "Go from your land . . ." (GENESIS 12:1)—following which it is stated, "Abram kept traveling further southward"—the mystical process of the rectification of divine sparks was launched. Subsequently, by decree of divine providence, individuals travel to the locations in which the divine sparks that these specific individuals must rectify await their redemption.

Saintly individuals with spiritual vision perceive the locations in which their divine sparks await their engagement, and they take the initiative to journey to those locations. The rest of us are left in the hands of the primary Cause behind all causes and the ultimate Reason behind all reasons: G-d orchestrates countless apparent causes and circumstances to bring specific individuals to the locations in which their predestined service of rectification is required.

FIGURE 5.2

Here are some strong clues by which to identify our mission(s) in this world:

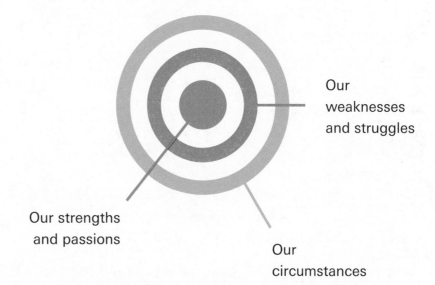

Our weaknesses and struggles

Our strengths and passions

Our circumstances

▼ **COBBLER'S WORKSHOP**
Max Liebermann, oil on wood,
Berlin, Germany, 1881–1882.
(Alte Nationalgalerie, Staatliche
Museen zu Berlin)

V. A LARGER PICTURE

Toward the start of this lesson, there was an exercise (5.1) designed to clarify current thoughts and feelings about reincarnation. At this point, having reviewed the above materials, it is possible to examine the earlier responses and determine their accuracy.

Undoubtedly, a primary reincarnation phobia—the fear of discovering that we are truly someone else, simply reincarnated—will have melted before the kabbalistic clarity that does not deny us our personal identity. On the contrary, the kabbalistic concept of reincarnation enhances our personal identity by providing us a unique purpose and meaning: an exclusive role to play *within the universal human mission*. This approach provides significant purpose and meaning, which is essential to emotional well-being.

Lastly, as humanity's collective mission rapidly approaches its glorious conclusion, the spiritual spotlight shines with additional focus on a particular segment of the population. These are souls who are destined to play an especially important role in scoring humanity's final, game-winning goal.

TEXT 13

MENTAL HEALTH REQUIRES A WILL TO MEANING

VIKTOR FRANKL, *MAN'S SEARCH FOR MEANING* (BOSTON: BEACON PRESS, 1992), P. 110

VIKTOR EMIL FRANKL, M.D., PHD 1905–1997

Psychiatrist, founder of logotherapy. Frankl was professor of neurology and psychiatry at the University of Vienna Medical School. During World War II, he spent 3 years in various concentration camps, including Theresienstadt, Auschwitz, and Dachau. Frankl was the founder of the psychotherapeutic school called logotherapy. Frankl authored 39 books, which have been published in 38 languages. His most famous book, *Man's Search for Meaning*, has sold over 9 million copies in the U.S. alone.

Thus it can be seen that mental health is based on a certain degree of tension, the tension between what one has already achieved and what one still ought to accomplish, or the gap between what one is and what one should become. Such a tension is inherent in the human being and therefore is indispensable to mental well-being. We should not, then, be hesitant about challenging man with a potential meaning for him to fulfill. It is only thus that we evoke his will to meaning from its state of latency.

▼ **EVENING MOOD**
Leis Schjelderup, oil on canvas. (Nordnorsk Kunstmuseum, Tromsø, Norway)

How does an understanding of the dynamics of reincarnation help us cope with tragedy? *Dr. Lisa Aiken* offers a perspective: *myJLI.com/soul*

TEXT 14

A SPECIAL MISSION FOR TODAY'S WOMEN

THE REBBE, RABBI MENACHEM
MENDEL SCHNEERSON, *LIKUTEI
SICHOT* 26, P. 375

אוּן דֶערְצוּ הָאבְּן נָשֵׁי וּבְנוֹת יִשְׂרָאֵל אוֹיךְ דִי גָאר וְוִיכְטִיקֶע שְׁלִיחוּת - צוּ
בְּרֶענְגֶען דִי גְאוּלָה הָאֲמִיתִּית וְהַשְׁלֵימָה, וְוִי גֶערֶעדְט מֶערֶערֶע מָאל, אַז כְּשֵׁם
וְוִי בַּא יְצִיאַת מִצְרַיִם אִיז "בִּשְׂכַר (בִּזְכוּת) נָשִׁים צִדְקָנִיּוֹת נִגְאֲלוּ אֲבוֹתֵינוּ
מִמִּצְרַיִם", אַזוֹי אִיז דָאס אוֹיךְ בְּכָל דּוֹר וָדוֹר, אוּן סְפֶּעצִיעֶל בְּדוֹרֵנוּ זֶה,
וֶועלְכֶער אִיז אַ גִלְגוּל פוּן דּוֹר יוֹצְאֵי מִצְרַיִם.

אוּן מ'זֶעט בְּטֶבַע נָשֵׁי וּבְנוֹת יִשְׂרָאֵל אַז בַּא זֵיי מֶער וְוִי בַּא אַנָשִׁים לֵייגְט
זִיךְ בְּפַשְׁטוּת צוּ אַרוֹיסְגֵיין מִיַּד פוּן גָלוּת אוּן מ'דַארְף זִיךְ מִיט זֵיי וֵוייגִיקֶער
אַמְפֶּערְן אַז מ'דַארְף שׁוֹין אִיצְט אַרוֹיס פוּן גָלוּת וְוִי מ'דַארְף זִיךְ מִשְׁתַּדֵל זַיין
מִיט אַנָשִׁים.

Jewish women and girls play an essential role in the highly critical mission of bringing about the true and complete Redemption. The women played an indispensable role in our Exodus from Egypt—indeed, our sages state that "our ancestors were redeemed from Egypt in the merit of the [deeds of the] righteous women" (TALMUD, SOTAH 11B). As we have discussed repeatedly, they fulfill this role in each subsequent generation. This is especially true of our present time, for we are the reincarnation of the generation that left Egypt.

Indeed, we can clearly observe that Jewish women and girls are naturally predisposed—far more readily than the menfolk—to the idea of immediately leaving the Exile. Less effort is required to convince them that we must leave this exile already than is required to inspire the men.

EXERCISE 5.2

1. From the various ideas offered in today's lesson, record the point that resonates with you most.

   _____

   _____

2. Identify a mitzvah to which you feel a strong connection, the one that might constitute the reason that your soul reentered this world.

   _____

   _____

HADLAKAT NEROT/CANDLE LIGHTING ➤
Zalman Kleinman, acrylic on canvas, New York, 1997.

KEY POINTS

1 Adam possessed the Jewish master soul that ultimately branched out into the 600,000 souls that received the Torah at Mount Sinai. All subsequent Jewish souls are offshoots of these soul-roots.

2 The 600,000 primary souls were each given a part of the world to perfect through the fulfillment of the 613 *mitzvot*. When a soul accomplishes its mission, it itself also gains rectification and elevation.

3 Every root soul must also study each of the Torah's four layers of teaching and uncover its unique part in Torah.

4 Few, if any, of the original souls completed all 613 *mitzvot* nor the required study during their original lifetimes. Reincarnation provides souls with additional opportunities to complete their missions and the rectification of the world and themselves.

5 When a person dies, all the refined elements of their soul return to Heaven. A new soul, built from the elements that were left unrectified, is then grafted from the stem soul and returned to this world.

6 As a general rule, our souls are reincarnations, but it is impossible to be conscious of or to accurately sense the experiences of our previous lifetimes.

7 Clues as to the nature of our soul's unique task in this world can be gleaned from (a) our strengths and passions, (b) our weaknesses and struggles, and (c) our unique life circumstances.

8 The kabbalistic view of reincarnation does not deny us our personal identity; each of us is a complete and unique individual who is simultaneously and integrally linked to a far greater reality. Reincarnation ascribes greater importance to our existence and provides each of us a unique role within the overall human mission.

ADDITIONAL READINGS

LIVING ON PURPOSE

BRAD KLONTZ

BRAD KLONTZ

Financial psychologist. Klontz is a founder of the Financial Psychology Institute and an associate professor of practice in financial psychology at Creighton University. He is a fellow of the American Psychological Association and has partnered with corporations, including JPMorgan Chase and H&R Block, to help raise awareness around issues related to financial health and financial psychology.

It's important to have a purpose. I have seen lives filled with loneliness and despair when no specific purpose has been embraced. On the other hand, I have seen drastic improvements in psychological well-being when people have identified a meaningful purpose.

Without purpose, what's the point of getting up every day? Life can't be just about growing-up, getting a job, taking a few vacations, retiring, and dying, can it? Is that why we are here on earth? I believe that we are each on earth for a special purpose, which is up to us to name. According to the American Heritage Dictionary, "purpose" is defined as: 1) the object toward which one strives or for which something exists; an aim or a goal, 2) a result or effect that is intended or desired; an intention, 3) determination; resolution, and 4) the matter at hand; the point at issue. Purpose in life is the intended result of our focus, determination, and intention. It is the entire point of our existence.

Many spiritual disciplines offer a framework to help followers define their life's purpose. Followers take comfort in the teachings and traditions of spiritual leaders and their insights into a higher power's purpose for them. Some believe that life is about striving to stay pure in mind and deed. Others emphasize that life should be enjoyed and experienced. Others say that life

is suffering, and our purpose is to detach from our egos and melt into the cosmos. Still others say that life should be about service to others. Regardless of the particular spiritual tradition or philosophical base, there is profound psychological value in clearly defining a customized purpose.

Why is purpose so important? A purpose sets the entire context for our lives. Without a clearly defined purpose, we are just a haphazard combination of goals and non-goals and actions and non-actions meandering through space and time. A purpose is a master plan for our life. Knowing our purpose helps us define our goals. It helps us avoid getting lost in the minutiae of daily life by keeping our eyes on the target. It can make life much more enjoyable and effortless. Purpose is not something that others choose for us; rather, it is something we must choose for ourselves. It emerges from an exploration of what we value most. When we are defining our purpose in life, it is important to not worry about how we will go about achieving it. When we identify and commit to our intentions, the opportunities and methods for achieving our purpose will begin to show up. In fact, they are often already in our lives, but we may not have noticed them because we were not paying attention. Defining our purpose helps us focus.

As long as your purpose fills you with passion, it can be simple and safe or grandiose and daring. My purpose is to help bring hope and healing to the world. All of my activities, intentions, and goals emerge from this basic purpose. What's your purpose? If you don't already know it, take time right now to define it.

1. Start by examining what you value most. Is it balance, faith, family, compassion, excellence, generosity, peace, connection to others, or something else?

2. Consider what you would hope others would say about you when they describe you, or what you would want to be written in your obituary. What legacy do you want to leave? You will be known for something. What do you want it to be?

3. Take a moment to write down your own special purpose. The simple act of writing things down, like goals and purpose, greatly increases their power in our lives. It doesn't have to be perfect, just write it down. You can hone it as you go.

4. Start each day and end each day by reciting it. Write it on a business card and carry it in your wallet or purse. In moments of fear, frustration, and sorrow, pull it out and read it. Doing so will help you keep things in perspective and remind you to stay focused on what is most important to you.

Don't waste any more time stumbling through life. Take time to identify your purpose and strive to let your purpose express itself each day in your work, your play, and your relationships. Living life on purpose will translate to better well-being for you, your family, and your world.

https://www.psychologytoday.com/us/blog/mind-over-money/201309/living-purpose

Reprinted with permission of the author

THE REINCARNATED PRINCE

BY RABBI TUVIA BOLTON

RABBI TUVIA BOLTON

Educator. Rabbi Bolton is a popular teacher, musician, composer, and storyteller. He is codirector and a senior lecturer at Yeshiva Ohr Tmimim in Kfar Chabad, Israel. Rabbi Bolton also writes popular weekly Torah articles that are translated into three languages and received by over fifteen thousand people each week.

Some three hundred years ago, the name of Rabbi Israel Baal Shem Tov spread throughout Europe as one who was willing to do anything, even perform miracles like Elijah and Moses, in order to help another, especially a fellow Jew.

One evening a middle-aged couple came with a desperate request; they wanted a child. Despite their prayers, good deeds and various remedies and treatments, they had failed to conceive a child in all the years of their marriage.

The Baal Shem Tov closed his eyes, put his face into his hands, lowered his head to the desk before him and his consciousness soared to the spiritual realms.

Minutes later he sat upright, looked at them sadly and said: "There is nothing I can do. Continue praying, continue your good deeds. May G-d have mercy, but it is beyond my ability to help you."

The woman burst into bitter tears; her husband turned his face aside and wept silently, his body shaking.

"No, no!" she cried. "I won't believe it. I will not accept no for answer. I know that when a *tzaddik* (righteous person) decrees, G-d must fulfill. I want a child!" Her cry pierced the walls and broke the holy master's heart.

He lowered his head again for many long minutes then looked up and said: "Next year you will have a child."

The couple was speechless. The man began trembling, took the Baal Shem Tov's hand and kissed it as his wife showered thanks and blessings. They backed out the door, bowing, weeping and praising G-d and His servant the holy Rabbi Israel.

Sure enough, two months later the woman conceived, and nine months thereafter gave birth to a beautiful baby boy.

The couple's joy increased day by day as the child grew. Their baby was beautiful! His eyes sparkled with life and his every smile filled their lives with warmth and happiness. At the age of one year, it was obvious he was something special; he was already walking and talking. As he approached the age of two they began looking for a tutor to begin teaching him Torah. They planned to take him to the Baal Shem Tov; they would show him what his blessing had brought.

But on the morning of his second birthday the child didn't wake up.

The neighbors came running when they heard the screams, but nothing could be done. As miraculously as the boy had come, so mysteriously and tragically had he departed this world.

The funeral was enough to make the heavens cry. After the week of mourning they returned to the Baal Shem Tov to inform him of the tragedy. But the Baal Shem Tov understood better than they could possibly have imagined.

"Your child," he said to the grieving parents, "contained a lofty soul that had made a huge sacrifice to save thousands of people. But this soul needed you to achieve its *tikkun* ('rectification') and become spiritually complete. That day, when you came to me, I looked into the heavens and saw that it was impossible for you to have children; but when I heard your cries and saw the depth of your pain, I realized that this special soul was destined to be yours for the short span of its return to physical life. Sit down, dear friends, I have a story to tell you."

■ ■ ■

Several hundred years ago lived a king who was childless. He was rich and powerful, but he desperately desired a son to carry on the lineage. He ordered that all his subjects hold daily prayers in their houses of worship that G-d should grant their sovereign an heir.

One of his advisors suggested that the reason the king was childless was because his Jewish subjects did not pray for him sincerely enough. The only way to make them do that, said this advisor, was to oppress them.

The next day the king issued a public proclamation stating that if the queen was not blessed with a child in the next three months, all the Jews would be expelled from his kingdom. With all the neighboring countries closed to Jewish settlement, the poor Jews had nowhere to go. Their cries and prayers rose from every synagogue in the land.

A call resounded through the heavens for a soul willing to descend into the spiritually desolate environment of the royal palace in order to save the Jews of that land. Finally, one very holy soul agreed to make the sacrifice.

Shortly thereafter, the queen became pregnant and soon gave birth to a son. The king was overjoyed and showered the Jews of his realm with presents and favors.

At the age of two, the child could already read and write, and when he was five years old he had surpassed all his teachers and learned all they had to teach. A master teacher—a priest whose fame as a genius and scholar had spread far and wide—was brought from afar to teach the prodigy.

This new tutor was of a different caliber altogether. It seemed that he had mastered every form of wisdom in the world and his very presence radiated a thirst for knowledge. The young genius could not get enough of his new teacher. He became more attached to him than even to his own father the king. He spent every moment of the day and most of the night with the tutor, absorbing more and more wisdom and learning. And the more he absorbed, the more he desired.

But the priest demanded his times of privacy. He had an agreement with the king that for two hours of every day he would lock himself in his room and no one, not even the king himself, was allowed to enter or disturb him in any way. It was on this condition that he accepted the task of teaching the prince.

But the prince was curious. He could not tolerate the idea that his beloved master was withholding something from him. He had to know everything!

One day, the young prince managed to hide himself in his teacher's room before the priest's daily two hours of seclusion. The priest entered the room, locked the door securely behind him, and searched the room thoroughly. Somehow he failed to discover the prince's hiding place and he proceeded in his strange daily ritual.

First he removed all the crosses from the walls and from around his neck, and put them in a box outside his window. Then he took out a large white woolen shawl with strings at the corners, wrapped it completely around his head and body, and began weeping like a baby.

Then he took out two small black boxes with long black straps attached to them, tied one to his left upper arm and the other above the middle of his forehead. After that he began to pray, swaying, singing and crying for over an hour. Finally, he took out a large Hebrew text and began reading from it in a sing-song voice, swaying back and forth all the time.

Suddenly, he stopped and listened intently. The faint but unmistakable sound of another person in the room had caught his ear. The priest was terrified. He jumped from his chair, hurriedly removed the black boxes and shawl, stuffed them in a drawer, and began to search the room. It did not take long for him to discover his young pupil, who had been observing everything with rapt fascination.

The priest begged the boy not to reveal what he saw. If the king found out he would certainly be beheaded. But the prince's curiosity had been aroused. He swore that he would never tell anyone what he saw in the room, but only if the priest would explain what he had just done and teach him what it was all about.

So the priest had no choice but to reveal that he was a Jew, doing what Jews have been doing for thousands of years: praying and studying the Torah and fulfilling its commandments. He had been compelled to hide his faith during one of the many decrees of forced conversions that Jews were subjected to in those times; now he was forced to assume the guise of an alien religion on the pain of death.

"You must teach me your ancient wisdom!" the prince insisted. "I knew that you were hiding something from me. In everything that you taught me, I always sensed that there was something more there, something deeper and truer, that you were withholding from me!" In vain did the "priest" plead that he would be subjecting them both to mortal danger. "If you refuse to teach me," the prince threatened, "I'll tell everyone what I saw in this room."

For several years they learned Torah together, until the boy announced that he wanted to convert to Judaism. His desire became so strong that teacher and pupil made up a story about going to Rome to further their studies. Instead of traveling to Rome, they escaped to another country where the boy converted and never returned to the palace again.

■ ■ ■

"The prince became a great and famous sage," the Baal Shem Tov concluded his story, "living a life of saintliness and good deeds. When he passed on from this world and his soul ascended to the heavens, it was the most luminous soul that had returned from earth in many generations. Only one blemish dimmed its shining perfection: the lingering effect of the fact that it had been conceived, borne, and fed for two years in the spiritually negative environment of the royal palace. All it lacked to attain the true heights of its glorious potential was for it to be conceived and return to earth, given birth to and weaned in the holy atmosphere of a righteous home.

"When I saw the depth of your holy desire for a child, I knew that you were worthy parents for this righteous soul."

Reprinted with permission from Chabad.org

REINCARNATION

BY RABBI DOVBER PINSON

RABBI DOVBER PINSON

Rabbi DovBer Pinson is the head of the IYYUN Kollel and Yeshiva, and he is the founder and dean of the IYYUN Center for Jewish Spirituality. He is a teacher of kabbalah and Jewish mysticism, and he lectures globally on these subjects. He has authored more than 30 books, many of which have been translated into multiple languages.

The concept of reincarnation seems to conflict with some of the basic tenets of Torah, such as the concepts of heaven and hell, eventual resurrection and general accountability for one's own actions. Assuming reincarnation suggests that the '*same*' soul journeys from one body into the next, reincarnation and personal immortality seem to contradict one another. How does reincarnation correlate with the notion of a personal, individual afterlife journey?

The question, "Where is the soul once it leaves the body?"—is a question that has been asked of and by Rabbis, philosophers and mystics for hundreds of years. Is the soul on a higher realm of existence somewhere 'up' there or does the soul reincarnate, re-embody and come to inhabit another human being down here? (*Teshuvas HaRashba,* Teshuvah 418. *Minchas Kenaos. Nishmas Chayim,* 4:15)

To reconcile this apparent contradiction we need to delve more deeply into the issue. The best place to begin would be with the first human beings, the first possessors of a human soul—Adam and *Chava*/Eve.

The Root Soul

Adam, the way he is described at the genesis of his creation, was both male and female. Physically or metaphysically speaking the prototypical human being, Adam, was neither all male nor all female,

he/she was both (Bereishis, 1:27. *Eiruvin*, 18a). Adam was therefore a synthesis of both the male and female genders, similar to, but not completely the same as a hermaphrodite or androgyne.

Today, these two aspects of the male/female dynamic are present in the protoplasm of all human cells, those of men and those of women. Considering that Adam was the first human being, the father/mother of the whole human species, all humans can trace their DNA to this one ancestor; he/she is the genetic embodiment of all further articulated gene sequences within the human line. Practically speaking, all people are understood by the Torah to be genetically related and descended from a single ancestral being much like modern biologists surmise—all forms of life ultimately descend, through the process of evolution and various mutations, from a single form of life.

A general Torah principle is that *physicality is merely a reflection of spiritual conditioning*. As Adam is viewed as the material parent of humanity, he/she is also the spiritual primogenitor. Adam's soul is the collective and universal soul from which all human souls emanate (*Shar HaGilgulim,* Hakdamah 12. Ramak, *Shiur Komah,* Chap. 2. See also *Medrash Rabbah,* Shemos, 40:3. *Tanchumah,* Ki Tissa, 12. *Tanya, Igeres HaKodesh,* 7). Adam's soul is therefore the source-soul from which all individualized souls are derivatives. Adam was a cosmic figure of sorts, containing elements of all the souls of every person who would eventually be born.

All souls are contained within the primordial soul of Adam, hence, once the eating from the Tree of the Knowledge of Duality occurred, followed by the ejection from Eden, the sparks within the collective soul of Adam were scattered throughout all worlds and all people. Ever since then the purpose of reincarnation is to restore the integral wholeness of the Root soul, thus creating a *Tikkun*/fixing/attunement of the mystical and primordial image of *Adam*/Humanity.

Putting the Puzzle Back Together

Adam, before eating from the Tree of Dualistic Knowledge, was at-one and unified, existing within the shade of the Tree of Life, basking within the glow of the Light of the Creator. Once Adam ate the fruit and identified with the reality of duality, separation occurred.

Let us delve a little deeper.

Before eating from and identifying with the "Tree of Knowledge of Good and Evil," which represents the world of opposites, the "body" and soul of Adam was one unified existence. There was no internal dichotomy and no separation between his body and soul. Adam existed in the garden of the "Tree of Life," defined as the reality of wholeness and Unity.

Even within the physical reality itself there was no separation, there was no separation between his body and the world outside of him. The body of Adam "stretched from one end of the earth to the other" (*Sanhedrin*, 38b). It was one, unified and "everywhere."

Being unified with the Tree of Life, the reality of Unity, Adam's body was a unified entity wherein even his fingers were not separated, but rather connected by skin, creating a mittened hand, as it were (*Seder HaDoros* 1, Eleph 2; 56–58). The skin of Adam was transparent, similar to the fingernails we have today (*Yalkut Shimoni* 15; 27. *Alshich*, Toras Moshe, Bereishis). The primordial "Body of Adam" had a shining, transparent skin (*Targum Yonasan. Pirkei Rabbi Eliezer*). Adam's body was even more brilliant than the light of the sun (*Medrash Vayikra*, 20:2. *Tikkunei Zohar*, Hakdamah. Note: *Baba Basra*, 58a).

The eating of the Tree of Knowledge in Eden caused a shrinking, a breaking apart of the one great body/soul into myriads of shards and sparks of light. The once unified body of Adam became pixelated into multiple pieces. Each shard became another specific and finite soul/spark. These shards/sparks are diminished from their original state for two reasons: 1) they are no longer a singular unified reality, and therefore as a result, 2) their individual lights are not as potent as they were when they were part of the whole.

As a particular finite expression of soul/spark from the primordial body/soul of Adam becomes embodied in a physical form, the task then becomes to fully actualize this distinct soul potential. One by one, through subsequent reincarnations and lives lived, all sparks become brilliant and bound together again. When a person lives his or her life and completely expresses their soul/spark, their particular shard of soul is *Zahir*/illuminated. After this soul completes its journey through physical life, the now illuminated soul/spark returns to the great Body/Soul of Adam.

After the eating and internalizing of duality, the Body/Soul of Adam fell apart; it became pixelated into many individual pieces, like a broken puzzle. Our job is to recreate the great Body of Adam, to put back the pieces of the puzzle so that it can brilliantly shine again.

Over time, each soul that has completed its task returns and thus recreates the one great and unified Body/Soul of Adam. Like pieces of the puzzle, each distinct soul expression is another part of the whole, and when all pieces of the puzzle are 'returned' and fit perfectly back into the primordial body of Adam we will enter, once again, into a unified reality sustained by the Tree of Life.

So far we have been describing and discussing the collective aspect of the Tree of Life, although every individual who lives his/her deepest truth also connects with the Tree of Life on a personal level.

The body is the physical imprint of the soul (*Choker U'Mekubal*, 1). Body and soul mirror and reflect each other. The literal structure of Adam's body was analogous to the spiritual form of his soul. As the body divided into various compartments, the same is true on some metaphysical level in regards to the soul. There are souls that are rooted in the head of Adam and there are souls that stem from the hands of Adam, there are souls from the heart and souls from the feet. Accordingly, 'head souls' are inclined toward intellectual pursuits and 'hand souls' show signs of physical dexterity, 'heart souls' brim with emotions and 'feet souls' are action or movement oriented. All in all, there is a particular soul-root within Adam for every individual distinct consciousness.

Family Souls

Herein is where the idea of group or family souls comes into play (*Sefer HaGilgulim,* 12. *Shiur Komah. Shit Alfei Shnin* 3. Shallah, *Kedushas HaGuf V'Damim. Tiferes Yonasan,* Vayigash). A group soul would be those individual souls that all share the same root within the primordial all-encompassing Body/Soul of Adam. As a physical representation of this truth they will gravitate toward each other in this temporal realm, either as a family, group, network, or more macrocosmically, as a nation. Physical nearness, whether via blood, friendship or even geographic location is indicative of spiritual connection. Souls that share a common root on a spiritual plane will transmigrate together on a physical level as well. These souls are bound together physically and spiritually by a common purpose, as they originated from the same archetype-aspect within the primordial Body/Soul of Adam.

An interesting detail regarding the immediate family dynamic is that although the nucleus of a family is constructed of souls who originate from the same broad area in the all-inclusive body/soul of Adam, still, not all members will share the exact same soul-root. At times a friend may share a closer soul-root than that of a relative. Diversity and individual expression within the context of the family unit is a result of the divergent sources and soul-roots of some of the members of the family.

Most members of a family will spring from the same area or same root of Adam's soul/body, but some souls will travel from other parts within the great body/soul of Adam and come to join a particular family unit for a specific incarnation and purpose (*Shar HaGilgulim,* 10. *Ohr Hachayim,* Ki Sisa 32:27). For this reason we find that within every family assemblage, although collectively they may share general common interests, some family members may go in different, and occasionally even opposite, directions.

Most of the family will gravitate toward one profession or live in one climate or environment, while there is always the one or two members of the family who seem to be singing their own tune and doing their own thing. For example, the whole family may be doctors or lawyers, while one child is a musician or painter.

A healthy unit is where each member of the family lives in accordance with their own particular soul inscription and where each member of the group is influenced and spiritually nourished by the individuality of the next, collectively creating a veritable rainbow of personalities and pursuits.

Parenthetically, many erroneously believe that if a child is born and named after a loved one the child will then automatically possess the same soul energy as the one who departed. True, we have many ancient teachings attesting to the ways in which our names affect our behavior (*Yumah,* 83b. *Berachos,* 7b. *Tanchumah,* Ha'azinu. *Zohar* 1, p. 58b). A certain number of these teachings also suggest that when parents name their children they do so with Divine inspiration and intuition so that the name will be suitable to the characteristics of the child's soul (*Shar HaGilgulim,* 23. *Emek HaMelech,* Shar 1:4. *Chesed LeAvraham,* 5:6. *Agrah DeKalah,* p. 107). Additionally, still other teachings indicate that when a child is named after a righteous person who has lived, that righteous soul who resides in the world of pure spirit is aroused and an affinity of souls is then forged between these two that can have positive results (*Noam Elimelech,* Bamidbar). Still, all this does not guarantee that a child who is named after someone else will inevitably have a spark of that soul. Though that can certainly occur, it is not the rule. Names are influential, but not necessarily definitive.

People Who Are Similar

Whereas family members may not all share the exact same soul root, there are others outside the family, community or even nation who do share the same spiritual DNA. Even outside the family there are souls who share roots within the great body/soul of Adam, and when these two meet up they will unavoidably and almost reflexively experience attraction and serious magnetism for each other; although it is not always necessarily a positively charged attraction (*Shar HaGilgulim,* 20).

When two similar souls encounter each other for the very first time there will often be a kind of aversion of or even dislike for one another. Being of the same ilk their internal chemistry is too much alike; it is like taking two objects with the same exact magnetic energy field and trying to fuse them together. These two souls may feel challenged by each other, if not consciously, then on a deeper level. A 'spiritual' type of jealousy may arise, pinning one soul against the next, struggling to see who can acquire more energy from their source.

If, however, these two individuals attain a more evolved measure of spiritual maturity and they are highly developed individuals who experience *Ruach Ha'Kodesh*/Divine intuition, then instead of an abhorrence and dislike a beautiful love can be nurtured and flourish between them (*Ibid. Pri Eitz Chayim,* Shar Hanhagos HaLimud. *Kehilas Yaakov,* Machlokas). Supposing these two powerful energy sources do in fact coalesce and manage to resonate with each other the vibrations that are created would be eminently more powerful. Much like light that is generated via friction and discord can be fiercer than light that is produced in harmony and uniformity.

Actualizing Our Soul-Potential

In relation to the concept of the body/soul of the cosmic Adam and the notion of a soul root that we have been discussing, our sages intuit that the human form is subdivided into six hundred and thirteen parts; two hundred forty-eight main organs and three hundred sixty-five principal veins and arteries. Which of the body parts or veins/sinews are included in this count

and which are left out was never fully disclosed. Perhaps this metabiological construct of the Rabbis is related to the *Neijing's* description of the 365 acupuncture points on the body. Either way, whether understood physically or metaphysically, this is the way the sages deciphered the human form. As soul animates body and spirit enlivens matter, the soul too, like the body, is comprised of six hundred and thirteen energies and attributes. And it is specifically through spiritually oriented activities that utilize the body that the soul is able to achieve its full crystallization, self-articulation and actualization. Although we must also keep in mind that as the soul is a spark of the Infinite, its essential core is neither reducible nor dividable.

Correlated to the six hundred and thirteen body parts and soul energies are the six hundred and thirteen Mitzvos of the Torah, which are comprised of the two hundred forty-eight body parts and the three hundred sixty-five days of the solar year (*Bechoros,* 45a. *Makos,* 23b. *Zohar* 1, p. 170b). Aligning oneself with the Mitzvos, which serve as the inner purpose and directives of creation, whether by actively participating in particular actions or refraining from others, allows the soul to soar to the most exalted and elated heights possible.

The full array of Mitzvos grants one the opportunity to fully bring to fruition all of the various aspects of soul as they are expressed through the body. Each distinct Mitzvah taps into another reservoir of spiritual-energy and sets the soul free, allowing for the soul to express itself in the most expansive way. By physically performing a particular Mitzvah the corresponding attribute within the soul is activated and as a result the soul as a whole attains an even greater and more comprehensive state of completion and articulation than when it existed as pure spirit prior to descending into human form.

Generally speaking, the Nefesh, Ruach and Neshamah unfold and become consciously felt in a progressive fashion. First a person develops on a level of Nefesh and then works his way up to Ruach, and then eventually graduates into the level of Neshamah. Only once the entire structure of Nefesh has evolved and been entirely articulated through the correlating Mitzvos, will the Nefesh level be transcended and included with that of Ruach. And then the same process repeats itself moving from Ruach to Neshamah. Reincarnation occurs when sparks of soul that were not fully articulated in one lifetime resurface in another human form to be worked on and fully expressed.

Mitzvos are the tools through which the soul attains excellence in this world. Theoretically, our aspirations should be to achieve excellence in all aspects of life, yet practically we achieve perfection—or as close to it as we can get—in only certain areas of our life. Every individual person has at least one Mitzvah that he or she is "*Zahir Tfei*/ultimately careful in performing" (*Shabbos,* 118b). *Zahir* can also be translated as illuminating or shining. This concept can then be understood as implying that there is at least one Mitzvah that every person is connected with; one positive area that he excels in. That one Mitzvah becomes the source of his or her personal radiance.

Overall every person displays some degree of uniqueness and specialty, even if it is only one area in life. There are some people, for example, who are remarkably compassionate and wonderful humanitarians, and yet they have a challenging time relating to their own family; while there are others who are fantastic in interfamilial relationships—i.e., they are good parents/children, brothers or sisters—but they experience difficulties when it comes to parting with their hard-earned money.

Whatever the Mitzvah is, it is that correlating energy within the soul that one becomes intimately connected with and joined to. In fact we find that the one, two or three areas that one excels in are the primary focus of that person's spiritual development and all other goals, aspirations and achievements flow from that particular domain. All of one's life, including their own interpretations of experiences and expressions, is founded on their own uniqueness and individuality.

Notice that whenever you are asked to capture or encapsulate in one or two words another person you will always discover something unique to say about them. For instance, employing some basic generic terms, one person you would say is gracious, another thoughtful, one is serious and responsible, another is lighthearted and cheerful, one is a good parent, and another is a good friend—each person expresses their own uniqueness. There are always traces of positivity within people and often this positive aspect of character is so powerful that it appears in everything else in that person's life as an extension and derivative of that particular trait.

Individual Personality

Individualized sparks of soul that a person connects with in this life become their 'own' soul—in this life and the next. As in life, when others think of this individual they think of him or her in a certain way; the same is true in death, the individuality within will continue to exist and extend eternally in the afterlife.

Individual/personal immortality is experienced when the soul of a person, the unique spark of a person's soul that they expressed in life, lives on for eternity in higher/deeper realms of existence. Having traveled through life the individualized spark of soul has now become ever more colorful, accumulating all of life's experiences and knowledge. In the afterlife that integral entity will journey onwards to ever increasing measures of awareness. What reincarnates into other human beings are the subconscious or 'beyond conscious' aspects that exist within the soul, the elements within the soul that were not activated or articulated.

Nothing is reoccurring. There is no repetition within creation and each person is born with the potential for a radical new expression.

The innate individuality, the spark of soul that fashioned the person's uniqueness, does not generally reincarnate. The *principium individuas* of a person, what makes people unique and guides them to their special destiny, will not re-embody. What reincarnates are the aspects of soul that one had little experience with, the elements of the multifaceted soul-energy that one had little association with. Clearly one's soul contained all the possible energies and the entire soul resided somewhere within the person, nevertheless, on a day-to-day level of awareness the person was only consciously affiliated with the uniqueness of his own soul, and nothing else. As such, it is this uniqueness of soul, coupled with a life full of memories that were imprinted on the soul that journeys on in the afterlife.

The soul 'divides' itself in the afterlife much as it did during life. Just as in this realm of existence there were sparks of soul that one connected with and there were others that remained dormant, in the afterlife this very same phenomenon continues. The sparks that were consciously activated in one's soul in this life remain with one's soul in the afterlife, while the other sparks reincarnate and gradually become individualized souls for other people. The unifying factor between all these incarnations is that they all collectively constitute 'one soul,' meaning that there is one overarching thematic interest, goal, drive and propensity that can be found in all manifestations of that 'one' soul.

Picture a tree with multiple branches. One tree with one root, yet with branches extending in all directions. Each of these individualized souls share the same root and are in essence part of one continuous unfolding field of consciousness; one soul, which unravels and becomes apparent throughout the course of many lives as individual spiritual energies are activated by different individual people.

The Spark That Contains the Whole

Though the soul keeps on dividing and subdividing itself, still, in each incarnation it retains integral wholeness and a sense of completion. Not only is the soul complete and all-comprehensive with all six hundred and thirteen energy forces as it had in the first incarnation, but subsequently in each incarnation the soul remains 'perfect' as it was in its previous embodiment. Even after the first possessor of soul passes away and the elements of soul that became exclusively his remain his, only the remainder of the soul reincarnates, and this 'remainder' is also complete. Think of the soul in terms of a hologram, where the part is like the whole and the whole is present within each part, every pixel mirroring the total picture.

As the collective spirit of Adam contains six hundred and thirteen soul energies, so too, all individual consciousness that stems from Adam's soul contains six hundred and thirteen aspects (*Sha'arei Kedushah* 1:1). The micro, or the part, is like the macro—the whole.

Additionally, each specific soul energy can be further divided into six hundred and thirteen aspects, and they in turn into another six hundred and thirteen. This is a dynamic referred to as *interinclusion*, wherein each part of a larger structure actually contains the whole structure in miniature within itself. The core of the soul is one with the Infinite and no matter how often infinity is divided it always remains infinite. Every 'slice' of infinity is infinite. Infinity cannot be divided (*Kuzari*, Maamor 5:18. *Chovos Halevavos, Shar HaYichud,* 5), and thus when you grasp a 'small parcel' of infinity you grasp the totality (*Keser Shem Tov*, 111. *Toldos Yaakov Yoseph*, Yisro. Yavatz, *Avos*, 4:2). Regardless of how often the soul is divided or subdivided it will always retain its signature shape and form as the general root soul; it will forever encompass all six hundred and thirteen branches of the single tree.

Practically, the fact that an individual's personality and primary soul-connection is the attribute of kindness does not necessarily mean that such a person is lacking in all other areas of life. It merely means that for him kindness is the center of his being, the foundation and root cause from which everything else in his life flows. The multiple multidimensional aspects of his soul are channeled and funneled through his individuality and uniqueness, his soul-connection of kindness.

Most, if not all people go through life and succeed in tapping into at least one aspect of soul. It seems that there is always one Mitzvah that is essential and vital to each person (Rayatz, *Safer Maamorim, Tof Shin Ches,* p. 240). There is always some positive life-affirming force, a *raison d'etre* that compels the human being to carry on and move forward through life. The individualized spark of soul that a person activates in this life through their one unique Mitzvah is what gains him/her their place in Gan Eden (Rambam, *Pirush HaMishnayos,* Sanhedrin, 10. *Avudraham,*

Hilchos Shabbos. Alshich, *Toras Moshe,* Shemini, 9; 5–6. *Mei Hashiloach* 1, p. 177), and is thus the part of their soul that remains his or hers throughout their afterlife. It is the uniqueness of self that will journey onwards for eternity.

Once the soul in its entirety, its divisions and sub-divisions, has been elevated, activated and articulated the soul will then cease to return into this earthly realm of existence. The soul will stop reincarnating. How long this process of elevation takes, whether it is in one lifetime or hundreds of lifetimes, essentially depends upon the individuals who possess that soul and what they do with it.

There is no limit or set amount of times the soul may descend, so long as even the slightest measure of development is being achieved during each subsequent incarnation (*Shar HaGilgulim,* 4. *Mishnas Chassidim,* Seder Nashim, Meseches Gilgul 2:3). When no perfection and elevation whatsoever has occurred in a lifetime, the soul will only descend another two times; it has three tries. If no perfection and elevation were reached in the subsequent two lifetimes the distinct soul will never reincarnate into another human being again (*Zohar* 3, p. 72b. *Tikkunei Zohar* 32. *Ramban,* Bereishis, 4:1. *Shivilei Emunah,* Nosiv 3. Chayit,

Ma'areches Elokus, 10. *Magid Mesharim, Iyov.* Alshich, *Devarim,* 7:9–10. *MaHarsha, Shabbos,* 152b). But even if a slight elevation is achieved in every subsequent incarnation, the soul will incarnate indefinitely. As long as there is work to do and work is being done, there are lives to lead.

The passage in the daily morning prayers, "The soul that You have given me is pure" (*Berachos,* 60b), is intended to be taken quite literally. Each soul that comes down to this world is pure, immaculate and unsoiled from any previous deeds of past incarnations. For the most part each person begins life with a clean slate. People are born innocent, neither good nor bad, holy nor evil, but simply innocent with the innate ability to choose their path. With regards to the spark of soul that belongs exclusively to each individual, this incarnation is considered the very first one; for it is the first time that these particular spiritual energies are combined in this proportion, making up this unique soul and articulating themselves in this novel manner.

Reincarnation and Judaism: The Journey of the Soul (Lanham, Md.: Rowman and Littlefield Publishers, Inc., 2004), ch. 7.

Reprinted with permission of the author

Lesson

LIFE IS SHORT-ISH
HOW DEATH INFORMS LIFE

By now we've come to appreciate death as the next phase in our ongoing personal missions. In our final lesson, we use what we've learned to revisit our priorities in this current phase and find ways to fill every moment with everlasting significance.

▲ THE GIRL I LEFT BEHIND ME
Eastman Johnson, oil on canvas, United States, 1870–1875.
(Smithsonian American Art Museum, Washington, D.C.)

I. DEATH BENEFIT

This chapter, the climax of *Journey of the Soul*, unwraps one of the greatest gifts afforded to us by all the information and insights collected in the previous chapters—a gift enabled by the fact that the dread of death is greatly mitigated by the previous clarifications of the nature of the soul and its pleasurable destination in the higher worlds.

EXERCISE 6.1

You have almost completed the journey into Judaism's approach to death, afterlife, reincarnation, etc. Take a moment to identify three ways that the perspectives we gained can influence one's life and its daily realities:

1. _____

2. _____

3. _____

◀ **SOWER AT SUNSET**
Vincent Van Gogh, impasto, oil paint on canvas, Arles, France, 1888. (Kröller-Müller Museum, Otterlo, Netherlands)

EXERCISE 6.2

Can you identify any benefits to occasionally contemplating our own mortality?

1. _____

2. _____

3. _____

TEXT 1

ACKNOWLEDG-ING DEATH CAN BE FREEING

ROBYN D. WALSER, PHD, *THE HEART OF ACT: DEVELOPING A FLEXIBLE, PROCESS-BASED, AND CLIENT-CENTERED PRACTICE USING ACCEPTANCE AND COMMITMENT THERAPY* (OAKLAND, CA: CONTEXT PRESS, 2019), CH. 4

ROBYN D. WALSER, PHD

Professor and Psychologist. Robyn Walser received her degrees in psychology from the University of Nevada. She is an associate clinical professor at the University of California, Berkeley, and works with the U.S. Department of Veterans Affairs' National Center for PTSD. Walser is a proponent of Acceptance and Commitment Therapy (ACT), a form of therapy that aims to help people cope with difficulties and trauma.

There is no exercise or reflection as potent, perhaps, as contacting one's ending. In confronting our own passing, we are better able, and more willing, to help others see the power of awareness of that which is inevitable—death—helping us to wake up to the tender colors of life and personal creation. . . .

In contemplating our own end, we recognize that there is still time for life in whatever time is left. Values are there to be lived until that last inevitable moment. To acknowledge this is freeing.

II. PRIORITIZING AND MAINTAINING FOCUS

From the Jewish viewpoint, occasionally contemplating our eventual passing has multiple benefits. Let's extrapolate them from the following texts.

TEXT 2A

"BE FOREVER SILENT . . ."

PSALMS 4:5

רִגְזוּ וְאַל תֶּחֱטָאוּ,
אִמְרוּ בִלְבַבְכֶם,
עַל מִשְׁכַּבְכֶם,
וְדֹמּוּ סֶלָה.

Be agitated and do not sin;
verbalize within your hearts
upon your beds
and be forever silent.

How do we transition from "good" to "very good"? Watch *Rabbi Dr. Yitzchak Breitowitz's* 3-minute response in "Facing Mortality": *myJLI.com/soul*

TEXT 2B

WEAPONIZING THE DAY OF DEATH

TALMUD, BERACHOT 5A

BABYLONIAN TALMUD

A literary work of monumental proportions that draws upon the legal, spiritual, intellectual, ethical, and historical traditions of Judaism. The 37 tractates of the Babylonian Talmud contain the teachings of the Jewish sages from the period after the destruction of the 2nd Temple through the 5th century CE. It has served as the primary vehicle for the transmission of the Oral Law and the education of Jews over the centuries; it is the entry point for all subsequent legal, ethical, and theological Jewish scholarship.

לְעוֹלָם יַרְגִּיז אָדָם יֵצֶר טוֹב עַל יֵצֶר הָרַע שֶׁנֶּאֱמַר, "רְגְזוּ וְאַל תֶּחֱטָאוּ".

אִם נִצְחוֹ מוּטָב, וְאִם לָאו יַעֲסוֹק בַּתּוֹרָה, שֶׁנֶּאֱמַר, "אִמְרוּ בִלְבַבְכֶם".

אִם נִצְחוֹ מוּטָב, וְאִם לָאו יִקְרָא קְרִיאַת שְׁמַע, שֶׁנֶּאֱמַר, "עַל מִשְׁכַּבְכֶם".

אִם נִצְחוֹ מוּטָב, וְאִם לָאו יִזְכּוֹר לוֹ יוֹם הַמִּיתָה, שֶׁנֶּאֱמַר, "וְדֹמּוּ סֶלָה".

We should always agitate our good inclination against our evil inclination, as it is stated, "Be agitated and do not sin."

If this vanquishes the evil inclination, all is good —but if not, we should occupy ourselves with Torah study, as it is stated, "Verbalize [Torah teachings until they enter] within your hearts."

If this vanquishes it, all is good —but if not, we should recite the Shema, as it is stated, "Upon your beds."

If this vanquishes it, all is good—but if not, we should remind ourselves of the day of death, as it is stated, "And be forever silent."

THERE'S MORE...

For several additional samples of Torah texts that discuss the need to at least occasionally contemplate one's mortality—and the benefits of this exercise—see below, Appendix A (p. 232).

END-OF-LIFE REGRETS

Perhaps the most sobering moments of a lifetime occur at its end. What are the thoughts of dying people as they stare at their own mortality? See Appendix B, Text 16 (p. 236), for a reading from a nurse who recorded the regrets of people she cared for in their final days.

QUESTIONS

Which do you consider of greater value—your time or your money? Explain your choice.

Are you living life in a manner that is consistent with the answer you just provided?

**THE SOUL OF THE SOULLESS CITY
('NEW YORK - AN ABSTRACTION')** ▶
Christopher R. W. Nevinson, oil on canvas,
London, U.K., 1920.
(Tate Britain Gallery, London)

On the difference between paralyzing and motivating fear, watch **Dr. Norman Blumenthal** in "The Benefits of Fear": *myJLI.com/soul*

TEXT 3

MONEY VS. TIME

JEWISH PROVERB, CITED IN
RABBI SHIMON FRANKFURTER,
SEFER HACHAYIM

**RABBI SHIMON FRANKFURTER
D. 1712**

Rabbinical scholar. Rabbi Shimon
Frankfurter was born in Schwerin,
Germany, and later settled in
Amsterdam, where he served as a
rabbi and an adviser to the Jewish
burial society. He authored and
published a work containing the
laws and prayers relevant to illness
and mourning. His son Moshe
republished it, with additional
prayers, under the title of *Sefer
Hachayim* (Amsterdam, 1716).

אָדָם דּוֹאֵג עַל אִיבּוּד דָּמָיו
וְאֵינוֹ דוֹאֵג עַל אִיבּוּד יָמָיו.
דָּמָיו אֵינָם עוֹזְרִים,
יָמָיו אֵינָם חוֹזְרִים.

Folks fret over a lost dime
and fail to fret over lost time.

But money provides no reprieve,
while time is impossible to retrieve.

A deeper understanding of time allows
us to better appreciate its value. *Rabbi
Yanki Tauber* explains in "The First
Creation": *myJLI.com/soul*

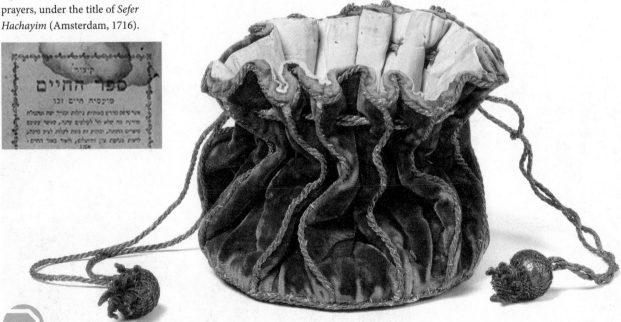

▲ **PURSE**
artist unknown, velvet, trimmed
with copper-gilt thread, France,
1660–1700. (Victoria and
Albert Museum, London)

TEXT 4

THE BENEFIT OF THE ANGEL OF DEATH

MIDRASH, *ELIYAHU RABAH*, CH. 16

TANA DEVEI ELIYAHU

A Midrashic work, sometimes referred to as *Seder Eliyahu*. Midrash is the designation of a particular genre of rabbinic literature usually forming a running commentary on specific books of the Bible. This work deals with the divine precepts, their rationales, and the importance of knowledge of Torah, prayer, and repentance. The work is divided into 2 sections *(sedarim)*: *Eliyahu Rabah* and *Eliyahu Zuta*.

אִלְמָלֵא מַלְאַךְ הַמָּוֶת, מָה אֲנַחְנוּ עוֹשִׂין לְאָבִינוּ שֶׁבַּשָּׁמַיִם?

צֵא וּלְמַד מֵעֲשָׂרָה דוֹרוֹת הָרִאשׁוֹנִים שֶׁהַקָּדוֹשׁ בָּרוּךְ הוּא הִשְׁפִּיעַ לָהֶן טוֹבָה מֵעֵין עוֹלָם הַבָּא, וְהֵם עָמְדוּ לְהַחֲרִיב אֶת כָּל הָעוֹלָם.

If not for [our fear of] the angel of death, what wrongs we would commit against our Father in Heaven!

Let us learn from the first ten generations of humanity: G-d showered them with abundant paradise-like goodness [including centuries-long lifespans], yet they were on the brink of destroying the world.

▼ **THE SUBSIDING OF THE WATERS OF THE DELUGE**
Thomas Cole, oil on canvas, United States, 1829.
(Smithsonian American Art Museum, Washington, D.C.)

Ric Elias was a passenger on Flight 1549, the plane that crash-landed in the Hudson River in 2009. Watch him in "3 Things I Learned While My Plane Crashed": *myJLI.com/soul*

TEXT 5

"LIVE EVERY DAY AS IF IT'S YOUR LAST SHOT"

MILES ALPERN LEVIN, *KEEP FIGHTING, STOP STRUGGLING: THE MILES LEVIN STORY* (MORGAN HILL, CA: BOOKSTAND PUBLISHING, 2012), PP. 10–11

MILES ALPERN LEVIN
1988–2007

Inspirational blogger. Following a cancer diagnosis in 2005, Levin began to post updates on an online forum to appraise his family and friends of developments related to his illness. Working out his feelings in writing on the blog, his charm, humor, spirit, and unceasing honesty drew the attention of readers from around the world. Miles passed away in August of 2007. His online posts were posthumously collected and published in *Keep Fighting, Stop Struggling: The Miles Levin Story.*

I went to the driving range the other day and I was thinking. . . .

I was thinking how you start out with a big bucket of golf balls, and you just start hitting away carelessly. You have dozens of them, each individual ball means nothing so you just hit, hit, hit. One ball gone is practically inconsequential when subtracted from your bottomless bucket. There are no practice swings or technique reevaluations after a bad shot, because so many more tries remain. Yet eventually you have to reach down towards the bottom of the bucket to scavenge for another shot and you realize that tries are running out. Now with just a handful left, each swing becomes more meaningful. The right technique becomes more crucial, so between each shot you take a couple practice swings and a few deep breaths. There is a very strong need to end on a good note, even if every preceding shot was horrible, *getting it right at the end means a lot.* You know as you tee up your last ball, "this is my final shot, I want to crush this with perfection; I must make this count." Limited quantities or limited time brings a new, precious value and significance to anything you do. Live every day shooting as if it's your last shot. I know I have to.

I found out today 5-year survival rates are just 30%.

EXERCISE 6.3

Allowing yourself a moment to contemplate between each response, record five meaningful endings to the following statement:

"Life is too short to . . ."

1. _____

2. _____

3. _____

4. _____

5. _____

Steve Jobs explains the implications of the fact that "Time Is Limited": *myJLI.com/soul*

▶ **THE CEMETERY**
Marc Chagall, painting, 1917 (Musée National d'Art Moderne, Paris)

III. THE GOLDEN YEARS

As we age, the importance of maximizing each day gains meaning and urgency. We are more acutely aware that our time is limited, and we develop a greater desire to make the most of each day. At the same time, and in direct contrast, many feel their abilities waning.

Conversely, Judaism's view of old age emphasizes that mining the vast treasures of one's golden years is indeed possible to achieve, and that not only are older people still capable, but in many ways they are *more* capable than their younger counterparts.

▼ OLD WOMAN READING
Jan Lievens, oil on panel, 1626–1633
(Rijksmuseum, Amsterdam)

TEXT 6

DO NOT WITHHOLD YOUR HAND IN THE EVENING

TALMUD, YEVAMOT 62B

רַבִּי יְהוֹשֻׁעַ אוֹמֵר: נָשָׂא אָדָם אִשָּׁה בְּיַלְדוּתוֹ, יִשָּׂא אִשָּׁה בְּזִקְנוּתוֹ. הָיוּ לוֹ בָּנִים בְּיַלְדוּתוֹ, יִהְיוּ לוֹ בָּנִים בְּזִקְנוּתוֹ. שֶׁנֶּאֱמַר (קֹהֶלֶת יא, ו), "בַּבֹּקֶר זְרַע אֶת זַרְעֶךָ וְלָעֶרֶב אַל תַּנַּח יָדֶךָ, כִּי אֵינְךָ יוֹדֵעַ אֵי זֶה יִכְשָׁר הֲזֶה אוֹ זֶה, וְאִם שְׁנֵיהֶם כְּאֶחָד טוֹבִים".

רַבִּי עֲקִיבָא אוֹמֵר: לָמַד תּוֹרָה בְּיַלְדוּתוֹ, יִלְמוֹד תּוֹרָה בְּזִקְנוּתוֹ. הָיוּ לוֹ תַּלְמִידִים בְּיַלְדוּתוֹ, יִהְיוּ לוֹ תַּלְמִידִים בְּזִקְנוּתוֹ. שֶׁנֶּאֱמַר, "בַּבֹּקֶר זְרַע אֶת זַרְעֶךָ וְגוֹ'".

Rabbi Yehoshua stated: Those who were married in their younger decades should nevertheless remarry in their old age. Those who had children while they were young should continue to have children in their older years. So it is stated, "Sow your seed in the morning, and do not withhold your hand in the evening. For you do not know which will prosper—whether this one or that, or whether they will be equally good" (ECCLESIASTES 11:6).

Rabbi Akiva stated: Those who studied Torah in their youth should continue to study in their old age. Those who had disciples in their younger years should continue to have disciples in their seniority. So it is stated, "Sow your seed in the morning," etc.

RETIREMENT GOALS

Additional retirement guidance, culled from Midrashic sources, is provided below in Appendix C, Text 17 (p. 237).

TEXT 7

RETIREMENT CAN BE DAMAGING FOR THE HEALTH

"RETIREMENT 'CAN DRASTICALLY DAMAGE HEALTH,'" *THE TELEGRAPH*, MAY 16, 2013

Retirement can cause a drastic decline in health, according to a new study.

Research by the Institute of Economic Affairs found that both mental and physical health can suffer [after retirement] . . . . The study—Work Longer, Live Healthier: The relationship between economic activity, health and government policy—shows there is a small boost in health immediately after retirement but that, over the longer term, there is a significant deterioration.

It suggests retirement increases the likelihood of suffering from clinical depression by 40 per cent and the chance of having at least one diagnosed physical condition by about 60 per cent.

The probability of taking medication for such a condition rises by about 60 per cent as well, according to the findings. People who are retired are 40 per cent less likely than others to describe themselves as being in very good or excellent health.

Redefining the purpose of life allows us to see old age from a different lens. *Rabbi Yanki Tauber* explains this concept in "Retirement: The Folly and the Opportunity": *myJLI.com/soul*

FIGURE 6.1

PREVALENCE OF COMMON MENTAL DISORDERS IN MEN AND WOMEN

JULIAN W. BUXTON, ET AL., "THE MENTAL HEALTH OF EARLY RETIREES: NATIONAL INTERVIEW SURVEY IN BRITAIN," *SOCIAL PSYCHIATRY AND PSYCHIATRIC EPIDEMIOLOGY*, 40 (2005), PP. 99–105.

JULIAN W. BUXTON

Julian W. Buxton is a British researcher. Working at the University of Cambridge's Department of Public Health and Primary Care, Buxton has published studies regarding retirement and its effects on mental health.

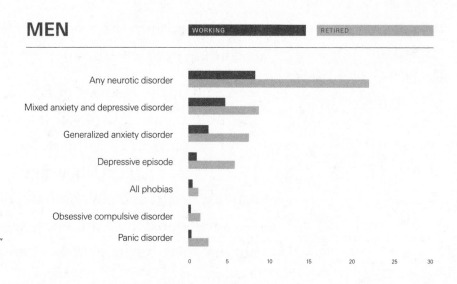

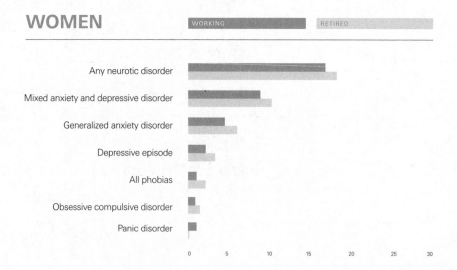

TEXT 8

CONSTRUCTIVE DESTRUCTION

TALMUD, MEGILAH 31B

אִם יֹאמְרוּ לְךָ זְקֵנִים "סְתוֹר", וִילָדִים "בְּנֵה", סְתוֹר וְאַל תִּבְנֶה.
מִפְּנֵי שֶׁסְּתִירַת זְקֵנִים בִּנְיָן, וּבִנְיַן נְעָרִים סְתִירָה.

If the elders advise you to destruct
and the youth to construct
—heed the counsel of the elders.

Because destruction [upon the advice]
of elders is constructive and construction
[upon the advice] of youth is destructive.

▼ **OLD MAN AND BABY**
Jozef Israëls, oil on canvas, Puebla, Mexico, 1880–1899.
(The Walters Art Museum, Baltimore, MD)

IV. A FATAL GLITCH

The previous chapters introduced insights into death, life, the soul, and the body—revolutionary ideas that, among numerous other benefits, led us to come to terms with death and mortality. However, those ideas *accept* the premise of death.

It is now the time to take the bold step of questioning that premise: the inevitability of death. Can mortality be an avertible feature of the human condition?

To make sense of this seemingly nonsensical question, we must examine the beginning of time and the effects of the first recorded transgression of G-d's will—Adam's infamous eating from the Tree of Knowledge.

TEXT 9A

THE CONSEQUENCE FORETOLD

GENESIS 2:16–17

וַיְצַו ה' אֱלֹקִים עַל הָאָדָם לֵאמֹר: "מִכֹּל עֵץ הַגָּן אָכֹל תֹּאכֵל. וּמֵעֵץ הַדַּעַת טוֹב וָרָע לֹא תֹאכַל מִמֶּנּוּ, כִּי בְּיוֹם אֲכָלְךָ מִמֶּנּוּ מוֹת תָּמוּת".

G-d commanded man, saying,
"Of every tree of the garden you may freely eat.
But do not eat from the Tree of Knowledge of Good and Evil,
for on the day that you eat from it,
you will certainly die."

TEXT 9B

CONSEQUENCE FULFILLED

IBID., 3:19

בְּזֵעַת אַפֶּיךָ תֹּאכַל לֶחֶם עַד שׁוּבְךָ אֶל הָאֲדָמָה כִּי מִמֶּנָּה לֻקָּחְתָּ. כִּי עָפָר אַתָּה וְאֶל עָפָר תָּשׁוּב.

By the sweat of your brow you shall eat bread,
until you return to the ground
—for you were taken from it.
For you are dust, and you will return to dust.

TEXT 10

DEATH ERADICATED

ISAIAH 25:8

בִּלַּע הַמָּוֶת לָנֶצַח וּמָחָה ה' אֱלֹקִים דִּמְעָה מֵעַל כָּל פָּנִים.

G-d will eradicate death forever
and wipe the tears off every face.

TEXT 11

SPIRITUAL DEATH RESULTS IN PHYSICAL DEATH

THE REBBE, RABBI MENACHEM MENDEL SCHNEERSON, *SEFER HAMAAMARIM MELUKAT* (CLASSIC EDITION) 2, PP. 277–278

RABBI MENACHEM MENDEL SCHNEERSON 1902–1994

The towering Jewish leader of the 20th century, known as "the Lubavitcher Rebbe," or simply as "the Rebbe." Born in southern Ukraine, the Rebbe escaped Nazi-occupied Europe, arriving in the U.S. in June 1941. The Rebbe inspired and guided the revival of traditional Judaism after the European devastation, impacting virtually every Jewish community the world over. The Rebbe often emphasized that the performance of just one additional good deed could usher in the era of Mashiach. The Rebbe's scholarly talks and writings have been printed in more than 200 volumes.

דְּהַמִּיתָה בָּעוֹלָם שֶׁנַּעֲשְׂתָה עַל יְדֵי חֵטְא עֵץ הַדַּעַת הִיא מְסוּבֶּבֶת מֵהַחֵטְא עַצְמוֹ.

וְהָעִנְיָן הוּא, דְּעִנְיַן הַחַיּוּת הוּא בִּקְדוּשָׁה דַּוְקָא, מַה שֶׁאֵין כֵּן הָרַע וְהַטּוּמְאָה (הֵיפֶךְ הַקְּדוּשָׁה) הֵם מָוֶת, וְלָכֵן, מִכֵּיוָן שֶׁעַל יְדֵי חֵטְא עֵץ הַדַּעַת נִתְעָרֵב רַע בְּהָאָדָם, מָוֶת רוּחָנִי, מִזֶּה נִשְׁתַּלְשֵׁל בּוֹ גַם מִיתָה כְּפְשׁוּטָהּ.

The condition of death that was introduced to the world through the sin of the Tree of Knowledge was a natural consequence of the very sin itself.

To explain: Life is associated exclusively with holiness. Unholiness, on the other hand, is death. As a result of the sin of the Tree of Knowledge, unholiness—spiritual death—mingled with the human identity, from which the condition of physical death is a natural eventual consequence.

REMEDYING THE PRIMORDIAL GLITCH

For a further reading—in which a Chasidic master describes how our approach to everyday life can be instrumental in eradicating death spiritually, which leads to the erasure of mortality—see Appendix D, Text 18 (p. 238).

TEXT 12

A FOUNDATIONAL BELIEF

MAIMONIDES, *COMMENTARY ON THE MISHNAH*, SANHEDRIN, INTRODUCTION TO CH. 10 (*PEREK CHELEK*)

RABBI MOSHE BEN MAIMON (MAIMONIDES, RAMBAM) 1135–1204

Halachist, philosopher, author, and physician. Maimonides was born in Córdoba, Spain. After the conquest of Córdoba by the Almohads, he fled Spain and eventually settled in Cairo, Egypt. There, he became the leader of the Jewish community and served as court physician to the vizier of Egypt. He is most noted for authoring the *Mishneh Torah,* an encyclopedic arrangement of Jewish law; and for his philosophical work, *Guide for the Perplexed*. His rulings on Jewish law are integral to the formation of halachic consensus.

וּתְחִיַּית הַמֵּתִים יְסוֹד מִיסוֹדוֹת תּוֹרַת מֹשֶׁה רַבֵּינוּ,

אֵין דָּת וְאֵין קֶשֶׁר עִם הָאוּמָה הַיְּהוּדִית לְמִי שֶׁאֵינוֹ מַאֲמִין בְּכַךְ.

The Resurrection of the Dead is a foundation of the Torah of Moses; one cannot maintain a connection to the Jewish religion and the Jewish nation without this belief.

TECHIYAT HAMETIM ▶
Baruch Nachshon, acrylic on canvas, Chevron, 2018. (nachshonart.com)

REINCARNATED SOULS

The previous chapter explored the Jewish view on soul reincarnation, whereby most souls return to this world numerous times, inhabiting a new body with each stay. Accordingly, the present topic of resurrection raises a question:

If a soul visits this world three times, for example, each time being provided with an entirely different human body for the duration of three distinct lifetimes, then which of these bodies will be resurrected on behalf of that soul? The first? The final? For an explanation, see Appendix E, Text 19 (p. 240).

TEXT 13

ZION WILL BE RESURRECTED, AND SO WILL WE

THE REBBE, RABBI MENACHEM MENDEL SCHNEERSON, *IGROT KODESH* 25, PP. 4–5

נְקוּדַת נֶחָמָה . . . מִתְבַּטֵּאת בַּנֻּסַּח הַמָּסוֹרָתִי וְהַמְקוּדָּשׁ עַל יְדֵי עֲשִׂירִיּוֹת דּוֹרוֹת שֶׁל תּוֹרָה וּמָסוֹרָה שֶׁל עַמֵּנוּ -

הַמָּקוֹם יְנַחֵם אֶתְכֶם בְּתוֹךְ שְׁאָר אֲבֵלֵי צִיּוֹן וִירוּשָׁלַיִם.

אֲשֶׁר בְּהִתְבּוֹנְנוּת רִאשׁוֹנָה תְּמוּהַּ הַקִּישּׁוּר שֶׁבֵּין שְׁנֵי הָעִנְיָנִים. אֶלָּא. . . כְּמוֹ שֶׁבְּוַדַּאי וּבְוַדַּאי יִבְנֶה הַשֵּׁם חָרְבוֹת צִיּוֹן וִירוּשָׁלַיִם וִיקַבֵּץ נִדְחֵי יִשְׂרָאֵל מִכָּל קַצְוֵי תֵּבֵל עַל יְדֵי מָשִׁיחַ צִדְקֵנוּ וִיבִיאֵם בְּרָנָּה לִרְאוֹת בְּשִׂמְחָתָהּ שֶׁל צִיּוֹן וִירוּשָׁלַיִם,

כָּךְ הוּא לְלֹא סָפֵק בְּנוֹגֵעַ לְאָבֵל הַיָּחִיד,

אֲשֶׁר יְקַיֵּים ה' דְּבָרוֹ וְהָקִיצוּ וְרַנְּנוּ שׁוֹכְנֵי עָפָר, וְתִגְדַּל הַשִּׂמְחָה, שִׂמְחָה אֲמִתִּית, בְּהִפָּגְשָׁם כּוּלָּם יַחַד בְּעֵת תְּחִיַת הַמֵּתִים.

A kernel of consolation . . . is captured in the traditional, hallowed statement of consolation that has been used [to comfort mourners] by tens of generations of our nation's communities that followed the Torah tradition:

May the Omnipresent console you among the other mourners of Zion and Jerusalem.

At first glance, the association of these two concepts [Jerusalem's destruction and a personal loss] is perplexing. The reality, however, is that . . . we have perfect confidence that G-d will rebuild the ruins of Zion and Jerusalem; He will gather the dispersed remnants of Israel from the ends of the earth through our righteous Mashiach, and He will bring them in gladness to witness the joy of Zion and Jerusalem.

We are equally confident that the same is true with regard to our personal bereavement: G-d will fulfill His promise that "those that dwell in the dust shall awake and joyfully sing." Great indeed will be the happiness and rejoicing then, when all will meet together after the Resurrection of the Dead.

EXERCISE 6.4

1. Record the point from today's lesson that resonated with you most.

_____

_____

2. Recognizing that life is limited, what can you do to better optimize your time?

_____

_____

KEY POINTS

1 Our exploration of death and the afterlife through the Torah's lens reduces our fear and unease, allowing us to consider our mortality without panic.

2 Some believe that because we eventually die, nothing is overly important. But Judaism insists that because we die, each moment of life is of supreme importance—and should be devoted to matters of eternal relevance. Considering our mortality motivates us to focus on what really matters.

3 Our natural illusion of immortality spurs us to consider time as dispensable—we care more about wasted money than wasted time. Reflecting on life's finitude replaces this illusion with an urgency to take advantage of each moment.

4 We are designed to be productive beings— "retirement" is not a Jewish concept. As our brute powers wane, we should transition to mentoring, sharing our wisdom and experience, etc.

5 Before the sin of the Tree of Knowledge, the body was the soul's extension, and their desires were synced. Sin destroyed that dynamic, causing spiritual death—the misalignment of body and soul. Physical death is the outgrowth of spiritual death.

6 We rectify spiritual death by realigning everything with its purpose—ignoring the superficial layers of a thing (its body) and instead focusing on its inner truth and purpose (soul). Upon completing this rectification, physical death will no longer be part of the human condition.

▼ **TEMPLE—THE SOUL OF JERUSALEM**
Alex Levin, oil on canvas, Jerusalem, Israel, 2019.

APPENDIX A

TEXT 14A

THREE THINGS TO CONSIDER

ETHICS OF THE FATHERS 3:1

ETHICS OF THE FATHERS (*PIRKEI AVOT*)

A 6-chapter work on Jewish ethics that is studied widely by Jewish communities, especially during the summer. The first 5 chapters are from the Mishnah, tractate Avot. Avot differs from the rest of the Mishnah in that it does not focus on legal subjects; it is a collection of the sages' wisdom on topics related to character development, ethics, healthy living, piety, and the study of Torah.

עֲקַבְיָא בֶּן מַהֲלַלְאֵל אוֹמֵר:
הִסְתַּכֵּל בִּשְׁלשָׁה דְבָרִים וְאֵין אַתָּה בָא לִידֵי עֲבֵירָה.
דַּע מֵאַיִן בָּאתָ, וּלְאָן אַתָּה הוֹלֵךְ, וְלִפְנֵי מִי אַתָּה עָתִיד לִתֵּן דִּין וְחֶשְׁבּוֹן.
מֵאַיִן בָּאתָ? מִטִּפָּה סְרוּחָה.
וּלְאָן אַתָּה הוֹלֵךְ? לִמְקוֹם עָפָר רִמָּה וְתוֹלֵעָה.
וְלִפְנֵי מִי אַתָּה עָתִיד לִתֵּן דִּין וְחֶשְׁבּוֹן?
לִפְנֵי מֶלֶךְ מַלְכֵי הַמְּלָכִים הַקָּדוֹשׁ בָּרוּךְ הוּא.

Akavya son of Mahalalel would say:
"If you reflect upon three things
you will not approach sin:
know your origins, your destination,
and before Whom you are destined to provide
a [personal] judgment and an accounting.

"From where did you originate?
From a putrid drop [of seed].

"Where are you headed?
To a [resting] place of dust, maggots, and worms.

"Before Whom are you destined to provide
a [personal] judgment and an accounting?
Before the supreme King of kings,
the Holy One, blessed be He."

TEXT 14B

LOSS OF APPETITE FOR TEMPORAL PLEASURES

RABBI YONAH OF
GERONA, AD LOC.

**RABBI YONAH OF GERONA
D. 1263**

Spanish rabbi and Talmudist. Rabbi
Yonah from Gerona, Catalonia,
was a cousin of Nachmanides. He
is renowned for his outspoken
critique of Maimonides's works,
and for later recanting his
opposition and vowing to travel
to Maimonides's grave in Israel
to beg his forgiveness. He left
France, but was detained in
Toledo, Spain, where he stayed
and became one of the greatest
Talmudists of his time. He is best
known for his moralistic works
on repentance and asceticism.

"וּלְאָן אַתָּה הוֹלֵךְ? לִמְקוֹם עָפָר רִמָּה וְתוֹלֵעָה". וְכִי תַחְשׁוֹב בְּלִבְּךָ לְאָן אַתָּה הוֹלֵךְ, לֹא תַחְפּוֹץ בְּכָל הַתַּעֲנוּגִים, כִּי לְרִמָּה אַתָּה טוֹרֵחַ. גַּם כָּל עוֹשֶׁר וְכָבוֹד תִּבְזֶה בְּעֵינֶיךָ וְכָל טוֹבָה תַּבְהִיל כִּי הַכֹּל הֶבֶל וּרְעוּת רוּחַ. וְעַל עִנְיָן זֶה עָשָׂה שְׁלֹמֹה הַמֶּלֶךְ סֵפֶר קֹהֶלֶת וְהִתְחִיל, "הֶבֶל הֲבָלִים", לְהַבְהִיל כָּל טוֹבָה וְכָל יָקָר. וְאַחַר שֶׁהִבְהִיל אֶת הַכֹּל אָמַר (קֹהֶלֶת יב, יג), "סוֹף דָּבָר הַכֹּל נִשְׁמָע, אֶת הָאֱלֹקִים יְרָא וְאֶת מִצְוֹתָיו שְׁמוֹר כִּי זֶה כָּל הָאָדָם".

Where you are headed? To a [resting] place of dust, maggots, and worms. If you contemplate your eventual destination, you will lose your cravings for corporeal pleasures because all the effort you exert in your pursuit of material pleasures is to the greater advantage of the maggots. You will also come to despise mortal honors and be turned off by material bounty, for it is all inconsequential, vanity, and ultimately worthless. This contemplation inspired King Solomon to compose the Book of Ecclesiastes, which opens with the words, "[All is] utterly meaningless" and whose goal is to highlight the sheer insignificance of all that is [superficially considered] good and precious.

Only after establishing the meaninglessness of all [mortal desires] does Solomon ultimately declare, "The end of the matter, all having been heard: fear G-d and observe His commandments, for this is a person's entire [purpose]" (ECCLESIASTES 12:13).

TEXT 15

QUESTIONING CONVENTION

RABBI YOSEF YITZCHAK
SCHNEERSOHN, *SEFER
HAMAAMARIM* 5710, P. 118

**RABBI YOSEF YITSCHAK SCHNEERSOHN
(RAYATS, FRIERDIKER REBBE,
PREVIOUS REBBE) 1880–1950**

Chasidic rebbe, prolific writer,
and Jewish activist. Rabbi Yosef
Yitzchak, the 6th leader of the
Chabad movement, actively
promoted Jewish religious practice
in Soviet Russia and was arrested
for these activities. After his release
from prison and exile, he settled
in Warsaw, Poland, from where he
fled Nazi occupation and arrived
in New York in 1940. Settling in
Brooklyn, Rabbi Schneersohn
worked to revitalize American
Jewish life. His son-in-law, Rabbi
Menachem Mendel Schneerson,
succeeded him as the leader
of the Chabad movement.

דְּיֶשְׁנָם כַּמָּה דְבָרִים בָּאָדָם שֶׁהוּא נוֹהֵג וְעוֹשֶׂה כֵּן וַיַּיילֶע אַזוֹי טוּט
וֶועֶלְט, וְהַדְּבָרִים הָאֵלֶּה הֵם כְּמוֹ חוּק שֶׁבִּלְתִּי מְזִיזִים אוֹתוֹ מִמְּקוֹמוֹ לְפִי
דְכֵן הוּא הַנְהָגַת הָעוֹלָם, וּכְמוֹ בְּכַמָּה עִנְיְנֵי נִימוּס וְהַדּוֹמֶה כו' . . .

וּכְמוֹ עַל דֶּרֶךְ מָשָׁל זְמַנֵּי הָאֲכִילָה וּזְמַנֵּי הַשֵּׁינָה, הִנֵּה מִצַּד הֶרְגֵּשׁ
הָעוֹלָם הֵם קְבוּעִים בְּעִתִּים וּזְמַנִּים, וְגַם כְּשֶׁצָּרִיךְ לְהִתְעַסֵּק בְּמִקָּח
וּמִמְכָּר וּמַשָּׂא וּמַתָּן, הִנֵּה זְמַנִּים הָאֵלּוּ עַל פִּי הָרוֹב בִּלְתִּי נִיזָּזִים
וּבִלְתִּי נִידָחִים כְּלָל וְעִיקָר, וּזְמַנֵּי הַקְּבִיעוּת שֶׁל תּוֹרָה וּתְפִלָּה הֵם
נִדָחִים וְאֵין לָהֶם קֶבַע, וְיֵשׁ שֶׁהֵם נִדָחִים חַס וְשָׁלוֹם לְגַמְרֵי.

הִנֵּה הָאָדָם אֲשֶׁר נוֹתֵן אֵיזֶה חֶשְׁבּוֹן לְנַפְשׁוֹ, הַאִם יֵשׁ אֵיזֶה חָכְמָה בְּהַנְהָגָה
כָּזוֹ? דְּמִי הוּא הַיוֹדֵעַ עִתּוֹ וּזְמַנּוֹ? וּכְדְאִיתָא בְּמִדְרָשׁ רַבָּה (דְּבָרִים רַבָּה
ט, ג) "אֵין אָדָם שַׁלִּיט לוֹמַר הַמְתִּינוּ לִי עַד שֶׁאֶעֱשֶׂה חֶשְׁבּוֹנוֹתַי וְעַד
שֶׁאֲצַוֶּה לְבֵיתִי כו'". וְאֵיךְ יִתֵּן כָּל נַפְשׁוֹ עַל דָּבָר שֶׁאֵין בּוֹ מַמָּשׁ כְּלָל, וְעַל
הָעִיקָר מָה שֶׁהָיְתָה הַכַּוָונָה בִּירִידַת נִשְׁמָתוֹ לְמַטָּה הוּא שׁוֹכֵחַ לְגַמְרֵי.

There are so many conventions that we follow
blindly, simply because everyone around us
does so. We take them very seriously, as if these
principles are carved in stone—for no reason other
than because society does so. Think of the many
rules of etiquette, protocol, and the like. . . .

One prime example is our schedules for meals and
sleeping hours. The prevailing attitude of society is
that these matters cannot budge. Even if important
business matters clamor for attention, by and large our
items of personal care remain rigidly rooted in place.
By stark contrast, our hours scheduled for Torah study
and prayer are all too easily waived; they rarely remain
fixed, and they are sometimes displaced altogether.

Consider honestly: Is there any wisdom to such an approach? Can we accurately predict when our time will come? As the Midrash (*DEVARIM RABAH 9:3*) puts it: "No one is able to control the angel of death and tell it, 'Wait for me to settle my accounts and instruct my household. . . .'" So how can we allow ourselves to be rigidly devoted to utterly meaningless matters, while completely forgetting about our most critical objective—the mission for which our souls descended into this world in the first place?

◄ MALACH HAMAVET (PURSUIT BY THE ANGEL OF DEATH)
Zalman Kleinman, acrylic on canvas, New York.

APPENDIX B

TEXT 16

NURSE REVEALS MOST COMMON END-OF-LIFE REGRETS

SUSIE STEINER, "TOP FIVE REGRETS OF THE DYING," *THE GUARDIAN*, FEBRUARY 1, 2012

A palliative nurse who has counselled the dying in their last days has revealed the most common regrets we have at the end of our lives. And among the top, from men in particular, is "I wish I hadn't worked so hard."

Bronnie Ware is an Australian nurse who spent several years working in palliative care, caring for patients in the last 12 weeks of their lives. She recorded their dying epiphanies in a blog called *Inspiration and Chai*, which gathered so much attention that she put her observations into a book called *The Top Five Regrets of the Dying*.

Ware writes of the phenomenal clarity of vision that people gain at the end of their lives, and how we might learn from their wisdom. "When questioned about any regrets they had or anything they would do differently," she says, "common themes surfaced again and again."

The top five regrets of the dying, as witnessed by Ware:

1. "I wish I'd had the courage to live a life true to myself, not the life others expected of me."

2. "I wish I hadn't worked so hard."

3. "I wish I'd had the courage to express my feelings."

4. "I wish I had stayed in touch with my friends."

5. "I wish that I had let myself be happier."

APPENDIX C

TEXT 17

FIND WORK!

AVOT DERABBI NATAN 11:1

AVOT DERABBI NATAN

A commentary on, and an elaboration of, the Mishnaic tractate Avot, bearing the name of Rabbi Natan, one of the sages of the Mishnah. The work exists in two very different versions, one of which appears in many editions of the Talmud.

רַבִּי יְהוּדָה בֶּן בְּתֵירָא אוֹמֵר: מִי שֶׁאֵין לוֹ מְלָאכָה לַעֲשׂוֹת, מַה יַּעֲשֶׂה?
אִם יֵשׁ לוֹ חָצֵר חֲרֵבָה אוֹ שָׂדֶה חֲרֵבָה, יֵלֵךְ וְיִתְעַסֵּק בָּהּ,
שֶׁנֶּאֱמַר (שְׁמוֹת כ, ח), "שֵׁשֶׁת יָמִים תַּעֲבֹד וְעָשִׂיתָ כָל מְלַאכְתֶּךָ".
וּמַה תַּלְמוּד לוֹמַר "וְעָשִׂיתָ כָל מְלַאכְתֶּךָ"?
לְהָבִיא אֶת מִי שֶׁיֵּשׁ לוֹ חֲצֵרוֹת אוֹ שָׂדוֹת חֲרֵבוֹת, יֵלֵךְ וְיִתְעַסֵּק בָּהֶן.

Rabbi Yehudah son of Beteira would say:
People who have no [need for] work,
what should they do?
If they own a yard or field that is desolate,
they should go and tend it,
as it is stated, "Six days you shall work and perform all your labor" (EXODUS 20:8).
What does the clause "All your labor" add to the verse?
That even [if we have no work,
we should find a way to engage in labor,
such as restoring] a desolate yard or field."

APPENDIX D

TEXT 18

CHOOSING LIFE

ADAPTED FROM RABBI SHALOM
DOVBER SCHNEERSOHN, *SEFER
HAMAAMARIM* 5659, PP. 30–31

**RABBI SHALOM DOVBER SCHNEERSOHN
(RASHAB) 1860–1920**

Chasidic rebbe. Rabbi Shalom
Dovber became the 5th leader
of the Chabad movement
upon the passing of his father,
Rabbi Shmuel Schneersohn.
He established the Lubavitch
network of *yeshivot* called Tomchei
Temimim. He authored many
volumes of Chasidic discourses
and is renowned for his lucid
and thorough explanations
of kabbalistic concepts.

וְהִנֵּה כְּשֶׁיִּתְבּוֹנֵן הָאָדָם בְּכָל זֶה, אֵיךְ שֶׁבְּכָל דָּבָר יֵשׁ אוֹר וְחַיּוּת הָאֱלֹקִי, וְהָעִיקָר
הוּא הָאוֹר הָאֱלֹקִי שֶׁבּוֹ, וְהַנִּבְרָאִים בֶּאֱמֶת בְּטֵלִים לְהָאוֹר הָאֱלֹקִי שֶׁבָּהֶם
וּלְשָׁרְשָׁם וְלִמְקוֹרָם הַמְהַוֶּוֹם כו', עַל יְדֵי זֶה יִתְעוֹרֵר בְּרָצוֹן וּתְשׁוּקָה וְאַהֲבָה
גְדוֹלָה לֶאֱלֹקוּת, שֶׁזֶּה יִהְיֶה כָּל חֶפְצוֹ וּמְגַמָּתוֹ רַק בֶּאֱלֹקוּת לְבָד, וְלֹא יִרְצֶה
בְּחִיצוֹנִיּוּת וְגַשְׁמִיּוּת הָעוֹלָם שֶׁהֵם מָוֶת מִצַּד עַצְמָם, הַוִּוֹים וְנִפְסָדִים כו', רַק
יִרְצֶה בְּהַחַיּוּת הָאֱלֹקִי שֶׁהוּא הָעִיקָר כו', וּמִכָּל שֶׁכֵּן שֶׁאֵין צָרִיךְ לְהַפְרִיד אֶת
הַדָּבָר הַגַּשְׁמִי. דְּהֲרֵי נִתְבָּאֵר לְעֵיל דְּהַגַּשְׁמִי בָּטֵל בֶּאֱמֶת אֶל הָאוֹר וְהַחַיּוּת
הָאֱלֹקִי, אָמְנָם עַל יְדֵי שֶׁהָאָדָם מְחַשֵּׁב אֶת הַגַּשְׁמִי לְדָבָר בִּפְנֵי עַצְמוֹ, דְּהַיְינוּ
בְּמַה שֶּׁרוֹצֶה לֶהָנוֹת מִגּוּף הַדָּבָר הַגַּשְׁמִי, עַל יְדֵי זֶה מוֹרִיד וּמַפְרִיד אוֹתוֹ. דְּגַם
אֶת הָעוֹלָם נָתַן בְּלִבּוֹ שֶׁל אָדָם כו', וְלָכֵן חֵטְא עֵץ הַדַּעַת גָּרַם פֵּירוּד בִּכְלָלוּת
הָעוֹלָם, כְּמוֹ כֵן כָּל אֶחָד וְאֶחָד עַל יְדֵי שֶׁרוֹצֶה לֵהָנוֹת מֵהַדָּבָר הַגַּשְׁמִי מִצַּד
עַצְמוֹ הֲרֵי הוּא מַפְרִיד אוֹתוֹ, וּלְהֵיפֶךְ כְּשֶׁרוֹצֶה בָּהָאֱלֹקוּת שֶׁל הַדָּבָר הַגַּשְׁמִי הֲרֵי
הוּא מַעֲלֶה אוֹתוֹ, וְהַיְינוּ שֶׁיִּהְיֶה נִרְאֶה וְנִגְלֶה בּוֹ אֵיךְ שֶׁהוּא בָּטֵל כו'.

Everything that exists has a soul—divine light and
energy—which constitutes its primary reality. Each
created entity is subordinate to the divine light that it
harbors, and it is nullified to the divine source upon
which its existence depends.

If we contemplate this, we will experience longing
and a powerful love for divinity; all of our desire
and yearning will be directed to connecting
with G-d. We will not desire the superficiality
and materiality of created entities, for on their
own, these elements are death—materials that
deteriorate and decompose with time. Rather,

we will be interested in connecting exclusively with the divine energy within each entity. . . .

"G-d placed the universe into the human heart" (ECCLESIASTES 3:11), meaning that our approach to materiality impacts its reality: If we desire to benefit from the tangible elements of an entity, we lend independent significance to that entity's physicality. As a result, it is divorced from its spiritual core and dragged into the realm of the spiritually disconnected. This occurred in a global sense when the first sin—the sin of the Tree of Knowledge—produced a universal disconnect from divinity. And it is repeated in microcosm each time we seek strictly material pleasure or gain, thereby disconnecting that matter or experience from divinity. Instead, we should seek its divine core, thereby sublimating its material shell, by placing it overtly at the service of its divine purpose.

▼ **THE TREE OF LIFE (DETAIL)**
Gustav Klimt, painting, study for later mosaic,1905. (Museum für angewandte Kunst, Vienna)

APPENDIX E

TEXT 19

WHEN A SOUL IS REINCARNATED IN MULTIPLE BODIES

RABBI CHAIM VITAL, *SHAAR HAGILGULIM*, INTRODUCTION 4

RABBI CHAIM VITAL
C. 1542–1620

Lurianic kabbalist. Rabbi Vital was born in Israel, lived in Safed and Jerusalem, and later lived in Damascus. He was authorized by his teacher, Rabbi Yitschak Luria, the Arizal, to record his teachings. Acting on this mandate, Vital began arranging his master's teachings in written form, and his many works constitute the foundation of the Lurianic school of Jewish mysticism. His most famous work is *Ets Chaim*.

אִם בַּפַּעַם הָא' . . . לֹא זָכָה לְתַקֵּן אוֹתָהּ (הַנֶּפֶשׁ) כּוּלָהּ וּמֵת . . . בְּעֵת תְּחִיַּת הַמֵּתִים אֵין לוֹ לַגּוּף הָא' אֶלָּא אוֹתוֹ הַחֵלֶק הַפְּרָטִי (שֶׁל הַנֶּפֶשׁ) אֲשֶׁר תִּיקֵּן הוּא בַּחַיִּים.

וְלָכֵן כְּשֶׁמִּתְגַּלְגֶּלֶת הַנֶּפֶשׁ הַזֹּאת בְּגוּף אַחֵר לְהַשְׁלִים תִּיקּוּנָהּ . . . בְּחִינַת הַחֲלָקִים שֶׁל הַנֶּפֶשׁ שֶׁנִּתַקְּנוּ בְּגוּף הַזֶּה הַשֵּׁנִי . . . הֵם לָזֶה הַגּוּף הַב' בִּזְמַן הַתְּחִיָּה.

If the first time [a soul entered this world] . . . it did not merit to achieve full rectification before passing away . . . then at the time of Resurrection [of the Dead], that particular body will be entitled to receive only the specific percentage of the soul that it did succeed in rectifying during its lifetime.

When the same soul is subsequently reincarnated into a second body to complete its rectification . . . only the portion of the soul that was rectified in the second body . . . will return to serve as the soul of that second body when it arises at the Resurrection [of the Dead].

ADDITIONAL READINGS

ON THE RESURRECTION

BY RABBI ARYEH KAPLAN

RABBI ARYEH KAPLAN
1934–1983

American rabbi, author, and physicist. Rabbi Kaplan authored more than 50 volumes on Torah, Talmud, Jewish mysticism, and philosophy, many of which have become modern-day classics. He is best known for his popular translation and elucidation of the Bible, *The Living Torah*; and his translation of the Ladino biblical commentary, *Me'am Lo'ez*.

In order to understand the significance of the Resurrection *(Techiyas Hameisim)* it would be instructive to look at the first two blessings of the Amidah *(Shemoneh Esrei)*, a prayer that is recited three times daily by every Jew.

The first blessing of the Amidah deals with our relationship to G-d; indeed, one can say that it establishes our relationship with G-d for the rest of this fundamental prayer. Thus the first blessing speaks of G-d as, "the Great Mighty, Awesome, Highest G-d, Who bestows bountiful kindness, Who is Master of all, Who recalls the love of the Patriarchs and will bring a redeemer to their children's children. . . ."

The second blessing begins with the words, "You are eternally Mighty, O G-d, You bring the dead back to life. . . ." The second blessing of this most important prayer thus deals with the Resurrection. From this alone, one would see that it is a key teaching of Judaism.

The Meaning of Life

The first two blessings of the Amidah actually deal with the two most important concerns of man regarding his own existence. The two primary questions that a person can ask are:

(1) What is the meaning of life?

(2) What happens after life in this world ends?

The first blessing of the Amidah brings us into contact with the answer to the first question. The meaning of life is defined by G-d's existence and our relationship to Him. If a person can establish a relationship to the One Author of all existence, then his own existence will have meaning.

However, no matter how meaningful life would be, if it would all end with death, its meaning would only be temporary. Therefore, the second blessing of the Amidah gives us the answer to the second question, "What happens after life in this world ends?" It also teaches that when one finds meaning in life, it is permanent, not temporary. Although life in this world may be temporary, there is another life, beyond the Resurrection, which will be permanent.

Influence of the Patriarchs

A key teaching of Judaism is that the actions of the Patriarchs, Abraham, Isaac, and Jacob, continue to serve as a spiritual inheritance to their descendants today. Every Jew is to some degree markedly influenced by the past acts of the Patriarchs.

Again, this is evident in the first blessing of the Amidah, which begins with the words, "Blessed are You, O L-rd our G-d, G-d of our fathers, G-d of Abraham, G-d of Isaac, and G-d of Jacob. . . ." Here, we attempt to elevate our own conception of G-d to that of the Patriarchs.

In order to understand this, it would be useful to repeat a teaching of the Baal Shem Tov (founder of Chassidism). He asks, why does the Amidah begin by saying, "Our G-d, G-d of our fathers"? The first term implies that we have discovered His existence by our own efforts—He is "our G-d." The expression, "G-d of our fathers," however, implies that we were taught about His existence. Thus, the two phrases seem to contradict each other. The Baal Shem Tov explains that every person must develop his own perception of G-d, since it is something that cannot be communicated totally to another. Hence, we speak of Him as "our G-d." But still, one must be able to determine whether one's perception of G-d is authentic, and one must therefore relate it to the perceptions of past generations. We thus add, "G-d of our fathers." Both are needed: the person's individual perception, and the historical perception of past generations. And since the paradigm of perception of the Divine was that of the Patriarchs, Abraham, Isaac, and Jacob when we say, "G-d of Abraham, G-d of Isaac, and G-d of Jacob," we acknowledge that our ultimate goal would be to reach their level of spiritual perception.

Four Degrees of Closeness to G-d
Moreover, in the last four words of the blessing of the Patriarchs, we establish an increasingly closer relationship with the Divine. In these words we address G-d as: "King, Helper, Rescuer, and Shield." Each of these words relates to a degree of closeness to G-d.

First, we speak to G-d as our "King." A king rules over his subjects, and in a general sense, is concerned with their welfare. However, the king is not available to help each subject on an individual basis, except in the most general terms. Therefore, a person who relates to G-d as "King" is quite distant from Him.

The next level is that of a helper (ozer). Imagine a situation where you are in financial straits and need a loan. You could not go to the king for it, but you could go to someone to whom you feel close. Such a person is your "helper." The relationship between a person and a "helper," then, is much closer than his relationship to a king.

The third level is that of rescuer (moshia). A helper can send assistance from a distance, but a rescuer must be right there on the spot. If a person is drowning, then his rescuer must be close enough to jump in and save him. So the level of rescuer is closer than that of the helper.

Finally, the fourth level is that of shield (magen). A rescuer can be a few hundred feet away when the person needs him. However, when an arrow is shot at a person, his shield must be directly in front of him, to intercept the arrow. Therefore, when a person has a conception of G-d as his "Shield," his perception is that of G-d right in front of him and surrounding him from all sides, protecting him from all danger.

The first person to attain this fourth level was Abraham. G-d explicitly told him, "Do not fear, Abram, I am your Shield" (Genesis 15:1). We recognize that Abraham reached the ultimate of this level of closeness to G-d when we conclude the first blessing, "Blessed are You, O L-rd, Shield of Abraham." We strive to attain this degree of closeness with G-d, using Abraham as the paradigm.

This was also the level attained by King David, and hence, the *Haftarah* blessings contain a section which concludes, "Blessed are You, O L-rd, Shield of David." David was on this level when he said, "I have placed the L-rd before me at all times" (Psalms 16:8).

In any case, after completing the first blessing of the Amidah, one may wonder why the relationships that the Patriarchs had with G-d should be significant, since they belong to a generation that is dead and buried. If the Patriarchs are dead and we are alive, how can we relate to their spiritual experiences?

The second blessing of the Amidah therefore speaks of the Resurrection. It teaches that death is not a permanent situation, and that the experiences of the Patriarchs are as alive today as they were during their actual lifetimes.

Two Conceptions of the Resurrection

There are two basic opinions regarding the Resurrection, those of the Rambam (Maimonides), and the Ramban (Nachmanides).

The Rambam's opinion is that when a person dies, he immediately goes to *Olam Haba* (the "World to Come" or the "Future World"), so called because it comes after life in this world. Thus, according to the Rambam, the "World to Come" promised in Torah literature involves only the soul, and is completely spiritual.

According to the Rambam then, the Resurrection, of necessity, involves a *temporary* return to the physical plane. Some advance a possible reason for the Resurrection, that the righteous will be able to see the Messianic world with physical eyes. In any case, according to the Rambam, the resurrected dead will die once again and will return to the "World to Come."

The Ramban, on the other hand, maintains that the World to Come is the world that will exist after the Resurrection, and that it will be a world that includes both body and soul. This is also the opinion of the *Zohar* and of most of the major Kabbalists. According to this opinion, a whole person consists of body and soul, and therefore, a person cannot attain maximum perception of the Divine without his body as well as his soul. Thus, the Resurrection is a key element in G-d's ultimate reward for mankind. It is seen as the inception of the World to Come.

This opinion states that when a person dies, his soul goes to the "World of Souls" (*Olam Haneshamos).* There it has a certain degree of perception of the Divine, and it waits there until the Resurrection. It is only after the Resurrection, however, in the World to Come, that this perception reaches its ultimate.

The Meaning of Death

The first mention of death in the Torah is in relation to the Tree of Knowledge, where G-d tells Adam, "And from the Tree of Knowledge of Good and Evil, do not eat from it, for on the day you eat from it, you will be bound to die" (Genesis 2: 17). Hence, on the simplest level, death is seen as punishment for Adam's original sin.

It is significant that in the very next verse, G-d says, "It is not good for man to be alone, I will make him a helpmate as his counterpart" (ibid. 2: 18). On a simple level, this means that once the possibility of death exists, G-d must make arrangements for the continuation of the species. When the possibility of death came into existence, then Adam would have to have a wife if mankind was not to become extinct with his death.

However, this can also be understood on a much deeper level. From a number of Midrashic sources, we see that the spiritual realm is looked upon as masculine, while the physical world is feminine. Thus, in the overall scheme of creation, the spiritual realm fertilizes the physical while the physical realm acts as the womb, through which G-d's purpose is brought to fruition.

Life, of course, is the connection of the body and the soul. Since the body, as part of the physical realm, is feminine and the soul masculine, death is a separation of the masculine from the feminine. Hence, after the possibility of death came into existence in the world, G-d said, "It is not good for man to be alone"—it is not good for the soul, the masculine component of the body-soul unit, to be isolated from bodily existence through death.

Thus, there are two male-female relationships that a person can have. One is immortality, while the other is marriage. Either one can guarantee the existence of the species. If man was to lose immortality, then he would have to marry and beget children.

The Tree of Knowledge was closely related to the male-female relationship; indeed, "knowledge" to some degree defines the male-female relationship. In Hebrew, "knowledge" is *daas,* a word which connotes "togetherness" and "unity." Thus, the Torah says "Adam knew his wife, Eve . . ." (ibid. 4:1).

Therefore, before eating of the Tree of Knowledge, "the man and the woman were naked, but they were not ashamed of themselves" (ibid. 2:25). Since the male-female relationship was perfect there was no cause for shame (see Ramban, etc.). And indeed, in the Torah we see that the relationship between man and woman was damaged by eating from the Tree of Knowledge, as G-d told Eve, "To your husband will be your desire, and he will dominate you" (ibid. 3:16).

If life itself is a male-female relationship, then after man ate from the Tree of Knowledge and damaged this relationship, death was inevitable. It was for this reason that death was punishment for the first sin.

The World to Come, however, is seen as a time when all the effects of Adam's sin will be eradicated. Thus, the relationship between body and soul will also be perfected. Therefore, it will (according to the Ramban and the Kabbalists) be a time when man will live immortally with body and soul together.

The Mystery of Life

One can look at the entire Amidah as being the vehicle through which a person perfects his life. In the Amidah one develops a relationship with G-d and with life, and then asks G-d to provide everything needed for the good life.

Indeed, that is one reason that the Amidah has eighteen blessings. The Amidah is called the *Shemoneh Esrei,* which literally means "eighteen." The Hebrew word for "life" is *chai,* which has a numerical value of eighteen (see *Avodas Hakodesh).*

This may be yet another reason why the Resurrection is the second blessing of the Amidah. Living in the physical world, we may see ourselves as spiritually dead. Therefore, as soon as we develop a close relationship with G-d in the first blessing, we ask that He resurrect us spiritually. This is then accomplished through the eighteen (which equals *chai,* life) blessings of the Amidah. By drawing ourselves close to G-d, we can experience a taste of the World to Come.

The Aryeh Kaplan Reader (New York: Mesorah Publications, 1983), pp. 184–188.

Reprinted with permission of the publisher

SWALLOWED UP FOREVER

BY YAAKOV BRAWER, PHD

DR. YAAKOV BRAWER

Scientist and professor. Dr. Yaakov Brawer is professor emeritus on the Faculty of Medicine at McGill University in Montreal. He lectures on neuroendocrinology and Chasidism. He has authored two books on Chasidic philosophy, *Something From Nothing* and *Eyes That See.*

From every incident in a person's life, one can acquire profound insight into the service of the Creator. So says the holy Baal Shem Tov. Fortified by this idea, I began my descent in the morgue elevator of the Department of Anatomy and Cell Biology at McGill University.

As the director of a neuroscience course, I was responsible for the annual inventory of brain prosections used in the student laboratory. These were stored in containers at the back of "the cold room," a sort of walk-in refrigerator, which also happened to house some forty cadavers awaiting the scalpels of the first year medical students.

I am uncomfortable with these yearly expeditions. The departmental morgue is no place for a nice *Chassidisher Yid* (Chassidic Jew). In fact, in my opinion, it is no place for anyone. Why then, did providence arrange things so that I had to go there? What sage wisdom in the service of my Creator was I supposed to attain in that dismal place?

I completed the inventory with customary dispatch and happily left the cold room to its silent occupants. While ascending in the elevator, I began to wonder if there might not be exceptions to the Baal Shem Tov's maxim. Later that day, however, the meaning behind the trip to the morgue dawned on me in the form of a question: What is the difference between the denizens of the morgue, and the students,

colleagues, technicians, and secretaries scurrying about on the floors above?

Lest the reader dismiss this thought as the morbid musing of a crackpot, I must emphasize that it is firmly rooted in Chassidic teaching. Indeed, it represents one of the most perplexing paradoxes in Chassidic literature, namely that anything destined to die and deteriorate is dead and deteriorated, while it is yet alive. I had wrestled with this conundrum in the past without success and I had long since shelved it away in a remote region of my brain reserved for intractable enigmas. The morgue experience, however, recast the question in visual imagery that demanded reconsideration. How was it possible to relate, much less equate those young, happy, healthy, rambunctious students with the inhabitants of the cold room?

Life as an Add-On

It is, of course, clear from the Torah perspective, that life and death define states considerably more complex and subtle than the simplistic physical notions held by the secular world. A creature does not necessarily have to be biologically defunct in order to be properly identified by Torah as "dead." Conversely, departed souls of the so-called dead, experience life far more intensely than do their earthly "living" counterparts.

What, then, is life? Inasmuch as G-d is not only the ultimate but the sole reality, life, quite simply, is G-dliness or Divinity. The degree to which an entity partakes of and is identified with G-dliness determines the extent to which it is alive. The divine soul, for example, is intrinsically and eternally alive because its very being is an uninterrupted extension of pure G-dliness. The body, on the other hand, is dissociated from the Divine source of its own existence, and its life is thus bestowed from without, as it were. Bodies, unlike souls, are not innately G-dly and are not, therefore, inherently alive.

The life of the body is a little like the weight of an object. Although we regard weight as an innate characteristic, it is really an alien property imposed externally by the gravitational force of the earth. Indeed, in space, an object has no weight. Since the body, per se, is not transparent to G-dliness, its life is only borrowed. It is an external feature bestowed provisionally in order to afford the body limited existence in this world. The fact that bodies are animated indirectly by transcendent levels of G-dliness precludes their awareness of the Divine source of their own being, which results in a powerful impression of independence.

This state of affairs pertains to the entire realm of *kelipot* ("shells"), which comprise most things and creatures in this material world. The process that gives rise to, and sustains the world of *kelipah* (also referred to as the *sitra achra*, "other side") differs fundamentally from the manner in which Divinity channels life to creations in the domain of holiness, such as souls or sacrosanct angelic beings. G-d extends life to the side of holiness by means of ten divine attributes or *sefirot*, whereas *kelipot* are animated through the agency of eleven *sefirot* referred to in the language of Kabbalah as the "eleven crowns of impurity."

The reason the realm of Kelipah requires an "extra" *sefirah* becomes clear once we understand the necessity for *sefirot* altogether. We can best appreciate the significance of *sefirot* by drawing an analogy to the soul.

The soul, as an emanation of G-dliness, is a simple (uncompounded) unified essence, which is, nonetheless, capable of expressing itself in a variety of specific ways. The attributes (*sefirot*) of the soul, such as wisdom, understanding, kindness, etc., are the particular abilities through which the soul-essence achieves this diversity of self-expression. Similarly, G-dliness transcends particularization, definition or limitation, whereas the creations that it animates are finite and multifarious. It is through the agency of *sefirot* that the infinite, unitary, supernal source of all life (G-dliness) can be expressed in distinct modes in order to sustain and vitalize a multiplicity of finite beings.

In the realm of holiness, G-dliness fuses with the *sefirot* and thereby acquires definitive characteristics such as kindness, or justice. A well-known analogy for this process is light passing through a colored glass. Although the light remains light, it has acquired the restrictive property of "color." Similarly, Divine Will shining through each of the ten *sefirot* represents a direct and continuous extension of G-dliness (life) that has acquired the limiting features necessary to engender a variety of finite creations.

In contrast, G-dliness (life) is detached from the "other side," and thus relates to the *sefirot* of *sitra achra* at a distance, so to speak. Its influence encompasses them but is not invested within them. The Divine light that indirectly vitalizes the *sitra achra* is thus accounted as an eleventh "separate" *sefirah*.

Since G-dliness is the very soul or life force of *sefirot*, the *sefirot* of the *sitra achra*, in a sense, have no soul, and they can, therefore, be considered "dead." It follows that the *kelipot* that derive from these *sefirot* are also "dead," even while they cavort about in this world.

A Practical Application

Because life is a peripheral rather than an integral feature of the body, it is hardly surprising that the body, as well as all other manifestations of *kelipah*, must eventually die in actual fact. A practical consequence of this is that bodily pleasures and worldly terrors are transient and insubstantial, and we must not be seduced by the former or immobilized by fear of the latter.

A powerful recent object lesson is the sudden, inexplicable demise of the Soviet Union. Anyone who watched the West quiver in fear when Khrushchev banged his shoe on the table at the U.N., or who cowered beneath his grade-school desk during an air raid drill, knows the monster that was the Soviet Union. The USSR was fully capable of destroying the entire world on a whim. Then, one day, for no apparent reason, it utterly vanished. It did not gradually deteriorate, it did not collapse under the weight of its own success, and it was not a casualty of strategic or political miscalculation. At the height of its influence, it just disintegrated.

Although the world was stunned by the totally unexpected dissolution of the USSR, students of Chassidut should not have been surprised. The USSR was, after all, a *kelipah*, immense, obstreperous, and intimidating, but a *kelipah* nonetheless, and *kelipot*, as we know, have no life. Thus, once the USSR had fulfilled whatever role the Almighty had in mind for it, in accordance with its true nature, it simply ceased to exist.

This is all good and well, but it only partially addresses our original paradox, which is that anything destined to die and deteriorate is dead and deteriorated (*nifsad* in Hebrew), while it is yet alive. We can now understand that since *kelipot* are not essentially and intrinsically alive, the designation "dead" accurately describes their status even while they exist in this world. But what do we do with the term "deteriorated"? Although an entity can be considered dead even before it palpably expires, how can something be deteriorated before it deteriorates? Deterioration, unlike death, refers to a purely physical condition.

Furthermore, despite the fact that *kelipah* is founded on a mirage, the misery that *kelipot*, such as the USSR, are able to inflict on humanity during their earthly tenure is disturbingly authentic.

So, although the morgue experience had inspired me to focus attention on this classic riddle anew, my insight was no keener than when I had first encountered it years before. After a week of abortive mental gymnastics I was ready to abandon the question once again, when, while setting my alarm clock one evening, the answer suddenly crystallized.

Being vs. Becoming

My alarm clock is of the electrical digital variety on which the time is set by pushing a button that drives the number display. When the desired time is reached, one simply releases the button. As I gazed absently at the hours speeding by, I was jolted by a phenomenal discovery. Time designations are fictitious. It is never three o'clock, nor is it ever four o'clock, midnight or noon. Because the movement of the number display never ceases, the time may approach twelve or depart from twelve but it never is twelve. Even if it were possible to determine the exact position on a clock that indicates noon, since the second hand never stops at that position, it is never noon.

To put it another way, we can ask the question: for how long is it noon? for one second? one hundredth of a second? one thousandth of a second? Clearly it is noon for no measurable time, which is to say, it is never noon. The verb to "be," of which the word "is" is the third person singular present form, confers upon its subject the status of reality. This verb, therefore, can not apply to any entity governed by time. Since time-locked creations are in a state of incessant becoming, they never "are." An entity ceases "becoming" only when it escapes the inexorable course of time and achieves a final, immutable stable state. It can then be said to "be."

This then, explains why anything destined to die and deteriorate is dead and deteriorated while it is yet alive. The permanent, eternal, stable state of a *kelipah* is nonexistence. That is its reality, and its entire earthly duration is directed toward this condition. Once it totally deteriorates, all change ceases. It is no longer under the influence of time, which is to say that it is no longer becoming what it is ultimately supposed to be, but rather it now simply "is."

Intuitively, we appreciate this even without the foregoing explication. We know, for example, that the Almighty liberally stocks life with obstacles and trials with the express intention that we overcome them. The reality of obstacles, therefore, the end to which they are conceived, is negation. Evil exists only to be vanquished and darkness is created only to be dispelled.

Now that we understand why the physical integrity of *kelipah* is as illusory as is its life force, we can properly appreciate our own condition. Just as the reality of *kelipah* is death and disintegration, so is the reality of the Jewish people life, on both the spiritual and physical plane.

The Divine soul is a direct uninterrupted emanation of G-dliness, and since G-dliness is eternal, any concept of death is inapplicable to the soul. Moreover, the death of the body is merely a transient condition, just as life is a temporary phase for *kelipah*. The consummation of G-d's purpose in creating the universe is *z'man techiah*, the time of resurrection of the dead. At this point physical change will cease as the Divine Will that drove existence toward perfection is realized. We will then be what we have been in the process of becoming these thousands of years, and what we were intended to be from the outset.

What About the World?

There is yet one remaining loose end. When that glorious day arrives, in what sort of world will we live? Our world, at present is described in the Tanya as a world "filled with *kelipah* and *sitra achra*," the ultimate stable state of which is nonexistence. What then, will remain of the physical universe, and more specifically, our home planet when G-d's supreme purpose is realized?

Obviously, the universe, including our world, will continue to exist if for no other reason than that we (body and soul) will need a place to live. Moreover, inasmuch as the physical universe is the ultimate expression of G-d's creative ability, simple common sense dictates that it is neither ephemeral nor illusory. Indeed, the Torah (Isaiah, 45:18) tells us as much: "Not for dissolution did He create it, but to be inhabited."

In fact, the eternal nature of the universe is even now apparent in the immutability of natural law and in the constant endless pattern of celestial movement. Throughout the natural order one detects the infinitude that is the signature of the Almighty. The limitlessness of G-d's generative power is even discernible in living beings. Although individuals die, the species to which they belong are perpetuated without end.

It would appear then, that the world as a manifestation of G-d's supernal Will is very much "alive" and will remain so. How do we reconcile this with the fact that the ingredients of worldly existence consist mostly of kelipah?

Understanding Kelipah

The problem is easily resolved once we refine our concept of *kelipah*.

The term *kelipah* literally means a "shell" or a "rind." To what extent does the shell represent the reality of a nut? Clearly, the shell is a minor, if necessary component. We do not buy walnuts because we are enamored of their shells. Yet although the significant feature of a nut is obviously the fruit, it is the shell that endows the nut with its characteristic appearance.

Similarly, *kelipot* do not constitute the reality of anything in this world. They are merely external garments that conceal the particular expressions of G-d's creative will that bring worldly beings into existence. By masking the Divine light that is the true essence of created beings, *kelipot* simulate a schism between Creator and creation. Indeed, the effect of *kelipah* may be so powerful that not only is the unity of G-d with creation obscured, but the very existence of Justice and a Judge may appear doubtful. When confronted with the apparent triumph of emphatic evil, it is not always easy to remember that *kelipah* is only a deceptive, lifeless husk.

Although the world is indeed filled with *kelipot*, since they constitute only the most superficial dimension of any given creation, they really do not add up to much at all. Moreover, it is only this superficial exterior that has no connection with life and for which nullity is its absolute terminal condition.

Indeed, the temporary (hence, unreal) death and deterioration experienced by the body serves to free it of its *kelipah* aspect, such that at *techiat hamaitim* (the resurrection of the dead), the body will be reestablished in its essential pure condition. In the case of the righteous, who have purified their bodies of the dross of *kelipah* through their divine service, the body does not undergo deterioration altogether. When, following the advent of Moshiach, the veneer of *kelipah* dissipates, G-d's living creative will will be revealed as the underlying reality of all being.

It was in order to learn this lesson, that Providence sent me year after year to the morgue, until I finally caught on. How can I be so certain? Simple. A few months following this episode, the department built cabinets for the brain prosections adjacent to the student laboratory, and I have never had to return.

Reprinted with permission from Chabad.org

ACKNOWLEDGMENTS

We are grateful to the following individuals for helping shape *Journey of the Soul*:

Journey of the Soul is a revision of a course by the same title that the Rohr Jewish Learning Institute (JLI) featured in 2015. **Rabbi Naftali Silberberg** designed and authored the original course and spearheaded its current revision. **Rabbi Yakov Gershon**—of JLI's Machon Shmuel: The Sami Rohr Research Institute—provided extensive Judaic research for the revision.

The course was originally conceived and developed and then revised with guidance and direction from **Casey Skvorc, PhD,** a leading member of JLI's CAB for The Wellness Institute. The JLI curriculum team was fortunate to draw on his vast erudition, experience, and expertise in the area of mental health to develop a scholarly and relevant learning experience. Thanks to **Elka Jacobs-Pinson, PsyD,** and **Malka Katzman, LMSW,** for assisting with the editing of the revision and to **Rabbi Shmuel Gomes** for assisting with the mental health research.

In partnership with the **Albert Einstein College of Medicine**, we are pleased to be able to offer this course for credits from the American Psychological Association (APA) and the AMA's Accreditation Council for Continuing Medical Education (ACCME). We are indebted to **Dr. Casey Skvorc** and **Rabbi Edward Reichman, M.D.,** for their dedicated collaboration and patient guidance throughout the process. Special thanks to **Mindy Wallach** for coordinating the accreditation and to **Shulamis Nadler** for her administrative assistance.

The following individuals contributed to the development of the course's initial release: **Rochel Holzkenner, Rabbi Eli Raksin, Rabbi Yanky Raskin, Chava Shapiro,** and **Rabbi Shmuel Super**. The following instructors served as the Instructor Advisory Board for the earlier version of this course: **Rabbis Yisroel Mangel, Sholom Raichik,** and **Avrohom Sternberg**. They spent many hours reviewing the course materials with the JLI team and provided numerous useful suggestions.

For the course's current, revised and enhanced iteration, the Instructor Advisory Board consists of the 400 instructors who taught the original course and provided JLI with their detailed feedback and suggestions via the dedicated instructor's message boards and in the post-course survey. Their brilliant suggestions led to sweeping changes and significant improvements to the course.

With this course, we are pleased to debut our redesigned, upgraded, full-color textbook! The redesign, completed in record time, was spearheaded by **Rabbi Zalman Abraham**, who led the devoted and talented design, layout, and imagery team that consists of **Shayna Grosh, Rabbi Zalman Korf, Shternie Zaltzman, Rivky Fieldsteel,** and **Rabbi Levi Weingarten**, skillfully coordinated by **Rochel Karp**.

Rivki Mockin streamlined and ensured the smoothness and timeliness of the content production. **Chana Dechter,** JLI Flagship's outgoing administrator, along with **Naomi Heber,** the incoming administrator, capably oversaw the entire project. **Mussi Abelsky, Shayna Grosh, Mushka Grossbaum, Chaya Mintz,** and **Mashie Vogel**

provided editorial assistance, and **Rakefet Orobona, Mimi Palace, Shmuel Telsner,** and **Ya'akovah Weber** enhanced the quality and accuracy of the writing with their proofreading. **Rabbi Mendel Sirota** directed the book's printing and distribution.

We'd like to warmly thank **Avi Webb** for leading the vision for the marketing of this course and **Mushka Kanner** and **Shifra Tauber** for creating and designing the course marketing materials.

Chany Block, Baila Goldstein, Mushka Lisker, and **Rivka Rapoport** designed the aesthetically pleasing PowerPoint presentations, and **Moshe Raskin** and **Getzy Raskin** produced the videos. The video scripts were masterfully written by **Rabbi Yaakov Paley.**

We are immensely grateful for the encouragement of JLI's visionary chairman, and vice-chairman of *Merkos L'Inyonei Chinuch*—Lubavitch World Headquarters, **Rabbi Moshe Kotlarsky**. Rabbi Kotlarsky has been highly instrumental in building the infrastructure for the expansion of Chabad's international network and is also the architect of scores of initiatives and services to help Chabad representatives across the globe succeed in their mission. We are blessed to have the unwavering support of JLI's principal benefactor, **Mr. George Rohr**, who is fully invested in our work, continues to be instrumental in JLI's monumental growth and expansion, and is largely responsible for the Jewish renaissance that is being spearheaded by JLI and its affiliates across the globe.

The commitment and sage direction of JLI's dedicated Executive Board—**Rabbis Chaim Block, Hesh Epstein, Ronnie Fine, Yosef Gansburg, Shmuel Kaplan, Yisrael Rice**, and **Avrohom Sternberg**—and the countless hours they devote to the development of JLI are what drive the vision, growth, and tremendous success of the organization.

Finally, JLI represents an incredible partnership of more than 2,000 *shluchim* and *shluchot* in more than 1,500 locations across the globe, who contribute their time and talent to further Jewish adult education. We thank them for generously sharing feedback and making suggestions that steer JLI's development and growth. They are our most valuable critics and our most cherished contributors.

Inspired by the call of the **Lubavitcher Rebbe**, of righteous memory, it is the mandate of the Rohr JLI to provide a community of learning for all Jews throughout the world where they can participate in their precious heritage of Torah learning and experience its rewards. May this course succeed in fulfilling this sacred charge!

On behalf of the Rohr Jewish Learning Institute,

RABBI EFRAIM MINTZ
Executive Director

RABBI YISRAEL RICE
Chairman, Editorial Board

Rosh Chodesh Kislev, 5781

THE ROHR JEWISH LEARNING INSTITUTE

**AN AFFILIATE OF MERKOS L'INYONEI CHINUCH,
THE EDUCATIONAL ARM OF THE CHABAD-LUBAVITCH MOVEMENT**
832 EASTERN PARKWAY, BROOKLYN, NY 11213

CHAIRMAN
Rabbi Moshe Kotlarsky
Lubavitch World Headquarters

PRINCIPAL BENEFACTOR
Mr. George Rohr
New York, NY

EXECUTIVE DIRECTOR
Rabbi Efraim Mintz

EXECUTIVE COMMITTEE
Rabbi Chaim Block
S. Antonio, TX

Rabbi Hesh Epstein
Columbia, SC

Rabbi Ronnie Fine
Montreal, QC

Rabbi Yosef Gansburg
Toronto, ON

Rabbi Shmuel Kaplan
Potomac, MD

Rabbi Yisrael Rice
S. Rafael, CA

Rabbi Avrohom Sternberg
New London, CT

ADMINISTRATION
Rabbi Mendel Kotlarsky

ADMINISTRATOR
Rabbi Dubi Rabinowitz

**ADVISORY BOARD OF
GOVERNORS**

George Rohr
New York, NY

Yaacov and Karen Cohen
Potomac, MD

Yitzchok and Julie Gniwisch
Montreal, QC

Barbara Hines
Aspen, CO

Ellen Marks
S. Diego, CA

Daniel and Rosie Mattio
Mercer Island, WA

David Mintz
Tenafly, NJ

Dr. Stephen F. Serbin
Columbia, SC

Leonard A. Wien, Jr.
Miami Beach, FL

ACADEMIC ADVISORY BOARD
Dr. Lewis Glinert
Professor of Hebraic Studies and Linguistics
Dartmouth College

Rabbi Edward Reichman, M.D.
Professor of Emergency Medicine
Albert Einstein College of Medicine

Dr. Jonathan Sarna
Professor of American Jewish History
Brandeis University

Dr. Lawrence H. Schiffman
Professor of Hebrew and Judaic Studies
New York University

EDUCATIONAL CONSULTANTS
Mr. Michael Brandwein
Lincolnshire, IL
Speech and Communication Expert

Dr. Andrew Effrat
Amherst, MA
Professor, School of Education
University of Massachusetts, Amherst

Dr. David Pelcovitz
New York, NY
Professor of Education and Psychology
Yeshiva University

Dr. Chana Silberstein
Ithaca, NY

Dr. Casey Skvorc
Washington, DC
National Institutes of Health

RABBINIC ADVISORY BOARD
Rabbi Yossi Shusterman
Beverly Hills, CA
CHAIRMAN

Rabbi Mordechai Farkash
Bellevue, WA

Rabbi Mendel Lipskier
Sherman Oaks, CA

Rabbi Avrohom Sternberg
New London, CT

CURRICULUM DEVELOPMENT

Rabbi Mordechai Dinerman

Rabbi Naftali Silberberg
EDITORS IN CHIEF

Rabbi Shmuel Klatzkin, PhD
ACADEMIC CONSULTANT

Rabbi Yanki Tauber
COURSE DESIGNER

Rabbi Baruch Shalom Davidson
Rabbi Chaim Fieldsteel
Rabbi Eliezer Gurkow
Rabbi Berry Piekarski
Rabbi Shmuel Super
CURRICULUM AUTHORS

Rabbi Yaakov Paley
Rabbi Boruch Werdiger
WRITERS

Rabbi Ahrele Loschak
EDITOR, TORAH STUDIES

Rabbi Mendel Glazman
Mrs. Mushka Grossbaum
EDITORIAL SUPPORT

Rabbi Yakov Gershon
Rabbi Shmuel Gomes
RESEARCH

Rabbi Michoel Lipskier
Rabbi Mendel Rubin
EXPERIENTIAL LEARNING

Mrs. Rivki Mockin
CONTENT COORDINATOR

MARKETING AND BRANDING

Rabbi Zalman Abraham
DIRECTOR

Mrs. Mashie Vogel
ADMINISTRATOR

Rabbi Avi Webb
BRAND COPYWRITER

Ms. Rochel Karp
DESIGN ADMINISTRATOR

Mrs. Chaya Mushka Kanner
Mrs. Mussi Sharfstein
Mrs. Shifra Tauber
Rabbi Levi Weingarten
GRAPHIC DESIGN

Mrs. Chany Block
Mrs. Rivky Fieldsteel
Mrs. Shayna Grosh
Rabbi Zalman Korf
Rabbi Moshe Wolff
Mrs. Shternie Zaltzman
PUBLICATION DESIGN

Lazer Cohen
Yosef Feigelstock
Ms. Basya Hans
SOCIAL MEDIA

Rabbi Yaakov Paley
WRITER

Rabbi Yossi Grossbaum
Rabbi Mendel Lifshitz
Rabbi Shraga Sherman
Rabbi Ari Sollish
Rabbi Mendel Teldon
MARKETING COMMITTEE

MARKETING CONSULTANTS

JJ Gross
Israel

Joseph Jaffe
EVOL8TION
New York, NY

Warren Modlin
MEDNETPRO, INC.
Orange County, CA

Alan Rosenspan
ALAN ROSENSPAN & ASSOCIATES
Sharon, MA

Gary Wexler
PASSION MARKETING
Los Angeles, CA

JLI CENTRAL

Rabbi Isaac Abelsky
Rabbi Mendel Abelsky
Ms. Rochel Karp
Rabbi Motti Klein
Ms. Adina Posner
Mrs. Aliza Scheinfeld
ADMINISTRATION

Rabbi Mendel Sirota
AFFILIATE SUPPORT

Rabbi Shlomie Tenenbaum
PROJECT MANAGER

Mrs. Mindy Wallach
AFFILIATE ORIENTATION

Mrs. Chany Block
Mrs. Bunia Chazan
Mrs. Mushka Druk
Mrs. Baila Goldstein
Mrs. Mushka Grossbaum
Getzy Raskin
Moshe Raskin
Mrs. Mashie Vogel
MULTIMEDIA DEVELOPMENT

Rabbi Mendel Ashkenazi
Yoni Ben-Oni
Rabbi Mendy Elishevitz
Mendel Grossbaum
Rabbi Aron Liberow
Mrs. Chana Weinbaum
ONLINE DIVISION

Mrs. Ya'akovah Weber
LEAD PROOFREADER

Dr. Rakefet Orobona
Ms. Mimi Palace
PROOFREADERS

Rabbi Mendel Sirota
PRINTING AND DISTRIBUTION

Mrs. Musie Liberow
Mrs. Shaina B. Mintz
Mrs. Shulamis Nadler
ACCOUNTING

Rabbi Zalman Abraham
Mrs. Chana Dechter
Mrs. Shulamis Nadler
Mrs. Mindy Wallach
Mr. Yehuda Wengrofsky
DEVELOPMENT

Mrs. Musie Liberow
Mrs. Mindy Wallach
CONTINUING EDUCATION

JLI FLAGSHIP

Rabbi Yisrael Rice
CHAIRMAN

Mrs. Chana Dechter
Mrs. Naomi Heber
PROJECT MANAGER

JLI INTERNATIONAL

Rabbi Avrohom Sternberg
CHAIRMAN

Rabbi Dubi Rabinowitz
DIRECTOR

Rabbi Berry Piekarski
ADMINISTRATOR

Rabbi Eli Wolf
ADMINISTRATOR, JLI IN THE CIS
IN PARTNERSHIP WITH
THE FEDERATION OF JEWISH
COMMUNITIES OF THE CIS

Rabbi Shevach Zlatopolsky
EDITOR, JLI IN THE CIS

Rabbi Nochum Schapiro
REGIONAL REPRESENTATIVE,
AUSTRALIA

Rabbi Avraham Golovacheov
REGIONAL REPRESENTATIVE,
GERMANY

Rabbi Shmuel Katzman
REGIONAL REPRESENTATIVE,
NETHERLANDS

Rabbi Avrohom Steinmetz
REGIONAL REPRESENTATIVE,
BRAZIL

Rabbi Bentzi Sudak
REGIONAL REPRESENTATIVE,
UNITED KINGDOM

Rabbi Shlomo Cohen
FRENCH COORDINATOR,
REGIONAL REPRESENTATIVE

NATIONAL JEWISH RETREAT

Rabbi Hesh Epstein
CHAIRMAN

Mrs. Shaina B. Mintz
DIRECTOR

Bruce Backman
HOTEL LIAISON

Rabbi Menachem Klein
PROGRAM COORDINATOR

Rabbi Shmuly Karp
SHLUCHIM LIAISON

Rabbi Mendel Rosenfeld
LOGISTICS COORDINATOR

Ms. Rochel Karp
Mrs. Aliza Scheinfeld
SERVICE AND SUPPORT

JLI LAND & SPIRIT
ISRAEL EXPERIENCE

Rabbi Shmuly Karp
DIRECTOR

Mrs. Shaina B. Mintz
ADMINISTRATOR

Rabbi Yechiel Baitelman
Rabbi Dovid Flinkenstein
Rabbi Chanoch Kaplan
Rabbi Levi Klein
Rabbi Mendy Mangel
Rabbi Sholom Raichik
STEERING COMMITTEE

SHABBAT IN THE HEIGHTS

Rabbi Shmuly Karp
DIRECTOR

Mrs. Shulamis Nadler
SERVICE AND SUPPORT

Rabbi Chaim Hanoka
CHAIRMAN

Rabbi Mordechai Dinerman
Rabbi Zalman Marcus
STEERING COMMITTEE

MYSHIUR
ADVANCED LEARNING INITIATIVE

Rabbi Shmuel Kaplan
CHAIRMAN

Rabbi Shlomie Tenenbaum
ADMINISTRATOR

TORAHCAFE.COM
ONLINE LEARNING

Rabbi Mendy Elishevitz
WEBSITE DEVELOPMENT

Moshe Levin
CONTENT MANAGER

Mendel Laine
FILMING

MACHON SHMUEL
THE SAMI ROHR RESEARCH INSTITUTE

Rabbi Zalman Korf
ADMINISTRATOR

Rabbi Gedalya Oberlander
Rabbi Chaim Rapoport
Rabbi Levi Yitzchak Raskin
Rabbi Chaim Schapiro
Rabbi Moshe Miller
RABBINIC ADVISORY BOARD

Rabbi Yakov Gershon
RESEARCH FELLOW

FOUNDING DEPARTMENT HEADS

Rabbi Mendel Bell
Rabbi Zalman Charytan
Rabbi Mendel Druk
Rabbi Menachem Gansburg
Rabbi Meir Hecht
Rabbi Levi Kaplan
Rabbi Yoni Katz
Rabbi Chaim Zalman Levy
Rabbi Benny Rapoport
Dr. Chana Silberstein
Rabbi Elchonon Tenenbaum
Rabbi Mendy Weg

FACULTY DIRECTORY

ALABAMA

BIRMINGHAM
Rabbi Yossi Friedman 205.970.0100

MOBILE
Rabbi Yosef Goldwasser 251.265.1213

ALASKA

ANCHORAGE
Rabbi Yosef Greenberg
Rabbi Mendy Greenberg 907.357.8770

ARIZONA

CHANDLER
Rabbi Mendy Deitsch 480.855.4333

FLAGSTAFF
Rabbi Dovie Shapiro 928.255.5756

FOUNTAIN HILLS
Rabbi Mendy Lipskier 480.776.4763

ORO VALLEY
Rabbi Ephraim Zimmerman 520.477.8672

PHOENIX
Rabbi Zalman Levertov
Rabbi Yossi Friedman 602.944.2753

SCOTTSDALE
Rabbi Yossi Levertov 480.998.1410

TUCSON
Rabbi Yehuda Ceitlin 520.881.7956

ARKANSAS

LITTLE ROCK
Rabbi Pinchus Ciment 501.217.0053

CALIFORNIA

AGOURA HILLS
Rabbi Moshe Bryski
Rabbi Yisroel Levine 818.991.0991

ALAMEDA
Rabbi Meir Shmotkin 510.640.2590

BAKERSFIELD
Rabbi Shmuli Schlanger
Mrs. Esther Schlanger 661.331.1695

BEL AIR
Rabbi Chaim Mentz 310.475.5311

BURBANK
Rabbi Shmuly Kornfeld 818.954.0070

CARLSBAD
Rabbi Yeruchem Eilfort
Mrs. Nechama Eilfort 760.943.8891

CHATSWORTH
Rabbi Yossi Spritzer 818.718.0777

CONTRA COSTA
Rabbi Dovber Berkowitz 925.937.4101

CORONADO
Rabbi Eli Fradkin 619.365.4728

DANVILLE
Rabbi Shmuli Raitman 213.447.6694

ENCINO
Rabbi Aryeh Herzog 818.784.9986
Chapter founded by Rabbi Joshua Gordon, OBM

FOLSOM
Rabbi Yossi Grossbaum 916.608.9811

FREMONT
Rabbi Moshe Fuss 510.300.4090

GLENDALE
Rabbi Simcha Backman 818.240.2750

HUNTINGTON BEACH
Rabbi Aron David Berkowitz 714.846.2285

LA JOLLA
Rabbi Baruch Shalom Ezagui 858.455.5433

LAGUNA BEACH
Rabbi Elimelech Gurevitch 949.499.0770

LAGUNA NIGUEL
Rabbi Mendy Paltiel 949.831.8475

LOMITA
Rabbi Eli Hecht
Rabbi Sholom Pinson 310.326.8234

LONG BEACH
Rabbi Abba Perelmuter 562.621.9828

LOS ANGELES
Rabbi Leibel Korf 323.660.5177
Rabbi Dovid Liberow 424.261.8770

MALIBU
Rabbi Levi Cunin 310.456.6588

MARINA DEL REY
Rabbi Danny Yiftach-Hashem
Rabbi Dovid Yiftach 310.859.0770

NEWHALL
Rabbi Choni Marosov 661.254.3434

NORTH HOLLYWOOD
Rabbi Nachman Abend 818.989.9539

NORTHRIDGE
Rabbi Eli Rivkin 818.368.3937

OJAI
Rabbi Mordechai Nemtzov 805.613.7181

PACIFIC PALISADES
Rabbi Zushe Cunin 310.454.7783

PALO ALTO
Rabbi Menachem Landa 415.418.4768
Rabbi Yosef Levin
Rabbi Ber Rosenblatt 650.424.9800

PASADENA
Rabbi Chaim Hanoka
Rabbi Sholom Stiefel 626.539.4578

PLEASANTON
Rabbi Josh Zebberman 925.846.0700

POWAY
Rabbi Mendel Goldstein 858.208.6613

RANCHO CUCAMONGA
Rabbi Sholom B. Harlig 909.949.4553

RANCHO MIRAGE
Rabbi Shimon H. Posner 760.770.7785

RANCHO PALOS VERDES
Rabbi Yitzchok Magalnic 310.544.5544

RANCHO S. FE
Rabbi Levi Raskin 858.756.7571

REDONDO BEACH
Rabbi Yossi Mintz
Rabbi Zalman Gordon 310.214.4999

RIVERSIDE
Rabbi Shmuel Fuss 951.329.2747

S. CLEMENTE
Rabbi Menachem M. Slavin 949.489.0723

S. CRUZ
Rabbi Yochanan Friedman 831.454.0101

S. DIEGO
Rabbi Rafi Andrusier 619.387.8770
Rabbi Motte Fradkin 858.547.0076

S. FRANCISCO
Rabbi Gedalia Potash 415.648.8000
Rabbi Shlomo Zarchi 415.752.2866

S. MATEO
Rabbi Yossi Marcus 650.341.4510

S. MONICA
Rabbi Boruch Rabinowitz 310.394.5699

S. RAFAEL
Rabbi Yisrael Rice 415.492.1666

SOUTH LAKE TAHOE
Rabbi Mordechai Richler 530.314.7677

SUNNYVALE
Rabbi Yisroel Hecht 408.720.0553

TEMECULA
Rabbi Yonason Abrams 951.234.4196

THOUSAND OAKS
Rabbi Chaim Bryski 805.370.5770

TUSTIN
Rabbi Yehoshua Eliezrie 714.508.2150

UNIVERSITY CITY
Rabbi Yechiel Cagen 832.691.1825

VENTURA
Rabbi Yakov Latowicz 805.658.7441

WEST HILLS
Rabbi Avi Rabin 818.337.4544

WEST HOLLYWOOD
Rabbi Mordechai Kirschenbaum 310.275.1215

WEST LOS ANGELES
Rabbi Mordechai Zaetz 424.652.8742

YORBA LINDA
Rabbi Dovid Eliezrie 714.693.0770

COLORADO

ASPEN
Rabbi Mendel Mintz 970.544.3770

AURORA
Rabbi David Araiev 720.388.2704

DENVER
Rabbi Mendel Popack 720.515.4337
Rabbi Yossi Serebryanski 303.744.9699
Rabbi Mendy Sirota 720.940.3716

FORT COLLINS
Rabbi Yerachmiel Gorelik 970.407.1613

HIGHLANDS RANCH
Rabbi Avraham Mintz 303.694.9119

LONGMONT
Rabbi Yakov Borenstein 303.678.7595

VAIL
Rabbi Dovid Mintz 970.476.7887

WESTMINSTER
Rabbi Benjy Brackman 303.429.5177

CONNECTICUT

FAIRFIELD
Rabbi Shlame Landa 203.373.7551

GLASTONBURY
Rabbi Yosef Wolvovsky 860.659.2422

GREENWICH
Rabbi Yossi Deren
Rabbi Menachem Feldman 203.629.9059

MILFORD
Rabbi Schneur Wilhelm 203.887.7603

NEW HAVEN
Rabbi Mendy Hecht 203.589.5375

NEW LONDON
Rabbi Avrohom Sternberg 860.437.8000

STAMFORD
Rabbi Yisrael Deren
Rabbi Levi Mendelow 203.3.CHABAD

WEST HARTFORD
Rabbi Shaya Gopin 860.232.1116

WESTPORT
Rabbi Yehuda L. Kantor 203.226.8584

DELAWARE

WILMINGTON
Rabbi Chuni Vogel 302.529.9900

DISTRICT OF COLUMBIA

WASHINGTON
Rabbi Levi Shemtov
Rabbi Yitzy Ceitlin 202.332.5600

FLORIDA

ALTAMONTE SPRINGS
Rabbi Mendy Bronstein 407.280.0535

BAL HARBOUR
Rabbi Dov Schochet 305.868.1411

BOCA RATON
Rabbi Zalman Bukiet
Rabbi Arele Gopin 561.994.6257
Rabbi Moishe Denburg 561.526.5760
Rabbi Ruvi New 561.394.9770

BONITA SPRINGS
Rabbi Mendy Greenberg 239.949.6900

BOYNTON BEACH
Rabbi Yosef Yitzchok Raichik 561.732.4633

BRADENTON
Rabbi Menachem Bukiet 941.388.9656

CAPE CORAL
Rabbi Yossi Labkowski 239.963.4770

CORAL GABLES
Rabbi Avrohom Stolik 305.490.7572

CORAL SPRINGS
Rabbi Yankie Denburg 954.471.8646

CUTLER BAY
Rabbi Yossi Wolff 305.975.6680

DAVIE
Rabbi Aryeh Schwartz 954.376.9973

DELRAY BEACH
Rabbi Sholom Ber Korf 561.496.6228

FISHER ISLAND
Rabbi Efraim Brody 347.325.1913

FLEMING ISLAND
Rabbi Shmuly Feldman 904.290.1017

FORT LAUDERDALE
Rabbi Yitzchok Naparstek 954.568.1190

FORT MYERS
Rabbi Yitzchok Minkowicz
Mrs. Nechama Minkowicz 239.433.7708

HALLANDALE BEACH
Rabbi Mordy Feiner 954.458.1877

HOLLYWOOD
Rabbi Leizer Barash 954.965.9933
Rabbi Leibel Kudan 954.801.3367

KENDALL
Rabbi Yossi Harlig 305.234.5654

KEY WEST
Rabbi Yaakov Zucker 305.304.7713

LAKELAND
Rabbi Moshe Lazaros 863.510.5968

LONGWOOD
Rabbi Yanky Majesky 407.636.5994

MAITLAND
Rabbi Sholom Dubov
Rabbi Levik Dubov 470.644.2500

MIAMI
Rabbi Mendy Cheruty 305.219.3353
Rabbi Yakov Fellig 305.445.5444

MIAMI BEACH
Rabbi Yisroel Frankforter 305.534.3895

N. MIAMI BEACH
Rabbi Eli Laufer 305.770.4412

OCALA
Rabbi Yossi Hecht 352.330.4466

ORLANDO
Rabbi Yosef Konikov 407.354.3660

ORMOND BEACH
Rabbi Asher Farkash 386.672.9300

PALM BEACH
Rabbi Zalman Levitin 561.659.3884

PALM BEACH GARDENS
Rabbi Dovid Vigler 561.624.2223

PALM CITY
Rabbi Shlomo Uminer 772.288.0606

PALM HARBOR
Rabbi Pinchas Adler 727.789.0408

PALMETTO BAY
Rabbi Zalman Gansburg 786.282.0413

PARKLAND
Rabbi Mendy Gutnick 954.796.7330

PEMBROKE PINES
Rabbi Mordechai Andrusier 954.874.2280

PLANTATION
Rabbi Pinchas Taylor 954.644.9177

PONTE VEDRA BEACH
Rabbi Nochum Kurinsky 904.543.9301

S. AUGUSTINE
Rabbi Levi Vogel 904.521.8664

S. PETERSBURG
Rabbi Alter Korf 727.344.4900

SARASOTA
Rabbi Chaim Shaul Steinmetz 941.925.0770

SATELLITE BEACH
Rabbi Zvi Konikov 321.777.2770

SINGER ISLAND
Rabbi Berel Namdar 347.276.6985

SOUTH PALM BEACH
Rabbi Leibel Stolik 561.889.3499

SOUTH TAMPA
Rabbi Mendy Dubrowski 813.922.1723

SOUTHWEST BROWARD COUNTY
Rabbi Aryeh Schwartz 954.252.1770

SUNNY ISLES BEACH
Rabbi Alexander Kaller 305.803.5315

VENICE
Rabbi Sholom Ber Schmerling 941.493.2770

WELLINGTON
Rabbi Mendy Muskal 561.386.3090

WESLEY CHAPEL
Rabbi Mendy Yarmush
Rabbi Mendel Friedman 813.731.2977

WEST PALM BEACH
Rabbi Yoel Gancz 561.659.7770

WESTON
Rabbi Yisroel Spalter 954.349.6565

GEORGIA

ALPHARETTA
Rabbi Hirshy Minkowicz 770.410.9000

ATLANTA
Rabbi Yossi New
Rabbi Isser New 404.843.2464
Rabbi Alexander Piekarski 678.267.6418

ATLANTA: INTOWN
Rabbi Eliyahu Schusterman
Rabbi Ari Sollish 404.898.0434

CUMMING
Rabbi Levi Mentz 310.666.2218

GWINNETT
Rabbi Yossi Lerman 678.595.0196

MARIETTA
Rabbi Ephraim Silverman 770.565.4412

HAWAII

KAPA'A
Rabbi Michoel Goldman 808.647.4293

IDAHO

BOISE
Rabbi Mendel Lifshitz 208.853.9200

ILLINOIS

CHAMPAIGN
Rabbi Dovid Tiechtel 217.355.8672

CHICAGO
Rabbi Mendy Benhiyoun 312.498.7704
Rabbi Meir Hecht 312.714.4655
Rabbi Dovid Kotlarsky 773.495.7127
Rabbi Yosef Moscowitz 773.772.3770
Rabbi Levi Notik 773.274.5123

DES PLAINES
Rabbi Lazer Hershkovich 224.392.4442

ELGIN
Rabbi Mendel Shemtov 847.440.4486

GLENVIEW
Rabbi Yishaya Benjaminson 847.910.1738

GRAYSLAKE
Rabbi Sholom Tenenbaum 847.782.1800

HIGHLAND PARK
Mrs. Michla Schanowitz 847.266.0770

NAPERVILLE
Rabbi Mendy Goldstein 630.778.9770

NORTHBROOK
Rabbi Meir Moscowitz 847.564.8770

OAK PARK
Rabbi Yitzchok Bergstein 708.524.1530

PEORIA
Rabbi Eli Langsam 309.692.2250

SKOKIE
Rabbi Yochanan Posner 847.677.1770

VERNON HILLS
Rabbi Shimmy Susskind 847.984.2919

WILMETTE
Rabbi Dovid Flinkenstein 847.251.7707

INDIANA

INDIANAPOLIS
Rabbi Avraham Grossbaum
Rabbi Dr. Shmuel Klatzkin 317.251.5573

IOWA

BETTENDORF
Rabbi Shneur Cadaner 563.355.1065

KANSAS

OVERLAND PARK
Rabbi Mendy Wineberg................913.649.4852

KENTUCKY

LOUISVILLE
Rabbi Avrohom Litvin................502.459.1770

LOUISIANA

BATON ROUGE
Rabbi Peretz Kazen................225.267.7047

METAIRIE
Rabbi Yossie Nemes
Rabbi Mendel Ceitlin................504.454.2910

NEW ORLEANS
Rabbi Mendel Rivkin................504.302.1830

MAINE

PORTLAND
Rabbi Levi Wilansky................207.650.1783

MARYLAND

BALTIMORE
Rabbi Velvel Belinsky................410.764.5000
Classes in Russian

BEL AIR
Rabbi Kushi Schusterman................443.353.9718

BETHESDA
Rabbi Sender Geisinsky................301.913.9777

CHEVY CHASE
Rabbi Zalman Minkowitz................301.260.5000

COLUMBIA
Rabbi Hillel Baron
Rabbi Yosef Chaim Sufrin................410.740.2424

FREDERICK
Rabbi Boruch Labkowski................301.996.3659

GAITHERSBURG
Rabbi Sholom Raichik................301.926.3632

OLNEY
Rabbi Bentzy Stolik................301.660.6770

OWINGS MILLS
Rabbi Nochum H. Katsenelenbogen................410.356.5156

POTOMAC
Rabbi Mendel Bluming................301.983.4200
Rabbi Mendel Kaplan................301.983.1485

ROCKVILLE
Rabbi Shlomo Beitsh................646.773.2675
Rabbi Moishe Kavka................301.836.1242
Rabbi Levi Raskin................240.444.3345

MASSACHUSETTS

ANDOVER
Rabbi Asher Bronstein................978.470.2288

BOSTON
Rabbi Yosef Zaklos................617.297.7282

BRIGHTON
Rabbi Dan Rodkin................617.787.2200

CAPE COD
Rabbi Yekusiel Alperowitz................508.775.2324

HINGHAM
Rabbi Levi Lezell................617.862.2770

LONGMEADOW
Rabbi Yakov Wolff................413.567.8665

NEWTON
Rabbi Shalom Ber Prus................617.244.1200

SUDBURY
Rabbi Yisroel Freeman................978.443.0110

SWAMPSCOTT
Rabbi Yossi Lipsker................781.581.3833

MICHIGAN

ANN ARBOR
Rabbi Aharon Goldstein................734.995.3276

BLOOMFIELD HILLS
Rabbi Levi Dubov................248.949.6210

GRAND RAPIDS
Rabbi Mordechai Haller................616.957.0770

WEST BLOOMFIELD
Rabbi Elimelech Silberberg................248.855.6170

MINNESOTA

MINNETONKA
Rabbi Mordechai Grossbaum
Rabbi Shmuel Silberstein 952.929.9922

S. PAUL
Rabbi Shneur Zalman Bendet 651.998.9298

MISSOURI

S. LOUIS
Rabbi Yosef Landa 314.725.0400

NEVADA

LAS VEGAS
Rabbi Yosef Rivkin 702.217.2170

SUMMERLIN
Rabbi Yisroel Schanowitz
Rabbi Tzvi Bronchtain 702.855.0770

NEW JERSEY

BASKING RIDGE
Rabbi Mendy Herson
Rabbi Mendel Shemtov 908.604.8844

CHERRY HILL
Rabbi Mendel Mangel 856.874.1500

CLINTON
Rabbi Eli Kornfeld 908.623.7000

ENGLEWOOD
Rabbi Shmuel Konikov 201.519.7343

FAIR LAWN
Rabbi Avrohom Bergstein 201.362.2712

FORT LEE
Rabbi Meir Konikov 201.886.1238

FRANKLIN LAKES
Rabbi Chanoch Kaplan 201.848.0449

GREATER MERCER COUNTY
Rabbi Dovid Dubov
Rabbi Yaakov Chaiton 609.213.4136

HASKELL
Rabbi Mendy Gurkov 201.696.7609

HOLMDEL
Rabbi Shmaya Galperin 732.772.1998

MADISON
Rabbi Shalom Lubin 973.377.0707

MANALAPAN
Rabbi Boruch Chazanow
Rabbi Levi Wolosow 732.972.3687

MEDFORD
Rabbi Yitzchok Kahan 609.451.3522

MOUNTAIN LAKES
Rabbi Levi Dubinsky 973.551.1898

MULLICA HILL
Rabbi Avrohom Richler 856.733.0770

OLD TAPPAN
Rabbi Mendy Lewis 201.767.4008

RED BANK
Rabbi Dovid Harrison 718.915.8748

ROCKAWAY
Rabbi Asher Herson
Rabbi Mordechai Baumgarten 973.625.1525

RUTHERFORD
Rabbi Yitzchok Lerman 347.834.7500

SCOTCH PLAINS
Rabbi Avrohom Blesofsky 908.790.0008

SHORT HILLS
Rabbi Mendel Solomon
Rabbi Avrohom Levin 973.725.7008

SOUTH BRUNSWICK
Rabbi Levi Azimov 732.398.9492

TEANECK
Rabbi Ephraim Simon 201.907.0686

TENAFLY
Rabbi Mordechai Shain 201.871.1152

TOMS RIVER
Rabbi Moshe Gourarie 732.349.4199

VENTNOR
Rabbi Avrohom Rapoport 609.822.8500

WAYNE
Rabbi Michel Gurkov 973.694.6274

WEST ORANGE
Rabbi Mendy Kasowitz 973.325.6311

WOODCLIFF LAKE
Rabbi Dov Drizin 201.476.0157

NEW MEXICO

LAS CRUCES
Rabbi Bery Schmukler...................................575.524.1330

S. FE
Rabbi Berel Levertov...................................505.983.2000

NEW YORK

BAY SHORE
Rabbi Shimon Stillerman...................................631.913.8770

BEDFORD
Rabbi Arik Wolf...................................914.666.6065

BINGHAMTON
Mrs. Rivkah Slonim...................................607.797.0015

BRIGHTON BEACH
Rabbi Moshe Winner...................................718.946.9833

BRONXVILLE
Rabbi Sruli Deitsch...................................917.755.0078

BROOKLYN
Rabbi Nissi Eber...................................347.677.2276
Rabbi Dovid Okonov...................................917.754.6942

BROOKVILLE
Rabbi Mendy Heber...................................516.626.0600

CEDARHURST
Rabbi Zalman Wolowik...................................516.295.2478

COMMACK
Rabbi Mendel Teldon...................................631.543.3343

DIX HILLS
Rabbi Yaakov Saacks...................................631.351.8672

DOBBS FERRY
Rabbi Benjy Silverman...................................914.693.6100

EAST HAMPTON
Rabbi Leibel Baumgarten
Rabbi Mendy Goldberg...................................631.329.5800

ELLENVILLE
Rabbi Shlomie Deren...................................845.647.4450

FOREST HILLS
Rabbi Yossi Mendelson...................................917.861.9726

GREAT NECK
Rabbi Yoseph Geisinsky...................................516.487.4554

KINGSTON
Rabbi Yitzchok Hecht...................................845.334.9044

LARCHMONT
Rabbi Mendel Silberstein...................................914.834.4321

LITTLE NECK
Rabbi Eli Shifrin...................................718.423.1235

LONG BEACH
Rabbi Eli Goodman...................................516.897.2473

MONTEBELLO
Rabbi Shmuel Gancz...................................845.746.1927

NYACK
Rabbi Chaim Zvi Ehrenreich...................................845.356.6686

NYC KEHILATH JESHURUN
Rabbi Elie Weinstock...................................212.774.5636

NYC TRIBECA
Rabbi Zalman Paris...................................212.566.6764

NYC UPPER EAST SIDE
Rabbi Uriel Vigler...................................212.369.7310

NYC UPPER WEST SIDE
Rabbi Shlomo Kugel...................................212.864.5010

OCEANSIDE
Rabbi Levi Gurkow...................................516.764.7385

OSSINING
Rabbi Dovid Labkowski...................................914.923.2522

OYSTER BAY
Rabbi Shmuel Lipszyc
Rabbi Shalom Lipszyc...................................347.853.9992

PARK SLOPE
Rabbi Menashe Wolf...................................347.957.1291

PORT WASHINGTON
Rabbi Shalom Paltiel...................................516.767.8672

PROSPECT HEIGHTS
Rabbi Mendy Hecht...................................347.622.3599

ROCHESTER
Rabbi Nechemia Vogel...................................585.271.0330

ROSLYN
Rabbi Yaakov Reiter...................................516.484.8185

SEA GATE
Rabbi Chaim Brikman...................................917.975.2792

SOUTHAMPTON
Rabbi Chaim Pape...................................917.627.4865

STATEN ISLAND
Rabbi Mendy Katzman 718.370.8953

STONY BROOK
Rabbi Shalom Ber Cohen 631.585.0521

SUFFERN
Rabbi Shmuel Gancz 845.368.1889

YORKTOWN HEIGHTS
Rabbi Yehuda Heber 914.962.1111

NORTH CAROLINA

ASHEVILLE
Rabbi Shaya Susskind 828.505.0746

CARY
Rabbi Yisroel Cotlar 919.651.9710

CHARLOTTE
Rabbi Yossi Groner
Rabbi Shlomo Cohen 704.366.3984

GREENSBORO
Rabbi Yosef Plotkin 336.617.8120

RALEIGH
Rabbi Pinchas Herman
Rabbi Lev Cotlar 919.637.6950

OHIO

BEACHWOOD
Rabbi Shmuli Friedman 216.282.0112

CINCINNATI
Rabbi Yisroel Mangel 513.793.5200

COLUMBUS
Rabbi Yitzi Kaltmann 614.294.3296

DAYTON
Rabbi Nochum Mangel
Rabbi Shmuel Klatzkin 937.643.0770

OKLAHOMA

OKLAHOMA CITY
Rabbi Ovadia Goldman 405.524.4800

TULSA
Rabbi Yehuda Weg 918.492.4499

OREGON

PORTLAND
Rabbi Chaim Wilhelm 503.309.4490
Rabbi Mordechai Wilhelm 503.977.9947

SALEM
Rabbi Avrohom Yitzchok Perlstein 503.383.9569

PENNSYLVANIA

AMBLER
Rabbi Shaya Deitsch 215.591.9310

BALA CYNWYD
Rabbi Shraga Sherman 610.660.9192

DOYLESTOWN
Rabbi Mendel Prus 215.340.1303

LAFAYETTE HILL
Rabbi Yisroel Kotlarsky 484.533.7009

LANCASTER
Rabbi Elazar Green 717.368.6565

MONROEVILLE
Rabbi Mendy Schapiro 412.372.1000

NEWTOWN
Rabbi Aryeh Weinstein 215.497.9925

PHILADELPHIA: CENTER CITY
Rabbi Yochonon Goldman 215.238.2100

PITTSBURGH
Rabbi Yisroel Altein .... 412.422.7300 EXT. 269

PITTSBURGH: SOUTH HILLS
Rabbi Mendy Rosenblum 412.278.3693

READING
Rabbi Yosef Lipsker 610.921.1522

RYDAL
Rabbi Zushe Gurevitz 267.536.5757

WYNNEWOOD
Rabbi Moishe Brennan 610.529.9011

PUERTO RICO

CAROLINA
Rabbi Mendel Zarchi 787.253.0894

RHODE ISLAND

LINCOLN
Rabbi Aryeh Laufer 401.499.2574

WARWICK
Rabbi Yossi Laufer 401.884.7888

SOUTH CAROLINA

COLUMBIA
Rabbi Hesh Epstein
Rabbi Levi Marrus 803.782.1831

GREENVILLE
Rabbi Leibel Kesselman 864.256.1770

MYRTLE BEACH
Rabbi Doron Aizenman 843.385.2240

TENNESSEE

CHATTANOOGA
Rabbi Shaul Perlstein 423.490.1106

KNOXVILLE
Rabbi Yossi Wilhelm 865.588.8584

MEMPHIS
Rabbi Levi Klein 901.754.0404

TEXAS

AUSTIN
Rabbi Mendy Levertov 512.905.2778

BELLAIRE
Rabbi Yossi Zaklikofsky 713.839.8887

DALLAS
Rabbi Mendel Dubrawsky
Rabbi Moshe Naparstek 972.818.0770

EL PASO
Levi Greenberg 347.678.9762

FORT WORTH
Rabbi Dov Mandel 817.263.7701

FRISCO
Rabbi Mendy Kesselman 214.460.7773

HOUSTON
Rabbi Dovid Goldstein
Rabbi Zally Lazarus 281.589.7188
Rabbi Moishe Traxler 713.774.0300

HOUSTON: RICE UNIVERSITY AREA
Rabbi Eliezer Lazaroff 713.522.2004

LEAGUE CITY
Rabbi Yitzchok Schmukler 281.724.1554

MISSOURI CITY
Rabbi Mendel Feigenson 832.758.0685

PLANO
Rabbi Mendel Block
Rabbi Yehudah Horowitz 972.596.8270

S. ANTONIO
Rabbi Chaim Block
Rabbi Levi Teldon 210.492.1085
Rabbi Tal Shaul 210.877.4218

SOUTHLAKE
Rabbi Levi Gurevitch 817.451.1171

THE WOODLANDS
Rabbi Mendel Blecher 281.719.5213

UTAH

SALT LAKE CITY
Rabbi Benny Zippel 801.467.7777

VERMONT

BURLINGTON
Rabbi Yitzchok Raskin 802.658.5770

VIRGINIA

ALEXANDRIA/ARLINGTON
Rabbi Mordechai Newman 703.370.2774

FAIRFAX
Rabbi Leibel Fajnland 703.426.1980

GAINESVILLE
Rabbi Shmuel Perlstein 571.445.0342

LOUDOUN COUNTY
Rabbi Chaim Cohen 248.298.9279

NORFOLK
Rabbi Aaron Margolin
Rabbi Levi Brashevitzky 757.616.0770

RICHMOND
Rabbi Shlomo Pereira 804.740.2000

TYSONS CORNER
Rabbi Chezzy Deitsch 703.829.5770
Chapter founded by Rabbi Levi Deitsch, OBM

WASHINGTON

BELLINGHAM
Rabbi Yosef Truxton 360.224.9919

MERCER ISLAND
Rabbi Elazar Bogomilsky 206.527.1411
Rabbi Nissan Kornfeld 206.851.2324

OLYMPIA
Rabbi Yosef Schtroks 360.867.8804

SPOKANE COUNTY
Rabbi Yisroel Hahn 509.443.0770

WISCONSIN

BAYSIDE
Rabbi Cheski Edelman 414.439.5041

KENOSHA
Rabbi Tzali Wilschanski 262.359.0770

MADISON
Rabbi Avremel Matusof 608.231.3450

MEQUON
Rabbi Menachem Rapoport 262.242.2235

MILWAUKEE
Rabbi Levi Emmer 414.277.8839
Rabbi Mendel Shmotkin 414.961.6100

WAUKESHA
Rabbi Levi Brook 925.708.4203

ARGENTINA

BUENOS AIRES
Mrs. Chani Gorowitz 54.11.4865.0445
Rabbi Menachem M. Grunblatt 54.911.3574.0037
Rabbi Mendi Mizrahi 54.11.4963.1221
Rabbi Mendy Gurevitch 55.11.4545.7771
Rabbi Pinhas Sudry 54.1.4822.2285
Rabbi Shloimi Setton 54.11.4982.8637
Rabbi Shiele Plotka 54.11.4634.3111
Rabbi Yosef Levy 54.11.4504.1908

CORDOBA
Rabbi Menajem Turk 54.351.233.8250

SALTA
Rabbi Rafael Tawil 54.387.421.4947

S. MIGUEL DE TUCUMÁN
Rabbi Ariel Levy 54.381.473.6944

AUSTRALIA

NEW SOUTH WALES

DOUBLE BAY
Rabbi Yanky Berger 612.9327.1644

DOVER HEIGHTS
Rabbi Motti Feldman 614.0400.8572

NORTH SHORE
Rabbi Nochum Schapiro
Rebbetzin Fruma Schapiro 612.9488.9548

QUEENSLAND

BRISBANE
Rabbi Levi Jaffe 617.3843.6770

VICTORIA

CAULFIELD
Rabbi Mendel Groner 613.9532.7299

MOORABBIN
Rabbi Elisha Greenbaum 614.0349.0434

WESTERN AUSTRALIA

PERTH
Rabbi Shalom White 618.9275.2106

AZERBAIJAN

BAKU
Mrs. Chavi Segal................................994.12.597.91.90

BELARUS

BOBRUISK
Mrs. Mina Hababo.............................375.29.104.3230

MINSK
Rabbi Shneur Deitsch
Mrs. Bassie Deitsch...........................375.29.330.6675

BELGIUM

BRUSSELS
Rabbi Shmuel Pinson.........................375.29.330.6675

BRAZIL

CURITIBA
Rabbi Mendy Labkowski.....................55.41.3079.1338

S. PAULO
Rabbi Avraham Steinmetz...................55.11.3081.3081

CANADA

ALBERTA

CALGARY
Rabbi Mordechai Groner....................403.281.3770

EDMONTON
Rabbi Ari Drelich
Rabbi Mendy Blachman......................780.200.5770

BRITISH COLUMBIA

KELOWNA
Rabbi Shmuly Hecht..........................250.575.5384

RICHMOND
Rabbi Yechiel Baitelman.....................604.277.6427

VANCOUVER
Rabbi Dovid Rosenfeld.......................604.266.1313

VICTORIA
Rabbi Meir Kaplan............................250.595.7656

MANITOBA

WINNIPEG
Rabbi Shmuel Altein..........................204.339.8737

ONTARIO

LAWRENCE/EGLINTON
Rabbi Menachem Gansburg..................416.546.8770

MAPLE
Rabbi Yechezkel Deren.......................647.883.6372

MISSISSAUGA
Rabbi Yitzchok Slavin........................905.820.4432

NIAGARA FALLS
Rabbi Zalman Zaltzman......................905.356.7200

OTTAWA
Rabbi Menachem M. Blum...................613.843.7770

RICHMOND HILL
Rabbi Mendel Bernstein......................905.770.7700

THORNHILL
Rabbi Yisroel Landa..........................416.897.3338
Rabbi Moishe Schurder......................647.770.9351

THORNHILL WOODS
Rabbi Chaim Hildeshaim.....................905.881.1919

TORONTO AREA
Rabbi Sholom Lezell..........................416.809.1365

GREATER TORONTO REGIONAL OFFICE & THORNHILL
Rabbi Yossi Gansburg........................905.731.7000

WATERLOO
Rabbi Moshe Goldman.......................226.338.7770

YORK MILLS
Rabbi Levi Gansburg.........................416.551.9391

QUEBEC

CÔTE S.-LUC
Rabbi Levi Naparstek.........................438.409.6770

HAMPSTEAD
Rabbi Moshe New
Rabbi Berel Bell...............................514.739.0770

MONTREAL
Rabbi Ronnie Fine
Pesach Nussbaum.............................514.738.3434

OLD MONTREAL/GRIFFINTOWN
Rabbi Nissan Gansbourg
Rabbi Berel Bell...............................514.800.6966

S. LAZARE
Rabbi Nochum Labkowski..............514.436.7426

TOWN OF MOUNT ROYAL
Rabbi Moshe Krasnanski
Rabbi Shneur Zalman Rader..............514.342.1770

WESTMOUNT
Rabbi Yossi Shanowitz
Mrs. Devorah Leah Shanowitz..............514.937.4772

SASKATCHEWAN

SASKATOON
Rabbi Raphael Kats..............306.384.4370

CAYMAN ISLANDS

GRAND CAYMAN
Rabbi Berel Pewzner..............717.798.1040

COLOMBIA

BOGOTA
Rabbi Chanoch Piekarski..............57.1.635.8251

COSTA RICA

S. JOSÉ
Rabbi Hershel Spalter
Rabbi Moshe Bitton..............506.4010.1515

CROATIA

ZAGREB
Rabbi Pinchas Zaklas..............385.1.4812227

DENMARK

COPENHAGEN
Rabbi Yitzchok Loewenthal..............45.3316.1850

DOMINICAN REPUBLIC

S. DOMINGO
Rabbi Shimon Pelman..............829.341.2770

ESTONIA

TALLINN
Rabbi Shmuel Kot..............372.662.30.50

FRANCE

BOULOGNE
Rabbi Michael Sojcher..............33.1.46.99.87.85

DIJON
Rabbi Chaim Slonim..............33.6.52.05.26.65

LA VARENNE-S.-HILAIRE
Rabbi Mena'hem Mendel Benelbaz..............33.6.17.81.57.47

MARSEILLE
Rabbi Eliahou Altabe..............33.6.11.60.03.05
Rabbi Mena'hem Mendel Assouline..............33.6.64.88.25.04
Rabbi Emmanuel Taubenblatt..............33.4.88.00.94.85

PARIS
Rabbi Yona Hasky..............33.1.53.75.36.01
Rabbi Acher Marciano..............33.6.15.15.01.02
Rabbi Avraham Barou'h Pevzner..............33.6.99.64.07.70

PONTAULT-COMBAULT
Rabbi Yossi Amar..............33.6.61.36.07.70

SEINE-ET-MARNE
Rabbi Yossi Amar..............33.1.60.29.50.17

VILLIERS-SUR-MARNE
Rabbi Mena'hem Mendel Mergui..............33.1.49.30.89.66

GEORGIA

TBILISI
Rabbi Meir Kozlovsky..............995.32.2429770

GERMANY

BERLIN
Rabbi Yehuda Tiechtel..............49.30.2128.0830

DUSSELDORF
Rabbi Chaim Barkahn..............49.173.2871.770

HAMBURG
Rabbi Shlomo Bistritzky..............49.40.4142.4190

HANNOVER..............49.511.811.2822
Chapter founded by Rabbi Binyamin Wolff, OBM

GREECE

ATHENS
Rabbi Mendel Hendel 30.210.323.3825

GUATEMALA

GUATEMALA CITY
Rabbi Shalom Pelman 502.2485.0770

ISRAEL

ASHKELON
Rabbi Shneor Lieberman 054.977.0512

BALFURYA
Rabbi Noam Bar-Tov 054.580.4770

CAESAREA
Rabbi Chaim Meir Lieberman 054.621.2586

EVEN YEHUDA
Rabbi Menachem Noyman 054.777.0707

GANEI TIKVA
Rabbi Gershon Shnur 054.524.2358

GIV'ATAYIM
Rabbi Pinchus Bitton 052.643.8770

JERUSALEM
Rabbi Levi Diamond 055.665.7702
Rabbi Avraham Hendel 054.830.5799

KARMIEL
Rabbi Mendy Elishevitz 054.521.3073

KFAR SABA
Rabbi Yossi Baitch 054.445.5020

KIRYAT BIALIK
Rabbi Pinny Marton 050.661.1768

KIRYAT MOTZKIN
Rabbi Shimon Eizenbach 050.902.0770

KOCHAV YAIR
Rabbi Dovi Greenberg 054.332.6244

MACCABIM-RE'UT
Rabbi Yosef Yitzchak Noiman 054.977.0549

NES ZIYONA
Rabbi Menachem Feldman 054.497.7092

NETANYA
Rabbi Schneur Brod 054.579.7572

RAMAT GAN-KRINITZI
Rabbi Yisroel Gurevitz 052.743.2814

RAMAT GAN-MAROM NAVE
Rabbi Binyamin Meir Kali 050.476.0770

RAMAT YISHAI
Rabbi Shneor Zalman Wolosow 052.324.5475

RISHON LEZION
Rabbi Uri Keshet 050.722.4593

ROSH PINA
Rabbi Sholom Ber Hertzel 052.458.7600

TEL AVIV
Rabbi Shneur Piekarski 054.971.5568

JAPAN

TOKYO
Rabbi Mendi Sudakevich 81.3.5789.2846

KAZAKHSTAN

ALMATY
Rabbi Shevach Zlatopolsky 7.7272.77.59.49

KYRGYZSTAN

BISHKEK
Rabbi Arye Raichman 996.312.68.19.66

LATVIA

RIGA
Rabbi Shneur Zalman Kot
Mrs. Rivka Glazman 371.6720.40.22

LITHUANIA

VILNIUS
Rabb Sholom Ber Krinsky 370.6817.1367

LUXEMBOURG

LUXEMBOURG
Rabbi Mendel Edelman................352.2877.7079

MEXICO

S. MIGUEL DE ALLENDE
Rabbi Daniel Huebner................347.559.1304

NETHERLANDS

ALMERE
Rabbi Moshe Stiefel................31.36.744.0509

AMSTERDAM
Rabbi Yanki Jacobs................31.644.988.627
Rabbi Jaacov Zwi Spiero................31.652.328.065

EINDHOVEN
Rabbi Simcha Steinberg................31.63.635.7593

HAGUE
Rabbi Shmuel Katzman................31.70.347.0222

HEEMSTEDE-HAARLEM
Rabbi Shmuel Spiero................31.23.532.0707

MAASTRICHT
Rabbi Avrohom Cohen................32.48.549.6766

NIJMEGEN
Rabbi Menachem Mendel Levine................31.621.586.575

ROTTERDAM
Rabbi Yehuda Vorst................31.10.265.5530

PANAMA

PANAMA CITY
Rabbi Ari Laine
Rabbi Gabriel Benayon................507.223.3383

RUSSIA

ASTRAKHAN
Rabbi Yisroel Melamed................7.851.239.28.24

BRYANSK
Rabbi Menachem Mendel Zaklas................7.483.264.55.15

CHELYABINSK
Rabbi Meir Kirsh................7.351.263.24.68

MOSCOW
Rabbi Aizik Rosenfeld................7.906.762.88.81
Rabbi Mordechai Weisberg................7.495.645.50.00

NIZHNY NOVGOROD
Rabbi Shimon Bergman................7.920.253.47.70

NOVOSIBIRSK
Rabbi Shneur Zalmen Zaklos................7.903.900.43.22

OMSK
Rabbi Osher Krichevsky................7.381.231.33.07

PERM
Rabbi Zalman Deutch................7.342.212.47.32

ROSTOV
Rabbi Chaim Danzinger................7.8632.99.02.68

S. PETERSBURG
Rabbi Shalom Pewzner................7.911.726.21.19
Rabbi Zvi Pinsky................7.812.713.62.09

SAMARA
Rabbi Shlomo Deutch................7.846.333.40.64

SARATOV
Rabbi Yaakov Kubitshek................7.8452.21.58.00

TOGLIATTI
Rabbi Meier Fischer................7.848.273.02.84

UFA
Rabbi Dan Krichevsky................7.347.244.55.33

VORONEZH
Rabbi Levi Stiefel................7.473.252.96.99

SINGAPORE

SINGAPORE
Rabbi Mordechai Abergel................656.337.2189
Rabbi Netanel Rivni................656.336.2127
Classes in Hebrew

SOUTH AFRICA

CAPE TOWN
Rabbi Levi Popack................27.21.434.3740

JOHANNESBURG
Rabbi Dovid Masinter
Rabbi Ari Kievman................27.11.440.6600

SWITZERLAND

BASEL
Rabbi Zalmen Wishedski........................41.77.958.8418

LUZERN
Rabbi Chaim Drukman............................41.41.361.1770

THAILAND

BANGKOK
Rabbi Yosef C. Kantor...........................6681.837.7618

UKRAINE

BERDITCHEV
Mrs. Chana Thaler.................................380.637.70.37.70

DNEPROPETROVSK
Rabbi Dan Makagon..............................380.504.51.13.18

NIKOLAYEV
Rabbi Sholom Gotlieb...........................380.512.37.37.71

ODESSA
Rabbi Avraham Wolf
Rabbi Yaakov Neiman...............38.048.728.0770 EXT. 280

ZAPOROZHYE
Mrs. Nechama Dina Ehrentreu...............380.957.19.96.08

ZHITOMIR
Rabbi Shlomo Wilhelm..........................380.504.63.01.32

UNITED KINGDOM

BOURNEMOUTH
Rabbi Bentzion Alperowitz.....................44.749.456.7177

CHEADLE
Rabbi Peretz Chein...............................44.161.428.1818

LEEDS
Rabbi Eli Pink.......................................44.113.266.3311

LONDON
Rabbi Moshe Adler................................44.771.052.4460
Rabbi Mendel Cohen.............................44.777.261.2661
Rabbi Shneor Glitzenstein.....................44.792.585.7050
Rabbi Hillel Gruber...............................44.208.202.1600
Rabbi Chaim Hoch...............................44.753.879.9524
Rabbi Dovid Katz..................................44.207.624.2770
Rabbi Eli Levin......................................44.7540.461.568
Rabbi Yisroel Lew.................................44.207.060.9770
Rabbi Gershon Overlander.....................44.208.202.1600
Rabbi Shlomo Odze..............................44.791.757.3558
Rabbi Yossi Simon................................44.208.458.0416
Rabbi Bentzi Sudak..............................44.207.078.7469

MANCHESTER
Rabbi Levi Cohen..................................44.161.792.6335
Rabbi Shmuli Jaffe................................44.161.766.1812

URUGUAY

MONTEVIDEO
Rabbi Mendy Shemtov...........................598.2628.6770

JEWISH LEARNING INSTITUTE

The Jewish Learning Multiplex

Brought to you by the Rohr Jewish Learning Institute

In fulfillment of the mandate of the Lubavitcher Rebbe, of blessed memory, whose leadership guides every step of our work, the mission of the Rohr Jewish Learning Institute is to transform Jewish life and the greater community through the study of Torah, connecting each Jew to our shared heritage of Jewish learning.

While our flagship program remains the cornerstone of our organization, JLI is proud to feature additional divisions catering to specific populations, in order to meet a wide array of educational needs.

The Rohr **JEWISH LEARNING INSTITUTE**

a subsidiary of **Merkos L'Inyonei Chinuch,**
the adult educational arm of the Chabad-Lubavitch movement

TORAH STUDIES

Torah Studies provides a rich and nuanced encounter with the weekly Torah reading.

MYSHIUR
TALMUD LEARNING INITIATIVE

MyShiur courses are designed to assist students in developing the skills needed to study Talmud independently.

SINAI SCHOLARS SOCIETY

This rigorous fellowship program invites select college students to explore the fundamentals of Judaism.

JLI TEENS
YOUNG SMART JEWISH

IN PARTNERSHIP WITH CTEEN: CHABAD TEEN NETWORK

Jewish teens forge their identity as they engage in Torah study, social interaction, and serious fun.

ROSHCHODESH society

The Rosh Chodesh Society gathers Jewish women together once a month for intensive textual study.

TORAHCafé™

TorahCafe.com provides an exclusive selection of top-rated Jewish educational videos.

BRILLIANT LEARNING. NATURALLY.

NATIONAL JEWISH RETREAT

This yearly event rejuvenates mind, body, and spirit with a powerful synthesis of Jewish learning and community.

THE LAND & THE SPIRIT
JLI ISRAEL EXPERIENCE

Participants delve into our nation's past while exploring the Holy Land's relevance and meaning today.

JLI ACADEMY
PEDAGOGY · CURRICULUM · MARKETING

Select affiliates are invited to partner with peers and noted professionals, as leaders of innovation and excellence.

מכון שמואל

THE SAMI ROHR RESEARCH INSTITUTE

Machon Shmuel is an institute providing Torah research in the service of educators worldwide.